Community Benefits

THE CITY IN THE TWENTY-FIRST CENTURY

Eugenie L. Birch and Susan M. Wachter, Series Editors

A complete list of books in the series
is available from the publisher.

COMMUNITY BENEFITS

Developers, Negotiations, and Accountability

Jovanna Rosen

UNIVERSITY OF PENNSYLVANIA PRESS

PHILADELPHIA

Copyright © 2023 University of Pennsylvania Press

All rights reserved. Except for brief quotations used for purposes of review or scholarly citation, none of this book may be reproduced in any form by any means without written permission from the publisher.

Published by
University of Pennsylvania Press
Philadelphia, Pennsylvania 19104-4112
www.upenn.edu/pennpress

Printed in the United States of America on acid-free paper
10 9 8 7 6 5 4 3 2 1

Hardcover ISBN: 978-1-5128-2413-1
eBook ISBN: 978-1-5128-2414-8

A Cataloging-in-Publication record is available from the Library of Congress

To my mom and grandma

CONTENTS

Introduction   1

1. Nonresponsive Investment: The Atlanta Falcons
   Community Benefits Plan   15

2. Community Bypass: The Yesler Terrace Community
   Workforce Agreement   53

3. Managerial Disconnect: The Park East
   Redevelopment Compact   78

4. Fragile Accountability: The Metro Project
   Labor Agreement   111

5. Limits Learned: The Challenges and Opportunities
   of Benefits-Sharing Agreements   142

6. Toward an Accountable Future: Strategies
   for Community Benefits Delivery   158

Appendix 1. Benefits-Sharing Agreements: A New Frontier
for Development Conflict   177

Appendix 2. Methods   189

Appendix 3. Westside Neighborhood Prosperity Fund Grants
Funded by the Arthur M. Blank Foundation   198

Notes	203
References	229
Index	257
Acknowledgments	267

INTRODUCTION

Driven by economic growth, urban development, and renewed interest in urban life, American cities have undergone significant transformations in recent decades. These dynamics and the potential for significant profits have motivated developers[1] to pursue large-scale urban development projects: multimillion-dollar and sometimes billion-dollar projects, from stadiums to new light-rail transportation lines to mixed-use residential and commercial projects. New development, in turn, has transformed the built, social, and natural environments of the cities, neighborhoods, and communities in which it takes place. This wave of urban investment has amplified a real estate boom that, combined with stagnant wages and real estate speculation, drives a growing housing affordability crisis unfolding across many American cities. As a result, new urban investment raises legitimate concerns of neighborhood change, gentrification, and displacement in cities throughout the nation.

Many projects take place in historically underserved communities, where residents already grapple with contemporary and historical injustice, racial discrimination, institutional failures, and disinvestment, as well as rising inequality, escalating housing costs, and low-quality jobs. These communities are often the same ones that suffered harm from and limited participation in local development projects during and after urban renewal, despite their (often active) resistance. Many of these communities face renewed threats from this current wave of urban investment. As in the past, new urban development projects exert enormous pressure on low-income residents as they threaten to gentrify communities, displace existing renters, and exclude many residents from the prosperity they promise.

Community residents and advocates frequently express concern that these projects, which often rely on public funds or subsidies, will worsen urban economic and racial inequality by benefitting the absentee wealthy, rather than the local residents who have long worked to attract jobs, businesses, and amenities to their communities. Conversely, many of these projects also offer hope—a chance to bring long-sought investment into underserved neighborhoods. The difficult opportunity that has emerged for many community activists, then, is how they can work to *direct* investment to better capitalize on the local economic potential of these projects while minimizing local harm.

These dynamics and the struggle for community improvement launched a fight to control development. In the late 1990s and early 2000s, community advocates began to use their selective support for development projects, rather than resistance, to compel developers, labor unions, and local governments to meet at the negotiating table. Within a history of community exclusion and harm from urban development, community activists posed a simple but critically important question: Who would benefit from future local development? Communities sought to create tools to improve equity in the development process. They wanted to ensure that development projects dedicated local benefits, generated influential resident participation, and included effective oversight. In exchange, community activists offered their support for these often controversial projects. Their support could expedite development, which motivated developers and local governments to negotiate with communities.

These organizing efforts created the first negotiated local benefits distribution agreements, or *benefits-sharing agreements*, which have since become common across the country. Two main types have emerged: community benefits agreements (CBAs) and project labor agreements (PLAs) with community workforce provisions.[2]

A CBA is "a documented bargain outlining a set of programmatic and material commitments that a private developer has made to win political support from the residents of a development area and others claiming a stake in its future."[3] The first significant CBA, approved in 2001, governed the $2.5 billion Staples Center development in downtown Los Angeles. It included $390 million in public subsidies and tax rebates. In the agreement, the developer committed about $1.8 million in direct funding for job training, interest-free loans to affordable housing developers, and parks. The agreement also included provisions for local jobs, living wages, and affordable housing construction. In exchange for these local benefits, a coalition of community organizations supported the project during public hearings and through the environmental review process—a notoriously costly and unpredictable process in California.[4]

Since then, CBAs have become common across the country, governing projects such as the $11 billion Los Angeles International Airport expansion project, the $1.8 billion Yankee Stadium project in New York, the $321 million Consol Energy Center (now PPG Paints) hockey arena for the Pittsburgh Penguins, and the roughly $325 million Nashville Soccer Club stadium.[5] Cities including Pittsburgh and Detroit have also considered laws to systematize and mandate CBAs on public or costly projects, a policy that Detroit eventually passed.[6] The proliferation and expanded focus of CBAs demonstrates the extent to which these agreements and their benefits distribution goals have become central to contemporary urban governance.

PLAs are "collective bargaining agreements between contractors, or owners on behalf of contractors, and labor unions in the construction industry."[7] Relevant for this study are PLAs with community workforce provisions, or specifications within the agreement that dedicate local benefits, such as geographically or economically targeted hire. These agreements are sometimes called community workforce agreements.[8]

The first documented PLA to include community workforce provisions was the Port of Oakland PLA, formulated in the early 2000s. The agreement specified hiring local, disadvantaged workers, local contractors, and small businesses. It also included workforce training.[9] Since this agreement, most PLAs now include at least one community workforce provision.[10] Community workforce provisions frequently include geographically targeted hire (hiring local workers or workers who reside within a certain area), workforce development policies (e.g., skill-building policies such as apprenticeship requirements), "helmets to hardhats" provisions (to help veterans access construction careers), and disadvantaged business utilization requirements (to prioritize contracting with targeted businesses such as construction firms owned by individuals from minoritized groups). With the frequent inclusion of community workforce provisions, PLAs have become a prevalent regional organizing strategy.[11]

Prominent PLAs now exist for multibillion-dollar transportation, housing, and school construction projects across the nation, including in Seattle, Los Angeles, San Francisco, New York, and Boston.[12] Cities and public agencies are beginning to scale ad hoc PLAs to broader policies, in order to standardize agreement terms and oversight. For example, the City of Seattle Priority Hire Ordinance, approved in 2015, enacted a PLA for all city-funded projects above $5 million.[13] Master PLAs, which govern all projects within an agency, similarly create PLAs on multiple projects simultaneously, such as the Los Angeles Unified School District PLA, first approved in 1999.[14] Some research has examined these broader benefits policies, finding varying degrees of political support and community participation. Policies also produced different degrees of success in promoting equitable outcomes.[15]

Community Benefits: Developers, Negotiations, and Accountability draws evidence from four benefits-sharing agreements to respond to these important questions: What do benefits-sharing agreements produce, who benefits, and what factors lead to successful community benefits delivery? The stories of the studied development projects and the agreements that govern them—the Atlanta Falcons Community Benefits Plan, the Yesler Terrace Community Workforce Agreement in Seattle, the Park East Redevelopment Compact in Milwaukee, and the Los Angeles County Metropolitan Transportation Authority Project Labor Agreement—reveal the opportunities and limitations for using benefits-sharing agreements to foster community development through urban growth strategies. The book argues that these agreements risk falling short of their community benefits goals not just because of flawed agreement negotiations, but also because they are vulnerable to implementation failures. Rather, benefits-sharing agreements are often structured in ways that allow pro-development interests to move on before community benefits are realized. As a result, agreement implementation can become contested in ways that shape what these agreements deliver.

In this way, the agreements described here illustrate how pro-development interests can use benefits-sharing agreements to facilitate development and co-opt community engagement, without necessarily producing community outcomes. Pro-development interests generally pursue benefits-sharing agreements to expedite development, including to secure project approvals, funding, or necessary public support. Once they achieve this goal, developers and the actors who support their activities, often including local governments and unions, may retain little incentive to produce community outcomes. However, community benefits are often the last outcomes to materialize. Communities generally have little direct influence during implementation, unless participants carefully structure both agreement negotiations and implementation to ensure accountability. Therefore, the leverage that communities initially hold over developers—which inspires benefits negotiations—can decline as the project moves forward and before benefits delivery. These conditions can undermine developer commitment to community outcomes delivery, enabling implementation to diverge from community goals.

The agreements described in this book show how, without accountability, developers and other project proponents can figuratively *walk away from the negotiating table* once the development moves forward. This disregard for community benefits and priorities can leave communities solely responsible for benefits delivery during implementation, but with few viable avenues to ensure that outcomes materialize. In response, communities can organize to attempt to gain leverage to influence implementation. However, beyond the inherent difficulty of community organizing against urban growth interests, community enforcement over benefits delivery comes at a significant cost for underresourced participants. Therefore, benefits-sharing agreements risk leaving underserved communities with the burden of policy implementation, but with few resources to successfully achieve results.

Altogether, the agreements described in this book demonstrate the importance of accountability during agreement implementation. The story of the Mercedes-Benz stadium in Atlanta shows how developers and local government used a toothless agreement to marginalize community opposition. Without leverage, community advocates struggled to keep the city and the developer accountable to their goals—the challenge of *nonresponsive community investment*. The Yesler Terrace Community Workforce Agreement in Seattle reveals the effects of *community bypass*, where the Seattle Housing Authority and unions pursued the agreement to advance their own goals, without significant community engagement. The fragmented and limited implementation that emerged reflects the relative indifference to community outcomes that characterized this agreement from the very beginning. In Milwaukee, stakeholders avoided the process flaws that limited outcomes in Atlanta and Seattle. However, the economic recession of the 2000s delayed land development by a decade, allowing a crucial *managerial disconnect* to emerge and undermine agreement implementation. As a result, many of the original agreement participants moved on to fight new political battles, leaving local government staff responsible for agreement implementation without critical information, oversight, and resources.

In contrast, the Los Angeles case demonstrates the potential for carefully structured agreements to deliver results, though implementation may still prove difficult. The Los Angeles Metro Project Labor Agreement illustrates how benefits-sharing agreements can achieve a *fragile but persistent accountability* that ensures that developers and local government remain responsive to community benefits delivery during implementation. The Metro agreement created an effective, although fragile, accountability structure around the studied Crenshaw Line project. This structure resulted from the combination of oversight from the Metro Board of Directors, penalties for noncompliance, dedicated leadership, motivated agency staff and union leaders, and vigilant community enforcement. As a result, the Los Angeles agreement has produced many of the promised outcomes.

Together, these agreements show how equitable and inclusive agreement negotiation represents a necessary but not sufficient condition to deliver results for communities. While academic research and practitioner efforts related to the community benefits movement have largely focused on organizing, building community-labor coalitions, and the fight to get agreements approved, formulation processes represent only part of the story.[16] Rather, implementation is a critically important stage that influences what these agreements deliver, and who actually benefits. The cases further reveal certain elements that agreements require to achieve success during implementation: community participation, managerial connections, effective partnerships, responsiveness, and vigorous oversight with accountability mechanisms. However, as the cases show, creating these conditions is difficult, sometimes impossible, and hinges on fragile processes.

Throughout, this book shows how benefits-sharing agreements offer a fundamentally limited, though potentially beneficial, community development strategy: communities gain benefits in exchange for supporting impactful development projects, which often threaten to create more harm than dedicated benefits could possibly mitigate. Regardless, as explained in Chapter 5, the incremental benefits promised by these agreements may represent a significant and impactful victory given the existing, neoliberal urban political framework, which disproportionately favors the goals of urban elites.[17] When successful, benefits-sharing agreements can deliver meaningful improvements for residents and communities potentially impacted by the changes that urban growth poses. Therefore, the final chapter concludes by specifying conditions to ensure that benefits-sharing agreements produce positive change for impacted residents.

The Promise of Benefits-Sharing Agreements

Given the sincere hope and potential gain attached to community benefits organizing, it is crucially important to understand the fundamental challenges and unique opportunities associated with this strategy. Benefits-sharing agreements represent an important departure in organizing around urban development projects, in which community activists attempt to leverage urban growth and their influence in the land development process to promote community development goals through negotiated agreements. Community stakeholders generally intend for benefits-sharing agreements to intervene in urban development projects in two ways: (1) altered distributions of the project's costs and benefits, toward greater community benefits and reduced community harm, and (2) more equitable power distributions, accomplished through influential community participation in project approval and agreement negotiations.[18] Overall, community representatives seek to improve equity in urban development by creating new development processes and outcomes that explicitly advance the interests of affected residents, often from historically disinvested communities and neighborhoods.

These community development goals drove the efforts of early benefits-sharing agreement advocates, who explicitly responded to exclusion and inequity in urban development. Among these leaders, community activist Gilda Haas was instrumental in driving the Los Angeles Live agreement. Reflecting on this novel agreement, she emphasized that, "the goal of the CBA was *community control over development*, a goal that resides in a larger human rights development framework we call urban land reform—a people-centered development framework that establishes a right to the city for all."[19] The community surrounding the L.A. Live project and local organizers sought a legally binding benefits agreement to alter traditional land use practices. They hoped to fundamentally change a system that too often produced concentrated harm for local residents, from direct project impacts and larger neighborhood change, without creating significant improvement. In response, the agreement dedicated local benefits to ensure that affected residents shared in the prosperity that the project promised, particularly given the risk that the project would amplify ongoing gentrification and neighborhood change.[20]

Similar to each agreement discussed in this book, an organization affiliated with the Partnership for Working Families (PWF) helped develop and advance the L.A. Live agreement, in this case the Los Angeles Alliance for a New Economy (LAANE).[21] The PWF is a nationwide network of community organizations created to innovate and diffuse solutions to economic and environmental problems. The PWF and its affiliate organizations have driven the adoption of benefits-sharing agreements throughout the country, sharing information and expertise to promote widespread community benefits policy adoption.[22] Even though I did not select agreements based on their affiliation with the PWF, each of the agreements studied in this book involved affiliated organizations in some capacity, underscoring the centrality of this organizational network to the emergence of community benefits organizing nationally.

Concurrently, PLAs with community workforce provisions emerged in response to the historical harm and lack of benefit that low-income communities experienced from adjacent development. These agreements were also intended to respond to the routine exclusion of workers of color and women from construction unions. Community activists saw the Port of Oakland redevelopment as an opportunity to foster equitable development practices through local workforce development and greater community inclusion in the development process. Their organizing efforts secured the first PLA with community workforce provisions, intended to leverage the redevelopment project to create quality jobs, explicitly distributed to historically marginalized workers. Similar to the Los Angeles Live CBA, a PWF affiliate drove the Oakland PLA: the East Bay Alliance for a Sustainable Economy (EBASE).[23]

The PWF network was critical for information sharing between EBASE and LAANE, demonstrating the interconnectedness of these two agreement types, which were launched as part of a coordinated strategy intended to alter urban development processes and redistribute project benefits.[24] Importantly, labor agreements leverage the historical role that unions have played in advancing urban growth priorities in order to achieve negotiated community development outcomes.[25] This tactic reflects a growing shift toward community-labor coalitions as a strategy to enact progressive labor policy, to achieve higher labor standards and union jobs, while being more accessible to local workers through community workforce provisions.[26]

Community advocates like Gilda Haas and LAANE in Los Angeles pursued benefits-sharing agreements to demand (more) equitable development through dedicated local benefits and greater community influence over nearby development. These agreements build on the bargained development agreement model by inserting community interests and stakeholders into development negotiations. Advocates pursued these efforts to counter the historical exclusion of local residents from participating in and benefitting from nearby urban development projects. In this way, community activists have used benefits-sharing agreements to avoid repeating a planning history in which marginalized groups often faced immediate and cumulative harm from large-scale projects, including during and after urban renewal.[27] In theory, the final negotiated contract codifies these priorities, to govern how a development project proceeds. However, unlike development agreements, community advocates and unions primarily drive these new benefits-sharing agreements, with varying participation by local governments.[28]

Community activists encourage developers to negotiate benefits-sharing agreements by leveraging their influence with local elected officials and in the zoning and environmental approvals process, in which community opposition can jeopardize and delay projects, and drive up costs. Negotiated community benefits offer developers a means to expedite projects, which motivates them to come to the negotiating table.[29] Since large projects often include public subsidies or public contracts, the expectations and regulatory processes associated with public funding can further encourage developers to pursue benefits-sharing agreements as a means to demonstrate public support.[30] Negotiated agreements offer an opportunity for developers to address, at the outset, project opposition that may emerge throughout the development process. Instead, agreements can create support for controversial projects.[31] In this way, benefits-sharing agreements offer a means for developers and pro-growth interests to expedite development, while allowing communities to specify and extract the price that makes a development project sufficiently equitable to gain their support—at least in theory.[32]

In so doing, benefits-sharing agreements, and the organizing surrounding these policies, can alter urban governance processes. The agreements offer a means to either circumvent or supplement existing land use approval and policy formulation[33] procedures, in favor of deliberation[34] directly between stakeholders to create policies through consensus.[35] In theory, parties agree to a benefits distribution arrangement and a process that make the development acceptable to all signatories. After agreement approval, implementation—of both the project and the agreement—begins. Since early activists secured the first benefits-sharing agreements, communities across the nation have replicated this model, demanding that large-scale development projects produce targeted local benefits. While local governments and developers have bargained over development projects for decades, benefits-sharing agreements represent a new urban governance approach by explicitly attempting to cultivate influential community participation and outcomes during development negotiations, toward a more inclusive city.[36]

However, when the rubber has met the road of agreement implementation, many benefits-sharing agreements have faced critique for delivering few community benefits, for limiting influential community participation, and for producing only partial implementation. Results have sometimes reflected negotiation process failures, such as when developers have sought community participation solely in order to secure additional government subsidies that require such input, with little concern for influential and inclusive participation. Other agreements have faced new challenges during implementation, in which shifting conditions and priorities frustrate benefits delivery, with consequential impacts for community beneficiaries.[37] And yet, other agreements appear to deliver important community benefits and involve community participants in ways that influence how development proceeds.[38]

Even though outcomes and processes have varied widely, much remains unknown about what these agreements deliver, and for whom, and who controls benefits delivery. Regardless, benefits-sharing agreements have proliferated in urban governance, which underscores how important this strategy has become to planning, urban development, and community organizing for regional equity. As a result, these questions—*who ultimately benefits* from both the agreements and the projects in question, *how benefits delivery occurs*, and *what works* for benefits-sharing agreements to successfully produce community benefits—represent a critical inquiry for urban scholars, policy makers, and practitioners. Indeed, insight into these questions can help determine whether benefits-sharing agreements offer new opportunities for fostering equitable and inclusive practices in urban development, or whether these agreements simply offer another way for urban elites to advance projects to their disproportionate benefit.[39]

Community Benefits: Developers, Negotiations, and Accountability dives into four case studies to examine these questions. Each agreement shows the promise, perils, and pitfalls of community benefits and project labor agreements as a community development strategy. Examining them individually and comparatively shows the ways in which, even after an agreement gets signed, and even following successful negotiations, community beneficiaries risk not receiving promised benefits. Rather, without provisions to ensure accountability, developers and other pro-growth interests lack a structural incentive to produce community outcomes. These agreements suggest that implementation and outcomes frequently reflect the relative indifference, and sometimes active resistance, of pro-growth interests to community outcomes delivery. Therefore, this work reveals the careful conditions that must exist during both negotiation and implementation for agreements to produce results.

Chapter 1 describes the Atlanta Falcons Community Benefits Plan. Atlanta Falcons owner Arthur Blank's foundation and the City of Atlanta used a toothless agreement to marginalize opposition to the new $1.6 billion Mercedes-Benz stadium for the professional football team, funded with $200 million in public subsidies. They promised $30 million in direct investment to the neighborhoods surrounding the stadium. This problematic negotiation process extended into implementation. The Blank Foundation and the city implemented the agreement under a philanthropic model, where the foundation and the city managed benefits delivery by awarding grants. The grantmaking process lacked transparency and community influence. Both the top-down grantmaking process and the outcomes produced drew outcry from community activists. Even though community activists strategized to influence grant allocation, they had limited success, with the city and the Blank Foundation proving often nonresponsive to community pressure. This conflict illustrates the limitations for using benefits-sharing agreements to transform local relationships, distributions, and outcomes when powerholders use agreements as tokenistic or limited gestures. Therefore, the chapter reveals the challenge of *nonresponsive community investment*, where the community lacks influence over the way in which benefits-sharing agreements undertake local investment.

The Yesler Terrace Community Workforce Agreement, concerning a $1 billion public housing redevelopment project in Seattle, takes center stage in Chapter 2. Under this agreement, union construction jobs produced by the Yesler Terrace project were targeted toward public housing residents and local residents economically eligible for public housing. Specifically, the agreement was intended to bring new individuals into the construction trades and to create high-quality career opportunities for low-income public housing residents. The Seattle Housing Authority primarily pursued the agreement to demonstrate community inclusion on a controversial project and to improve the agency's public reputation. However, residents were more concerned with influencing how the impactful redevelopment project would proceed than with capturing the jobs produced. Therefore, agreement deliberations bypassed intended beneficiaries from the outset.

To ensure outcomes, unions targeted hiring to low-income workers who were already union members, to produce results consistent with the agreement terms. However, this strategy avoided the spirit of the agreement: to draw new, targeted workers into the trades and employ them on this project. Similar to the agreements in Atlanta and Milwaukee, the Yesler Terrace agreement illustrates how uncoordinated, toothless implementation can undermine outcomes. In this case, the Seattle Housing Authority and unions lacked a vested interest in hiring local workers in a manner that advanced the spirit of the agreement. This relative indifference, combined with the *community bypass* that continued into implementation, left no one focused on community outcomes delivery, consistent with the original agreement goals. Agreement implementation reflected this disconnect.

Chapter 3 tells the story of the Milwaukee County Park East Redevelopment Compact (PERC). Approved in 2004, the PERC has received significant attention in academic research because it was the first CBA codified as a local land use policy that governed more than one project. However, prior research stops short of examining what the lauded policy has actually delivered. In the decade after PERC approval, implementation fell largely to the county employees who administered the policy but lacked essential resources. In theory, the county board of supervisors has overseen agreement implementation. However, county representatives focused on fighting political and policy battles with conservative leaders, including former county executive and later Wisconsin governor Scott Walker. As a result, as development picked up after the recession, county representatives took a passive role in PERC implementation. Therefore, even though the PERC deliberations process produced an enforceable, ambitious policy, a crucial disconnect between agreement administrators and their oversight body emerged during a critical time in agreement implementation, which limited oversight and enforcement. Evidence reveals instances in which developers exploited this *managerial disconnect* to minimize their obligations under the PERC. These events show how, similar to the Atlanta case, Milwaukee development interests actively avoided delivering the community outcomes to which they agreed, absent enforcement pressure and vigilant oversight.

Chapter 4 details the story of a benefits agreement that was the most successful for the community in this book: the Metro PLA in South Los Angeles. The agreement governs $40 billion in transportation spending in Los Angeles County, including the $2.1 billion Crenshaw Line in South Los Angeles. The Metro PLA provides an important contrast to the other three examples. The Metro agreement on the Crenshaw Line has met or exceeded most outcomes. Community activists maintained vigilance during implementation by monitoring construction sites and reporting their findings. This watchdog effort, combined with strong leadership from elected officials on the Metro board of directors, motivated agency staff and contractors to remain focused on delivering community outcomes, under threat of penalties. This pressure, driven by community organizing and political oversight, forced all parties to remain focused on community outcomes delivery, even after their original, individual interests had been met.

The Metro case illustrates how carefully structured implementation, including community enforcement, responsive elected officials and local government staff, and structured accountability such as penalties for noncompliance, can encourage all actors to deliver on their original commitments. However, even with this effective implementation structure, the Metro PLA achieved only a *fragile accountability*. This accountability structure produced important results but required continued vigilance and dedication from both elected officials and underresourced community activists during implementation.

Chapter 5 synthesizes the lessons learned from these four case studies. The chapter draws from urban studies, planning, and public administration theory to establish how and why benefits-sharing agreements may systematically fail to produce community outcomes. In so doing, the chapter explains the systematic tendency for problems to arise during agreement formulation and implementation that limit accountability, such as nonresponsive community investment, managerial disconnects, and community bypass. Critically, power asymmetries between actors can frustrate agreement negotiations, implementation, and community outcomes delivery. Rather, as urban and planning theorists suggest, growth and capital interests still dominate local development, and communities alone generally lack the power to reject unwanted development or to fundamentally alter projects to their advantage, unless growth interests support their goals. Therefore, while these agreements represent an important land use innovation to potentially redistribute project benefits, they have not substantially altered *who* controls development, and *to what end*.

Since benefits-sharing agreements do not reconcile the fundamental power asymmetries in urban development, which bias toward growth, these agreements inherently risk delivering limited results to the communities that organize for benefits. Even if negotiations reach an agreement acceptable to all parties, pro-development interests generally get what they want when the agreement is signed. After this happens, pro-development interests can walk away from their commitments, minimizing or avoiding benefits delivery. With this departure, communities risk being figuratively *left at the negotiating table,* even as they organize to keep others accountable to their commitments. Indeed, in each agreement detailed here, including the Los Angeles Metro PLA, community participants were denied opportunities to share power with pro-development interests in the implementation process—and the lack of community power in implementation consistently proved consequential.

Even still, while benefits-sharing agreements deliver disparate and often limited outcomes for communities, they can produce meaningful benefits. However, agreement success does not just hinge on how agreement negotiations unfold. Rather, implementation represents a critical stage to determine the final policy outcomes produced. Successful benefits delivery requires accountability and some degree of power sharing with residents throughout implementation, to ensure that all stakeholders retain a vested interest in meeting community goals. Therefore, the question becomes, How can stakeholders undertake these agreements in ways that advance community goals during both agreement formulation and implementation, to create accountability? Before turning to that question directly in Chapter 6, Chapter 5 responds by identifying the systemic challenges underlying benefits-sharing agreements, clarifying why successful negotiations alone do not ensure results. This discussion helps explain why some agreements deliver on their community promises during implementation while others do not.

The final chapter offers a hopeful path forward through recommendations to improve agreements and their implementation. This analysis is intended to ensure that benefits-sharing agreements effectively deliver on the promises made to communities. To this end, Chapter 6 identifies strategies for communities to protect community benefits during both agreement formulation and implementation. Throughout, the lessons from Atlanta, Milwaukee, Seattle, and Los Angeles are crucial to understand both the perils and the possibilities for future benefits-sharing agreements.

CHAPTER 1

Nonresponsive Investment: The Atlanta Falcons Community Benefits Plan

Atlanta Falcons owner Arthur Blank began publicly planning to secure a new stadium for his National Football League (NFL) team in the early 2010s. The Home Depot cofounder worked with elected city officials and staff to obtain approval, rights to land, and financial support from the city. By 2013, after watching Blank promote a billion-dollar project in the historically disinvested Atlanta Westside, residents and activists saw an opportunity to act. They wanted to ensure that the high-profile project and its anticipated neighborhood impacts—widely viewed as a "done deal" to residents—enriched the lives of local people, not just politicians and the Atlanta business elite. After community advocates expressed concerns about the potential harm for residents, the city worked with community organizations and residents to form a committee to determine community benefits on the project. Community advocates hoped to secure a community benefits agreement to make certain that Blank and city elites were not the only ones to benefit from the new stadium and the city's $200 million project investment. City officials and the Atlanta Falcons viewed community benefits negotiations as a way to gain support from residents for the new stadium, deliver local benefits, and move the controversial project forward.[1]

However, after only five months of committee meetings, the body abruptly learned that its work had been ignored and its role deliberately bypassed. In November 2013 when Atlanta city councilmember Michael Julian Bond (son of the civil rights activist Julian Bond) was directly asked about the status of the policy under debate by the committee, he responded, "We can no longer amend this document because it is before City Council now." The committee had approved no plan. Members had not given their consent to any document or legal agreement. Residents believed they had been participating in a good-faith negotiation with Atlanta Falcons ownership and city officials, fighting for a legally binding agreement to dedicate community benefits. However, the project's timely progress and public financing hinged on the committee approving a community benefits policy on the project. Committee members knew that their leverage existed only until a policy was approved by the city council, when the project could move forward to construction.[2]

However, with Bond's remark, residents learned that stadium proponents had pushed through legislation without their knowledge. A seeming conspiracy of purposeful neglect rendered the local committee, its work, its opinions, and any agreements it tried to make immediately less powerful. The committee could no longer offer opinions or positions that would be legally binding. Residents feared that, without a legally enforceable agreement, the stadium would gentrify and harm the low-income neighborhood surrounding the stadium. In addition to neglecting community priorities, it seemed that the Atlanta Falcons and city officials had viewed community participation as a tokenistic gesture, rather than as a forum for meaningful debate about the project's neighborhood impacts. Perhaps the city and Blank hoped that mere engagement with the committee would encourage local support, but their collective actions showed no genuine concern for committee deliberations and community priorities.[3]

Community stakeholders expressed shock, frustration, and outrage at how local officials had intentionally circumvented public participation. Many of the roughly fifty resident attendees began chanting "Shame!" at Bond and other representatives. One resident exclaimed, "You wonder why we want an agreement? Because we don't trust you! And you proved yourself untrustworthy tonight!" Their anger was clear.[4]

The resident was articulating what so many in the community not only had feared but had experienced before. This was not the first time that a sports team and city officials in Atlanta had worked in tandem to promote their vision for the city, subsidizing megaprojects that would bring new investment to Atlanta, often directly at the expense of Atlanta Westside residents and Black residents in particular. For more than thirty years preceding this project, city leaders had consistently promised residents benefits from proposed new projects. Each time the developments delivered few tangible results. Rather, projects had often worsened conditions for residents, triggering displacement and deepening inequality. The fact that these projects were often directly subsidized by local government and assisted by governmental land use controls only heightened the community's sense of injustice. By 2013, the hope that many residents initially held over the new stadium was fractured when they witnessed, once again, that when urban elites and public officials conspire to advance their agendas, community advocates and residents often have few viable avenues to stop them.[5]

From the outset, the proposed stadium risked perpetuating a harmful pattern of impactful development projects within underserved Black communities on the Atlanta Westside. These projects illustrate a history of *nonresponsive community investment*, where the city's elites have pursued urban growth, local development, and investment in ways that often avoided influential community participation and ignored residents' expressed preferences. As historian Larry Keating documents in *Atlanta: Race, Class and Urban Expansion*, the Atlanta governing regime has long favored business and growth interests and failed to adequately support low-income, Black residents—including residents near the Georgia Dome. Local government officials and Atlanta elites have generally aspired to make the city a cosmopolitan center. They have advanced projects that promote that image, often at the expense of low-income, Black communities and that are undertaken without inclusive community involvement.[6] From the outset, the new stadium risked perpetuating that harmful legacy.

But why would city officials or the Atlanta Falcons organization even recognize community advocacy, formalize participation in a city-led committee, and negotiate community benefits in the first place? Why did they feel the need to engage with the community? Why did local residents and community activists put in any effort in the first place? Why did they think this time would be different?

The Atlanta Falcons stadium exemplifies several key themes in why growth interests aspire to channel community advocacy, why communities vie for benefits agreements, and how a variety of forces and factors can undermine community outcomes—even after policy approval. In Atlanta, tokenism and conspiratorial neglect in policy negotiations proved only the beginning. Once put into operation, the so-called community benefits plan, effectively created between the Atlanta Falcons and the local government and advanced without the consent of the local committee established for exactly this role, functioned as a form of top-down philanthropic investment that seemed as much an effort to control neighborhood investment as it was a plan for community benefit. This approach to agreement negotiations directly translated into policy implementation. Taken together, the history of Atlanta's preferential relationships with local elites such as sports franchises, the disregard for the local community as unqualified participants in local investment, and the clear pro-growth vision that the city and Atlanta Falcons advanced, even amid community resistance, showcases how community benefits agreements can promise much but fail to deliver.

The City That Should Have Known Better

In the decades preceding Blank's push for a new stadium, Atlanta residents had, on several occasions, jockeyed with city officials and the city's sports teams over renovations and local benefits. While city officials often dedicated benefits to and claimed to attempt to empower local communities, time and again the resulting projects lined the pockets of team owners while leaving worse housing and employment options for people in the local neighborhoods.

The first Atlanta–Fulton County stadium, built in the 1960s and once housing both the Braves and the Falcons, launched the sports megaproject development pattern in Atlanta. In 1963, when Mayor Ivan Allen Jr. sought to attract a professional baseball team, the owner of the Milwaukee Braves selected an urban renewal–cleared parcel near downtown Atlanta for its future stadium, in the Summerhill and Peoplestown neighborhoods. To pay for the new stadium, taxpayer money was diverted from existing parks and sports infrastructure in the city, funds that otherwise would have helped remedy a significant racial gap in the distribution of neighborhood sporting facilities. The stadium project included insufficient parking, which motivated many property owners to tear or burn down their houses, turning neighborhood blocks into parking lots. Peoplestown, to the south of the stadium, lost about one-quarter of its population from 1960 to 1970, and the percentage of Black residents increased from 49.8 percent to 89 percent. In this way, the Atlanta–Fulton County stadium fit into a broader pattern in the city of displacing residents for development projects that served citywide or regional goals.[7]

As urban renewal and major development and freeway projects tore apart communities and reshaped Atlanta in the 1950s and 1960s, Atlanta became a major organizing site of the civil rights movement. Martin Luther King, Jr., had deep ties to the city—he was born and raised on the Westside, where considerable stadium development has taken place in the decades since. The stadium-adjacent neighborhoods lie only about two miles from Dr. King's birth site and Ebenezer Baptist Church, where much of the Southern Christian Leadership Conference's civil rights–era activism took place. During the civil rights movement, the historically Black colleges on the Westside became major centers of student organizing activity. By the time Atlanta became a majority Black city in the 1970 census, the Black community's political influence had grown. Activists focused on pushing back against a history of political exclusion, institutionally sanctioned discrimination and neglect, and development projects that harmed their communities.[8]

In 1973, Atlanta elected its first Black mayor, Maynard Jackson. Mayor Jackson installed the neighborhood planning unit structure in Atlanta, which incorporates community participation into the political process to give residents a voice in local decision making and an influential role in developing the city's comprehensive plan. Neighborhood planning units are "citizen advisory councils that make recommendations to the Mayor and City Council on zoning, land use, and other planning-related matters."[9] As a result of this model, Atlanta has "a very strong citizen engagement component by design," though the model has faced criticism for generating uneven participatory outcomes.[10]

In the late 1980s, the city launched a new campaign with promises that this time would be different. The Atlanta Falcons pushed for their own stadium, coinciding with city officials' efforts to launch onto the world stage as a major cosmopolitan center by pursuing the 1996 Olympics. By 1989, the Falcons and the city had chosen a site near downtown to build the Georgia Dome.[11] Burns describes the events surrounding the Georgia Dome development in an article for *Atlanta Magazine*:

> Back in 1991, when the Georgia Dome was under construction, then-mayor Maynard Jackson and members of City Council (among them future mayor Bill Campbell), set up shop at the corner of Magnolia and Vine to hear from residents concerned about the Dome's impact on the neighborhood. Back then, the *Atlanta Journal-Constitution* reported on plans to build homes on vacant lots and offer job training to those living in the Dome's shadow. 'This is not a sideshow,' Jackson told the newspaper. "When that Dome opens up it's not going to be business as usual in Vine City . . . We want the sidewalks fixed and the streets properly paved to make Vine City as good as any other neighborhood."[12]

City representatives made a significant public commitment to use the Georgia Dome project to invest in Westside communities. The project was supposed to transform the physical area and deliver positive change for residents.

The Georgia Dome's community impacts deepened existing distrust between residents and local government and remain widely criticized. The Georgia Trust Fund, created in 1989 to manage community benefits, dedicated $8 million in loans for housing.[13] According to Invest Atlanta, the development authority managing the fund, the loans "were made to for-profit, nonprofit developers and homebuyers to provide for new and rehabilitated rental housing as well as homeownership opportunities. The repayment dollars for these loans revolves into a program income account and is used to make additional loans for eligible housing development in the Vine City and English Avenue communities."[14] However, by all accounts, even with this investment, the project did not provide lasting, transformative neighborhood benefits. As one local government representative said, "Now if we look into the community, you've no idea where [the money] went, right? . . . It went to this project, it went to that project, some of the buildings that were started never got finished . . . it didn't get to the people who needed it most."[15]

Local government and residents passed blame for the failures in the Dome's community impacts. Some argued that the program was flawed from the outset, citing requirements that nonprofits secure loans and have significant development expertise.[16] Many residents considered the investment doomed to fail because not enough resources were allocated to generate the promised improvement: "You give people just enough money so that they can't do what they need to do and say: got you! You didn't get it."[17] Others attributed the failures to misguided implementation, whereby residents lacked sufficient support to implement the technical components of community benefits delivery. Benefits targeted physical construction, and particularly new home construction, sometimes led by local religious leaders without development expertise. Across these perspectives, however, the consensus is clear: the Dome's community benefits did not create enduring, significant change.[18]

The 1996 Olympic Games continued this pattern of harmful development in Black communities. Atlanta won the Olympics bid in 1990, as the Georgia Dome development proceeded. Among the proposed projects was a new baseball stadium, to be built next to the existing one and to which the Atlanta Braves would move after the Olympics. Despite significant local impacts and widespread criticism, the Braves and the Atlanta Committee for the Olympic Games (ACOG) successfully limited public participation in the planning process. Their proposal made no significant attempt to avoid further harming a neighborhood that had already borne the impacts of the first baseball stadium project. While Peoplestown residents formed the community organization

Atlanta Neighborhoods United for Fairness (A'NUFF) to demand participation and transparency, they were excluded from influential participation in the stadium planning process. The city and county governments approved the stadium location chosen by ACOG and the Braves and gave management to the Braves. The Braves and ACOG successfully avoided environmental and traffic assessments and minimized their community benefits obligations, despite residents' strong objections.[19]

The Olympics development attempted to address equity concerns by directing some jobs created by the event to low-income residents. However, many challenged whether these benefits actually materialized for low-income residents at the same time that the event displaced people and businesses, exacerbating long-standing patterns of displacement and racial dispersion across the city. Rather, the event faced wide criticism for failed investment. Moreover, the Olympics-related housing development later became prohibitively expensive for low-income residents, which contributed to significant gentrification and displacement in neighborhoods like Summerhill. Intended to showcase Atlanta as a world-class city, the Olympics secured little lasting improvement for residents affected by the development. Rather, the Olympics became yet another case in a series of local, high-profile developments that promised much but delivered little for the communities in which development took place.[20]

The legacy of stadium construction in Atlanta has left its imprint on many of the Westside's low-income, predominantly Black neighborhoods. Decades of projects have significantly harmed communities and exacerbated inequality while providing few benefits. Across these projects, developers and the city disproportionately determined local development, with little input from surrounding communities—a pattern of nonresponsive community investment. As one longtime resident stated at the Atlanta city council meeting deliberating the new Falcons stadium, "We have 150 years of the business community running this city. They displaced people to build Turner Field. They displaced people to build the Atlanta Civic Center. And they displaced people to build the Dome, which is already serviceable. This city has a long history of being unfair."[21] Such treatment has only exacerbated the issues that Westside communities and residents face, with projects like the Georgia Dome cutting residents off from downtown and fragmenting communities. As the project progressed, residents worried that the new stadium would bring more of the same to their neighborhoods—concentrated harm but few benefits for existing residents.[22]

The Plan and the Place

In the decade following the Olympics, billionaire Arthur Blank entered this historical stream. After buying the Falcons in 2002, Blank sought a new stadium with modern amenities, including a retractable roof. While the Georgia Dome remained fully functional, then mayor Kasim Reed and other local elected officials were quick to support the new stadium proposal and to help the Falcons leverage public funds to finance the project. The Falcons' Georgia Dome lease was to end between 2017 and 2020, depending on bond repayment. City officials feared that the Falcons would move away from downtown or outside of the city altogether, as the Atlanta Braves baseball team had recently initiated a move to the suburbs. Beyond event revenue, many public officials saw a new stadium as an opportunity to promote the city's profile and capture new events, including a professional soccer team.[23]

Atlanta officials justified the project on its anticipated economic development impacts. The city expected construction of the new stadium to increase regional GDP by $155 million by creating 1,468 full-time-equivalent jobs and more than $71 million in personal income. Once completed, high-profile stadium events, including the Southeastern Conference Championship Game, were expected to generate between $111.6 million and $149.1 million in annual revenue for the state of Georgia. Advocates hoped that the new stadium would attract other high-profile events such as the Super Bowl (estimated at $187 million to $276 million in state revenue), the FIFA World Cup ($150 million to $250 million), and the BCS National Championship Game (now the College Football Playoff National Championship, $125 million to $201.7 million). Without the Falcons in the Georgia Dome, the Dome was estimated to lose between $1.5 million and 2.5 million each year, and the Georgia World Congress Center would lack funds for needed improvements. From the city's perspective, this deficit, combined with the additional tax revenue promised by the new stadium, underscored the need to make the new stadium deal work.[24]

City officials and the Falcons initially sought funding from the state government, but the state refused to contribute to a new stadium. Led by Mayor Reed, the City of Atlanta leveraged its hotel-motel tax to contribute $200 million to construct the new stadium. The city argued that the stadium would contribute back to the hotel-motel tax fund by attracting out-of-town tourists, though much of the project revenue would spill beyond Atlanta city boundaries. The remaining project funding would come from Falcons owner Arthur Blank. The state would receive $2.5 million annually in rent, with annual 2 percent rent increases. Blank was expected to gain substantial revenue from selling the stadium's naming rights and from game day sales, including tickets and concessions. Therefore, the project promised to further enrich Arthur Blank and promote citywide goals, with public dollars supporting these ends. Indeed, before the stadium was completed, it was already scheduled to host the 2019 Super Bowl championship game. The city attracted a new soccer team, Atlanta United, also owned by Arthur Blank. The team sold stadium naming rights to Mercedes-Benz, the luxury European car manufacturer, for an undisclosed amount, further illustrating the stark inequality that the project represents.[25]

Atlanta's economic and geographic inequality is well-documented, and the area around the new stadium exemplifies this divide. The Mercedes-Benz stadium, like the current Georgia Dome, was to be located within the historically disinvested Westside, near the Georgia World Congress Center and downtown, and adjacent to the Castleberry Hill, Vine City, and English Avenue neighborhoods.[26] With a growing income gap, Atlanta consistently has among the highest levels of inequality and concentrated poverty of all American cities. The Westside neighborhoods have among the highest poverty rates in the city, with residents facing food insecurity, low-quality housing, rising rents, and high crime rates.[27] As one community leader described, "in the shadow of the stadium, [there is] all of this human need."[28]

As the project began, most residents in the area surrounding the Georgia Dome and the new stadium were Black or African American, low-income, and relatively young. Approximately 45 percent earned less than $20,000 a year, and roughly two-thirds earned less than $40,000 (see Table 1). Unemployment was far higher in the neighborhoods near the Georgia Dome than at the county and state levels. Castleberry Hill, closest to downtown and the Georgia Dome, had relatively higher property values than the other neighborhoods adjacent to the Dome.[29]

Meanwhile, intense speculation abounded in these neighborhoods, driving rising rents across the Atlanta Westside.[30] Outside investors had begun to bet on the stadium, downtown development, and a hot real estate market to catalyze neighborhood change, to allow them to cash in on higher future property values. Speculation contributed to the uncertainty and risk facing residents as stadium planning got underway. Local businessman Rick

Table 1. Atlanta Neighborhood Demographics as Project Began

	United States	Georgia	Fulton County	Westside Tax Allocation District (TAD) Neighborhoods/ Community Improvement Fund Eligible Area
Population	314,107,084	9,907,756	967,100	9,274
Average Household Size	2.6	2.7	2.5	2.0
% White Alone	62.8%	55.0%	40.6%	16.0%
% Black or African American	12.2%	30.4%	43.5%	72.7%
% Hispanic or Latino	16.9%	9.1%	7.7%	5.5%
% with High School Diploma or Equivalency or Less, but No College (25 Years or Older)	41.7%	43.6%	27.5%	44.8%
% Households with Income Less than $20,000[31]	17.9%	20.0%	19.4%	44.9%
% Households with Income Less than $40,000	38.1%	41.5%	37.3%	68.8%
% Age 0–17 Years	23.5%	25.1%	23.5%	14.1%
% Age 18–24 Years	10.0%	10.2%	10.7%	26.6%
% Age 25–34 Years	13.5%	13.7%	16.5%	23.3%
% Age 35–44 Years	13.0%	14.0%	15.1%	12.1%
% Age 45–54 Years	14.1%	14.1%	13.9%	11.7%
% Age 55–64 Years	12.3%	11.5%	10.6%	6.8%
% Age 65–74 Years	7.6%	6.9%	5.7%	3.1%
% Age 75 and older	6.0%	4.5%	4.0%	2.3%
% Unemployed (Total)	9.2%	10.8%	11.1%	19.1%
% Unemployed (White)	7.9%	8.3%	5.7%	11.0%
% Unemployed (Black or African American)	16.1%	16.2%	18.2%	21.4%
% Unemployed (Hispanic or Latino)	11.0%	9.6%	8.3%	12.8%

Source: American Community Survey, 2010–2014 (5-Year Estimates). I estimated boundaries using Social Explorer and Westside TAD neighborhood maps from Invest Atlanta (Invest Atlanta, 2013c). The census tracts do not correspond exactly to the TAD boundaries, so I included census tracts comprised largely of the neighborhoods listed (tracts 25, 26, 35, 36, and 118). As such, the neighborhood classifications defined in this table are larger than the neighborhoods themselves. Except for the total populations, the numbers for the neighborhoods show the averaged amounts across tracts.

Warren, from the wealthy Buckhead neighborhood, purchased approximately 10 percent of the properties in English Avenue, some for only hundreds of dollars apiece. While waiting for the neighborhood property values to increase to make a fortune, Warren let his properties decay to the point where they housed drug deals and prostitution and accumulated extensive code violations. As an article in the *Atlanta Journal-Constitution* described,

> The sheer number [of properties he owns] means Warren holds much of the fate of this fragile neighborhood in his hands. Some say he's holding it hostage. . . . Privately, he has acknowledged that he and business partners acquired dangerous and derelict properties in hopes of a profit someday. . . . What's clear from Warren's track record is that he's a cunning investor who is setting the stage for a big payoff. As a result, he is changing the face of English Avenue more than any of its most influential politicians or churches, let alone the core group of residents fighting to revive the neighborhood. As blight closes in, properties are even cheaper to buy.[32]

With a history of failed real estate and other financial deals, Warren preyed on residents by renting decaying properties to them, then refusing to make improvements. Some sued, with one tenant winning a $22,000 judgment against him for hazardous conditions. In 2014, Warren frankly acknowledged that he expected soon to be the biggest violator of housing codes in Atlanta. At that time, at least eighty code enforcement complaints had been made since 2010, including many classified as "highly hazardous." Warren's actions exacerbated neighborhood housing issues to such an extent that he was sentenced to jail time for property code violations—a "rare" feat—though that same article noted that "you can get worse [punishment] for shoplifting."[33]

Many speculated that Warren was waiting for the neighborhood to reach the point where the city would be forced to intervene to improve conditions. He tried to secure a massive profit by attempting to sell two dozen properties to the Fulton County/City of Atlanta Land Bank for $667,500, with money from the Arthur M. Blank Family Foundation. The Blank Foundation, funded by Atlanta Falcons owner Arthur Blank, supported the land sale to alleviate property "blight" in the area surrounding the Georgia Dome. However, the mayor stepped in to end the deal. The mayor's spokeswoman said that allowing Warren such profit from his harmful speculation in English Avenue and Vine City would have represented a "slap in the face" to residents.[34]

Figures 1 and 2. Abandoned properties in neighborhoods surrounding the stadium, during stadium construction (photos by author).

The Con

As negotiations proceeded and neighborhood speculation unfolded, the stadium location became a central point of contention. The Falcons and Atlanta Mayor Kasim Reed identified two sites, directly to the north and the south of the existing dome. The Falcons and the mayor preferred the south site, closer to public transit and the convention center, which would require acquisition of two historic churches on the land: Friendship Baptist and Mount Vernon Baptist. The oldest Black Baptist church in Atlanta, Friendship Baptist was more than 150 years old. It was also the site where two prominent historically Black colleges were founded: Spelman College (founded as Atlanta Female Baptist Seminary) and Morehouse College. Early classes took place in the basement.[35]

Due to their histories and significance, many residents opposed moving the churches altogether. However, the Blank family negotiated with the congregations to purchase the land, with encouragement from the mayor. Talks did not proceed easily; negotiations with Mount Vernon Baptist Church stalled for some time after the two parties sought prices that differed by more than $14 million. When negotiations missed an established August 1, 2013, agreement deadline, the Falcons believed that the south site was no longer an option. However, Mayor Reed encouraged both parties to come back to the negotiating table, and the church eventually agreed to a sale. The Falcons paid $19.5 million for the Friendship Baptist Church property, and the Falcons and Georgia World Congress Center Authority paid $14.5 million for the Mount Vernon Baptist Church property. The project required acquisition of five other properties; four were sold near the appraised value, and one holdout owner sought $12.5 million for a property for which the Georgia World Congress Center Authority offered $1.26 million. The state used eminent domain to acquire the property.[36]

The events surrounding the sale of the churches and other land represented an important moment for some residents, who had hoped the communities would maintain a unified front to the city and developers. From their perspective, "the city did divide and conquer" and appeal to the differences across the various neighborhoods. Divisions fractured the neighborhoods' united front, allowing negotiators to gain traction and the development to proceed.[37]

The use of eminent domain and the mayor's strong commitment to the project showed many community residents that the project was going to move forward regardless of community resistance—as one leader put it, to "enrich those who are already rich." The question that remained was whether and how residents could also benefit. In this way, many community activists maintained that they could never control *whether* the development would occur, only *how* it would take place.[38] How negotiations proceeded over the development benefits package would further reveal the ways in which both the city and the Falcons acted to protect growth interests, repeatedly denying the community influence and oversight. These activities advanced a nonresponsive community investment approach, to limit and control community benefits commitments and outcomes.

Mobilizing for Community Benefits

The Atlanta Westside's local advocacy tradition, its tense history, and the legacy of institutional neglect inspired mixed expectations about the new Falcons stadium. With the new stadium, Larry Keating stated, "This is the fourth time we've built a stadium in a poor black neighborhood. That's wrong. And that tells people in those neighborhoods you don't count, just get out of my way. That's real ugly. That's a real punch in the nose."[39] Some hoped that the new stadium could be different—and that Atlanta could finally end this destructive development pattern. As Rebecca Burns cautiously noted in *Atlanta Magazine*, "Almost a quarter-century later, Atlanta gets a second chance to make good on those promises [from the Georgia Dome project]."[40] Entering this tense history with such a significant investment, the question of the stadium's community impacts and benefits became particularly important and contested. Negotiations quickly became a central arena for the community to address past grievances, address institutional distrust, and pursue better outcomes for residents. Their experiences shaped how the new stadium and community benefits negotiation would unfold.[41]

Recognizing the project's inevitability, community activists mobilized to leverage stadium approval for local benefits. Community advocates, including residents and organizations such as Georgia STAND-UP, part of the Partnership for Working Families, sought a community benefits agreement. After studying the experiences of other community organizing efforts nationwide, advocates hoped to avoid the disruptive, harmful path of previous development projects in the city and to include affected residents in both the planning process and outcomes—particularly in light of the stark inequality that the stadium represented. Georgia STAND-UP and local activists lobbied the mayor and city council members for an agreement, using their influence over elected officials voting on the stadium project to push for community benefits.[42]

Motivated by significant public opposition to the inclusion of public financing, the history of land development in Atlanta, and community pressure, city officials worked to attach community benefits to the stadium development. In a decisive move, council member Michael Julian Bond moved to require that the $200 million in bonds could not be issued until the city council and the mayor approved a community benefits package. This action created a key source of leverage for community activists, forcing stadium proponents to prioritize benefits negotiations to advance the stadium project. Throughout, community representatives claimed that the Blank Foundation and city representatives were not inspired to produce community benefits out of genuine concern for residents or political responsiveness, but rather out of "shame" that "the community next door" to the massive development remained so visibly underresourced.[43]

The Community Benefits Plan Committee, including city and neighborhood representatives, was formed in July 2013 to determine the community benefits package on which the stadium's progress hinged. In separate negotiations with the mayor's office, Invest Atlanta, the economic development branch of the city, and the Arthur Blank Foundation signed a memorandum of understanding in which the foundation agreed to allocate $15 million to community benefits. Invest Atlanta similarly committed $15 million, for a promised $30 million total investment in the area. The Community Benefits Plan Committee would shape how the $30 million would be spent. Invest Atlanta would facilitate the plan committee, involving elected officials, representatives from the mayor's office, and community representatives.[44]

Both Invest Atlanta and the Blank Foundation committed to calling for proposals for projects on which to spend the $30 million but retained the sole discretion to decide which projects would receive funding, broadly directed by the community benefits plan. Invest Atlanta could fund only capital projects because of institutional constraints, while the Blank Foundation could fund either capital projects or programming. Invest Atlanta also had commissioned a report undertaken by a consulting firm to provide guidance on how to best invest in the area—which residents argued did not sufficiently include their ideas and priorities. In this way, at the outset, both the city and the Blank Foundation sought to limit community control over the scale of community investment—the amount of money dedicated to community benefits—as well as how community investment would occur. Rather, the city and the foundation initiated a top-down grantmaking approach to community investment and funding dispersal, limiting the community's influence from the outset.[45]

The community benefits plan meetings quickly became a forum where community participants expressed considerable distrust of the city and the Blank Foundation, rooted in their past experiences. Community representatives looked to other community benefits agreements to inform their strategies, though experiences with the Georgia Dome project largely shaped their priorities, perspectives, and strategies. One community respondent stated the obligation that many felt: "this time, we wanted to be better stewards" of neighborhood development, to avoid "unmanaged gentrification" and displacement. This perspective motivated community representatives to focus, from the outset, on both the policy's terms and its enforceability, to ensure results.[46]

Negotiations soon centered on whether deliberations would produce a legally binding community benefits agreement, which community representatives actively sought to secure legal recourse in case the agreement terms were not delivered. Further demonstrating the extent of institutional distrust felt by residents, the community sought clawbacks to ensure that additional public funds would be withheld from funded projects that were not fulfilling their community obligations. City officials would not agree to a legally binding agreement, but rather sought a nonbinding community benefits plan, enforced by Invest Atlanta, to provide additional flexibility during implementation. City representatives also felt that a nonbinding plan could be approved and enacted more quickly because it would not have to meet legal requirements—thus expediting the stadium project. They cited research on community benefits agreements to show that even a legally binding agreement can fail to deliver promised benefits.[47]

Residents pushed back on these efforts to limit their oversight capacity, and the meetings became tense. One local government representative reflected on these early meetings by stating, "Our first meeting was tough because what you saw was the community purging all the attention and all the disappointment that they had been holding there for years ... what about this is going to be different? You guys just wanted to bring the stadium in here. And you don't care about anything else that's going on. And so, our first few meetings pretty much went nowhere. I mean, there were a couple of them where we just had to say, you know what, let's come back next week."[48] A different local government representative echoed this sentiment, and said that, "A few minutes after [the meeting] had begun, it had just degenerated into chaos. A lot of shouting, a lot of arguing. And it was really bad. And it was bad because the history over there is so bad. You really have to look at the [Georgia] Dome to really get an appreciation of the things that happened."⁴⁹ From the general perspective of stadium advocates, these discussions took valuable time away from detailing the plan specifics and moving forward with stadium construction. Since the bond funding could not be issued until the plan was approved, stadium proponents grew concerned that the community was delaying the stadium project's timely progress.⁵⁰

Meanwhile, local government representatives sought to maintain control over the benefits committee deliberations, despite active resistance by residents. City representatives cited the failed Georgia Dome investment as evidence that the community lacked the capacity to direct investment, which necessitated limited community control. As one local government official stated,

> you've got a community that is used to getting money, used to giving a lot of pressure and then having city hall kind of follow and say, what would it take . . . just leave us alone. But this time [was different], because of the dynamics of the people involved on the dome side, primarily on the Falcons and the Blank Foundation and Arthur Blank himself, and just a general sense that things just can't keep going the way that it has been going on. . . . The community, they wanted more money, they wanted money to do the things that they've said they've always wanted to do, what we were attempting to do. And they wanted it now, they didn't trust city hall, certainly they didn't trust the development authority. And they didn't trust each other. So, it was an extremely violent sort of situation.⁵¹

In this way, stadium proponents disregarded the community's expressions of past harm as unproductive behavior that hindered timely progress on a project that the city desperately sought to secure. This perspective further entrenched the community's demands for a legally binding agreement. As deliberations stretched over months, and construction risked further delays, local government representatives began to express concern at the pace of negotiations.⁵²

Soon enough, it was November 2013—when the fateful meeting would occur. Only five months after the committee began meeting, and with key issues still very much up for debate, city officials had advanced the plan to the city council—bypassing community negotiations and ensuring that the policy would not be legally binding.⁵³

A representative from the mayor's office maintained that the move was intended to allow the council to approve the plan before break and was merely a "placeholder" for the terms that the committee would later specify. However, this action moved the development forward, toward allowing the public bonds to be issued, and therefore undermined the community's key source of leverage. To many, the move further clarified that the committee never held real power to determine the agreement terms and raised objections of tokenism.[54]

Community stakeholders expressed shock, frustration, and outrage at how their local officials had deliberately circumvented public deliberation. Even some city representatives agreed with residents. City Council president Ceasar Mitchell stated, "I am afraid that a process already filled with distrust, from the outset, will now lose any remaining credibility needed to achieve a positive outcome so desperately needed. We have to put our heads together and find a way out of this mess."[55] As Yvonne Jones, the head of the Vine City and English Avenue neighborhood planning unit and a member of the Community Benefits Plan Committee, stated, "All this has been a sham. Whoever comes in, whatever they say. All we can do is hope now. It's just a hope and a prayer."[56] Community participants recognized that by advancing the proposal without reaching an agreement with community representatives, the city council had effectively nullified the influence of the committee formed expressly to ensure community participation and accountability on this controversial project. The move confirmed their original distrust.[57]

As the plan proceeded to the city council's Community Development Committee, many residents encouraged committee members to vote against the proposal. They contended that the process had misled residents and the plan was still too vague, since it did not clarify which projects would receive funding or how the money would be dispersed.[58] One group of community activists sued the city to halt the stadium project on multiple grounds, including that the city subsidies would not benefit Atlanta residents. They eventually lost the lawsuit. The development proceeded, albeit delayed.[59]

The Approval Aftermath

That the benefits package proceeded as a plan, and not an agreement, remained a point of contention for community participants, who worried about the policy's enforceability. One community representative argued that the "deadline-driven" process was set up to avoid real deliberation from the outset. Some held that the committee chair, Michael Julian Bond, "was the mayor's point guy to kind of shut things down, and kind of keep things in limited conversations and limited responses." Before a scandal led to ethics charges, Councilman Bond was rumored to want to run for mayor and therefore had a broader political agenda. Altogether, the approach illustrated the city's continued desire to exert control over the proceedings.[60]

Some pushed back against the city's involvement altogether and held that the community should have negotiated with Arthur Blank directly. As one community representative stated, "We should have been marching in there, in front of their homes ... it took us saying, hey, we want a representative from [the developer]. I don't recall a time Mr. Blank himself came to that community benefits meeting. He's a billionaire but it would have been a wonderful gesture, even if it was just a gesture, for him to come and say: I want $200 million to finance the stadium."[61] The Blank Foundation's limited direct community interactions during the community benefits plan process further illustrate the philanthropic organization's detachment from community deliberations—leaving the city as the influential intermediary and fundamentally shaping how events would proceed.

In contrast to the perspective of community activists, many local government participants expressed satisfaction at the benefits deliberation process and the final plan. According to one, the process "was not necessarily civil when we started, [but the community] got to a point where we were being constructive and moving forward and really putting our best ideas out there. We *got over the fact* that it wasn't to be an agreement and we moved on with the plan." Others echoed this sentiment. They expressed optimism about outcomes delivery and lasting community improvement, confident that their top-down community investment strategy would deliver the best results for the neighborhoods near the stadium—if not for current residents.[62]

Throughout, local government representatives directed the Atlanta Falcons community benefits plan deliberation despite the community's best efforts to control this process. Residents sought to control the investment to protect their vision for the neighborhoods and ensure benefits delivery, consistent with their goals. However, after the plan was fast-tracked, community representatives were unable to maintain significant influence over the Blank Foundation and local officials, who had prioritized expediting development over meeting resident priorities. As a result, the approved, toothless plan only provided guidelines for how the money would be spent, leaving enormous discretion to the Blank Foundation and Invest Atlanta, who consistently acted to limit community control. With the final plan in place, grantmaking and implementation began, to determine how the allocated money would be spent.

On the ground, as the stadium construction proceeded, residents expressed some sense that conditions had begun to improve. According to residents, English Avenue used to be dark at night, with drug deals occurring frequently. The lack of local housing and employment opportunities drove many residents to leave, and the population of the neighborhoods had declined before the stadium project emerged. But now, "the streets are lit up and they've tried to deal with the open drug market there. I think that's been a significant change. It's not perfect, but it's better than it was. And there is somewhat of a sense of order that people can't just do anything, like it was before." Many residents are committed to community advocacy and improvement, wary of gentrification, and resentful of the "unwholesome perception" of their community. As one individual stated, "the spirit of the people who remained, they all share a vision that, hey, this is a beautiful area, this is a beautiful community... They want to see their neighborhood preserved and uplifted. And a lot of people are dedicated to their vision." Active, underresourced churches, nonprofits, and other local institutions have remained committed to community development efforts throughout.[63]

However, physical improvements only heightened worries that gentrification would eventually displace the residents that have supported these neighborhoods for so long. Intense speculation by investors like Rick Warren illustrate the challenges that community residents have faced, including persistent poverty, crime, and health, safety, and environmental issues in the neighborhood—at the same time as residents believed that the area was at the brink of major transformation. Even though land values have remained relatively low, they have risen rapidly, so gentrification and displacement have posed a real, impending threat. Based on an analysis of data from the real estate website Zillow, a 2016 study conducted by Dan Immergluck found that the median rent increased 22 percent in English Avenue and 17 percent in Vine City since 2012. The sharpest increases occurred between December 2015 and July 2016, at the end of the study, when rents increased 14 percent in English Avenue and 9 percent in Vine City. These data suggest a quickening pace of neighborhood change—a worrisome trend for low-income renters. Concerns over affordability, gentrification, and displacement have persisted in the years since the stadium was built.[64]

As gentrification concerns abound, the City of Atlanta has worked with philanthropic partners to leverage investment in the Atlanta Westside to create a larger revitalization strategy, with both groups citing inequality as a pressing issue. Local government representatives recognized that the $30 million dedicated from the stadium would be "just not enough money" to create lasting improvement.[65] As Dan Cathy, the CEO of Chick-fil-A, which sponsors the Peach Bowl football game held at the stadium, said, "We're going to have limousines pulling in there where people are going to be eating caviar and shrimp cocktail, but across the street we got people digging through a trash can trying to find something for lunch. That's an issue for me. That's an issue for Arthur Blank as well."[66] At the same time, residents have pushed back, questioning whether local leaders are more worried about perception than in improving the lives of current residents.[67]

Regardless of their motivations, the city has looked to government and philanthropic funding, continuing its top-down community investment approach motivated, at least in part, by the belief that the Georgia Dome investment failed because of ineffectual community stewardship.[68] To this end, the city established the Westside Future Fund in 2014 to "serve as a catalyst for philanthropic and corporate support" and to coordinate neighborhood revitalization efforts. The mayor appointed the board membership, including the presidents of Spelman College, and the Blank Foundation; the president/CEOs of Jackmont Hospitality, Atlanta Life Financial, and United Distributors; the chairman and CEO of PulteGroup; a partner from Bain & Company, a global consulting firm; and Atlanta city council members Michael Julian Bond and Ivory Lee Young, Jr.[69] The stadium and related investment quickly helped catalyze development, including a proposal advanced by Georgia Tech for a $500 million, 60-acre mixed-use development at the northern site where the Falcons chose not to locate the new stadium.[70] The city also secured a $30 million Choice Neighborhoods Implementation Grant from the U.S. Department of Housing and Urban Development in September 2015.[71]

Similar to the stadium funding, the top-down philanthropic approach employed by the Blank Foundation and the city limited the ways in which community residents could inform funding strategies, develop capacity, direct investment, and generate grassroots change. Residents expressed fear that without community participation, investment strategies would advance large-scale neighborhood change with physical improvements that would only spur gentrification, displace residents, and exclude them from material benefit. One resident expressed concern that by not focusing on tenant protections and shielding residents from rising rents, "your goal is to make this a new place for new people. I've been involved in this community since before the day I got here. And at this moment in time, I actually feel like I'm living on the Arthur M. Blank Family plantation, and I really don't like that feeling."[72]

To this end, many residents strongly maintained that the community investment strategy coinciding with the new stadium intentionally avoided their influential involvement. As a result, it did not address residents' concerns about insufficient planning for the displacement and gentrification that they argued was beginning to take place. As Tim Franzen of the Housing Justice League in Atlanta told the *New York Times*, "Instead, it's like, we're going to develop it the way we want to develop it and develop it for who we want to develop it." For this reason, many residents feared that this nonresponsive, top-down investment strategy would ultimately raise housing costs and exacerbate harm by seeking neighborhood change rather than prioritizing community development strategies to support existing residents.[73]

With the Atlanta Falcons community benefits plan in place, construction on the Mercedes-Benz stadium began. The stadium was completed in 2017. The stadium was touted as a "game changer" for fans; it is "on target" to be the first NFL and Major League Soccer stadium to receive LEED platinum status from the U.S. Green Building Council for its sustainable design.[74] The stadium also includes 650 concession stands, a bar the size of the entire field, and "edible gardens" outside the field.[75] Originally anticipated to cost $1 billion, the total project cost reached an estimated $1.6 billion.[76] The stadium is owned by the Georgia World Congress Center Authority and "license(s) rights of use" to the Falcons. Owner Arthur Blank can earn stadium revenue from "tickets, premium seating, food and beverage, sponsorships, naming rights and parking."[77] After the Mercedes-Benz stadium was completed, the Georgia Dome was demolished. It was intended to be replaced with a luxury hotel, to be advanced after the stadium hosted the Super Bowl in 2019, and the already completed Home Depot Backyard. The Home Depot Backyard provides a premium tailgating space and year-round park, intended to minimize vacant lots in the surrounding neighborhoods and improve the game day experience.[78] Meanwhile, a 2017 report published in the *Guardian* found that the total public funding for the marquee stadium could one day reach $700 million—far exceeding the $200 million that justified the community benefits plan. This difference reflected the hotel-motel subsidy

Figure 3. Vine City neighborhood with completed Mercedes-Benz Stadium in background (photo by author).

clause language, which created an enduring fund to cover future "maintenance, operation, and improvement."[79]

Residents continued to contest the plan during implementation, but the nonresponsive approach to community investment produced mixed results—and limited community control.

In total, the Atlanta Falcons community benefits plan dedicates $30 million to community benefits in Vine City, English Avenue, Castleberry Hill, Marietta Street Artery, and the "Downtown Neighborhood Area, and surrounding areas." Invest Atlanta's $15 million dedication was to be dispersed through the Westside Tax Allocation District Community Improvement Fund. The $15 million from the Blank Foundation was to be a charitable contribution, spent through the Westside Neighborhood Prosperity Fund.[80]

The Atlanta Falcons community benefits plan broadly specifies that the money "provide community job training, affordable housing, environmental mitigations, special event enforcement programs, historic preservation, health and wellness programs and economic development." Specific recommendations include a community center with job training, education, youth programs, health and wellness programs, and business initiatives, as well as desired "catalytic projects," affordable housing, land banking, environmental mitigation, transportation improvements, zoning, historic preservation, green space, and provisions for community safety.[81] Because Georgia is a right-to-work state, the plan never envisioned that the stadium construction jobs would be unionized. The plan requires Invest Atlanta or a representative to report quarterly to the City of Atlanta Community Development/Human Resources Committee and to meet quarterly with the Community Benefits Plan Committee while providing implementation "updates" on the Invest Atlanta website.[82] It further specifies that Invest Atlanta hold application cycles beginning in January 2014 to allocate at least some of the funds to community initiatives. The plan includes no penalties for noncompliance and lacks a detailed implementation strategy.[83] Therefore, the plan distinctly lacks accountability mechanisms to community goals, preferences, and needs. Moreover, the Blank Foundation and Invest Atlanta retain sole discretion over how this money will be spent—much to the chagrin of many residents, who sought to specify the projects produced.[84]

Invest Atlanta and the Blank Foundation's Activities

Invest Atlanta hired an outside consultant to create the Westside TAD neighborhood strategic implementation plan. It combines local plans to "create a cohesive, sustainable vision for the Westside TAD neighborhoods that will guide future redevelopment" and "build human capital and increase job creation as an economic development strategy."[85] The plan formulation process involved community engagement, including resident and business outreach, neighborhood tours, interviews, and three community meetings from March to June 2013. The plan specifies recommendations for design, safety, transportation, stormwater management, job creation, and human capital. It also includes an implementation strategy, with a focus on neighborhood stabilization and job creation.[86]

Guided by this broad community plan and the benefits plan, Invest Atlanta sought projects to fund. In January 2014, Invest Atlanta issued a call for project proposals to developers and community groups. Invest Atlanta accepted applications for grants through the Westside TAD from January to April 2014.

Applications were to be "evaluated on their fit into the priority categories established in the Community Benefits Plan and their ability to accelerate quality-of-life improvements, leverage other public and private funding sources and attract new investment, jobs and residents."[87] Invest Atlanta provided only gap funding, usually up to 20 percent of total project costs, and projects therefore needed to find other funding sources for the remaining costs. This requirement created a very steep funding match for residents seeking resources.[88]

Further, during Community Benefits Plan Committee meetings, residents expressed concern that their ideas would not be taken seriously because of the formal proposal process, which favors groups with experience writing grants and applications. In response, Invest Atlanta offered forty hours of "technical assistance" to show the agency's "good faith" to improve resident competitiveness in the grantmaking process and enable community projects and projects identified by the plan to get selected.[89] Beyond the challenges associated with the grant application process, applications were partially evaluated based on project readiness, as well as the experience and financial strength of applicants. Taken together, these requirements favored wealthier, better-connected applicants—potentially from outside of the targeted neighborhoods—creating barriers that made it more difficult for residents to bring their projects to fruition.[90]

Invest Atlanta initially received eighteen applications. A committee from Invest Atlanta and the City of Atlanta selected eight projects to fund, totaling about $6.2 million of the $15 million that Invest Atlanta originally allocated to funding in the area. The largest initial allocation funded more than half the Quest Healthy Workforce Center, totaling more than one-fifth of Invest Atlanta's $15 million promised investment. The completed Quest community center, which opened in 2016, provides a physical space for job training, including to prepare residents to work in local jobs and jobs that the stadium's construction and activities would directly produce. Invest Atlanta helped fund the Quest complex construction. The Blank Foundation funded an existing job training and support services program, Westside Works, in partnership with the City of Atlanta and various training programs and community organizations. Representatives from both the community and the city cited the program and the Quest center as evidence that stadium-related investment had produced "some success."[91] By the time the Quest center opened, Westside Works had already placed roughly 350 people in jobs that, on average, paid $12 per hour in construction, technology, health care, and the service industry. This investment promoted the goals articulated in the benefits plan; the community sought workforce development opportunities to ensure that residents gained skills and

Table 2. Invest Atlanta Grants Through Community Improvement Fund to 2021

Project	Recipient	Project Type	Total Project Cost	Invest Atlanta Approved Funding
Quest Healthy Workforce Development Complex I & II	Quest Community Development	Community Center	$6,664,696	$3,468,162
Lindsay Street Park	Conservation Fund	Parks	$700,000	$222,000
Project Shield/Cameras	Atlanta Police Foundation	Security	$1,200,000	$1,200,000
Hagar CTM	Hagar Civilization Training Missionary	Housing	$675,000	$500,000
770 English Ave. Expansion	TBC Industries, Inc.	Employment	$400,000	$250,000
Owner-Occupied Rehab	Various	Housing	$1,000,000	$1,000,000
AUERC @ Proctor Creek	Community Improvement Association Environmental Resource Center, Inc.	Parks	$10,000,000	$100,000
Westside Financial Empowerment Center	Federation of Community Development Credit Unions	Financial Literacy and Services	$900,000	$100,000
Awesome, Inc.	Awesome, Inc.	Employment	$414,126	$166,126
English Avenue School Nine-Block Master Plan, Phase I	Greater Vine City Opportunities Program	Community Center	$3,422,670	$1,000,000
West Block Retail	H.J. Russell & Company	Retail	$5,255,633	$600,000
TBC Industries	TBC Industries	Business incubation	Not specified	$250,000
Westside Heritage Owner-Occupied Rehab program		Home rehabilitation	Not specified	$2,400,000

Project	Recipient	Project Type	Total Project Cost	Invest Atlanta Approved Funding
oaksATL Community Development, Inc. (for 891 North Avenue NW and 551 Lindsay Street NW)	oaksATL Community Development, Inc.	Affordable housing renovations	$500,000+	Up to $500,000
oaksATL Community Development, Inc. (for 584 Lindsay Street NW)	oaksATL Community Development, Inc.	Affordable housing renovations	$500,000+	Up to $500,000
oaksATL Community Development, Inc. (for 557 Lindsay Street NW)	oaksATL Community Development, Inc.	Affordable housing renovations	Not specified	Up to $534,000
Hagar CTM	Hagar Civilization Training Missionary	Affordable housing renovations	Not specified	$812,000
Total			$31,632,125	$13,602,288

Source: Invest Atlanta reporting: Invest Atlanta, 2021b; Invest Atlanta, 2020a; Invest Atlanta, 2020b; Invest Atlanta, 2018a; Invest Atlanta, 2018b; Invest Atlanta, 2017; Invest Atlanta, 2016b.

access to long-term career opportunities, beyond the immediate construction jobs created by the stadium project.[92]

Another set of grants funded community enterprises and businesses consistent with the city's local economic development goals. TBC Industries, a local media company, secured an early grant of $250,000, and Awesome, Inc., was awarded $166,126. The projects aligned with the local government's desire to augment its growing film industry and include English Avenue and Vine City in that growth. In the proposal process with Awesome, Inc., Invest Atlanta also secured internships for local youth from that enterprise, to enhance the investment's impact and develop human capital. The projects further promised workforce development, job training, and local entrepreneurship opportunities, consistent with the priorities espoused in the community benefits plan but also the city's economic development goals for the area. In addition, H. J. Russell & Company won a $600,000 grant for a commercial development project that would support local small business

Figure 4. Lindsay Street Park (photo by author).

development. The National Federation of Community Development Credit Unions also received $100,000 toward a financial empowerment center, to which the Blank Foundation also contributed money.[93]

A different set of grants funded neighborhood improvement projects, including Lindsay Street Park, which was the first public park in English Avenue.[94] The park project redeveloped six abandoned parcels, requiring environmental remediation, to form what one local reporter called "an oasis within the community."[95] Another news editorial held that the park project is "a model of what needs to happen" for the polluted creek and flood zone.[96] A $500,000 grant to Hagar Civilization Training Missionary redeveloped ten multifamily affordable housing units. A $1 million grant funded various home repairs across English Avenue and Vine City. A different grant conducted a feasibility plan for the Atlanta Urban Ecology Resource Center, but funded only 1 percent of the $10 million project. Finally—and most controversially—the Atlanta Police Foundation was awarded $1.2 million for police cameras in the neighborhoods. The police cameras were one of the few Invest Atlanta awards that received full funding.[97]

Since these initial grants, the remaining money has been spent at the discretion of the Invest Atlanta board, consistent with the benefits plan, largely on affordable housing–related projects. This includes a $2.4 million grant issued in May 2018 from the community fund to expand the Westside Heritage Owner-Occupied Rehab Program. The program helps local homeowners rehabilitate their homes. At the same time, Hagar Civilization Training Missionary received an $812,000 grant to convert seven properties in Vine City and English Avenue into twenty affordable units, made available to households earning 50 percent of the area median income.[98] In January and February 2020, the Invest Atlanta board approved $1,000,000 in grants, through two separate $500,000 allocations, for oaksATL Community Development, Inc., in coordination with Peace Preparatory Academy. The grants were designated to renovate thirty-one affordable multifamily apartment homes in English Avenue. In 2021, the board allocated up to $534,000 to oaksATL for a mixed-use development with affordable housing.[99] For those community members whose projects did not receive funding, however, their experiences exacerbated lingering resentment and distrust of the process. They questioned how future money would be spent.[100]

Invest Atlanta has overseen grant implementation, with later monetary disbursements contingent on adequate project progress. Invest Atlanta hired a project manager and outside staff to oversee the more technical parts, since the agency lacked the internal capacity to do so. If a project did not progress according to plan, as respondents noted did happen, Invest Atlanta staff noted that they delayed project disbursements until the project manager and funding recipients could get the project on track.[101] In this way, Invest Atlanta chose to directly select projects, monitor implementation, and enforce outcomes. However, its approach included little transparency and accountability to the larger public and the intended community beneficiaries.

To disperse its allocation, the Blank Foundation chose projects to fund with participation by Invest Atlanta and the community. As specified by the plan, the Blank Foundation called for grant applications for its Westside Neighborhood Prosperity Fund in 2014. The Blank Foundation noted that it would prioritize proposals that would "be catalysts for the community" and undertake additional community investment through a "coherent vision."[102] However, respondents emphasized that the funded proposals did not necessarily have to come from within the Westside communities or propose a place-based strategy focused on the Atlanta Westside. Nonprofits able to work in the targeted areas that met the eligibility criteria were allowed to submit proposals. This philanthropic grantmaking approach left significant discretion to the Blank Foundation, which committed to "favor[ing] groups that have the capacity to work with those who are already in the area" that could "strike an appropriate balance of both outside skills and expertise with local knowledge and understanding."[103]

The foundation committed and spent the entire $15 million by the end of 2019 (see Appendix 3), consistent with the benefits plan. At the end of 2017, the Blank Foundation had already awarded more than $10 million in grants, or more than two-thirds of their promised funding. At times, the Blank Foundation worked in coordination with Invest Atlanta, for example, by granting to the Quest Community Development Organization. Notably, two of the six largest grants were awarded to the Atlanta Police Foundation. Established as a public-private partnership, the Atlanta Police Foundation is focused on "driving out crime" and improving neighborhood safety to "make Atlanta the safest large city in the country."[104]

The Blank Foundation also prioritized capacity building, to help organizations already working in the community to "increase their impact" so that they could "play a larger role in creating the transformative change we all want to see."[105] To this end, the foundation worked with the Georgia Center for Nonprofits to enact Westside Momentum in January 2015, which extended a call for grants until February 13, 2015. Created by the Georgia Center for Nonprofits, and first piloted in 2011, Westside Momentum offered a "three-year capacity building initiative built to help nonprofits grow their respective community impacts." The grants were "open to all Westside-based nonprofit organizations and community initiatives looking to strengthen leadership, build infrastructure, and deepen collaborative efforts that can help restore the English Avenue, Vine City, [and] Castleberry Hill neighborhoods as vibrant and thriving communities."[106]

Westside Momentum created two programs: six organizations in the Core Group, and thirty-nine organizations in the Community Group. The Core Group received three-year "intensive" capacity-building and leadership training, with coaching and financial support.[107] In contrast, the Community Group received far less support, limited to mostly networking and training opportunities, which some recipients reportedly refused. With limited time and resources, many had reportedly hoped that the Blank Foundation would provide more direct support to local organizations and could not justify expending resources participating in the Community Group when they needed to focus on fundraising opportunities.[108]

The Blank Foundation selected grant recipients at its discretion, consistent with its approach to the benefits plan, which exacerbated tension with community residents who sought to control how the promised investment was spent. When the Blank Foundation issued the call for proposals, many community-based nonprofits that had "been working and struggling in the community for awhile" applied for the funds, as well as outside organizations proposing to begin working in the community. The Blank Foundation pursued funding some organizations outside the community, with whom community members argued the foundation had already established relationships.[109]

Community activists "took [the foundation] to task about" funding outside organizations at the expense of "growing people internally" to the community. Many emphasized the distrust that the foundation's actions generated, as it undermined the intent underlying the community benefits plan: to generate "spending *for* the community, not *on* the community."[110] One community representative described resident response to finding out that the call for grants was open beyond the community, "I'm going to tell you straight up that what you just did, that is not what we asked for. What you just did, in putting a call to outreach to every damn non-profit in the City of Atlanta, was to dilute and disempower the people who have the relational capacity to actually get out there and get the work done in favor of your friends . . . [this] was the total opposite of what the community asked for. That's exploitation on wholesale. So, we had to stop that." According to this individual, once the community confronted the Blank Foundation, the foundation was "responsive, but you know, it hasn't been *willing* responsiveness."[111] In other words, from their perspective, the Blank Foundation responded to community pressure only reluctantly as plan implementation got underway, after the community demanded responsiveness, and not out of any structured or proactive accountability. Residents consistently sought to ensure that local benefits would materialize consistent with their goals and to the advantage of existing residents, rather than to catalyze neighborhood change that may contribute to eventual displacement. Their determination to pursue responsive investment was motivated by lingering distrust from decades of planning and investment that excluded and harmed existing residents, including negotiations for the benefits plan, where community oversight was deliberately limited.[112]

Similar to Invest Atlanta, the Blank Foundation approached community investment with minimal community participation, transparency, and accountability, creating a philanthropic investment approach that lacked responsiveness to community beneficiaries. Rather, the investment was based on the organization's vision and priorities from the very outset, with the plan supporting their discretion over funding. The Blank Foundation funded projects separately from Invest Atlanta, though Invest Atlanta coordinated with the Blank Foundation on occasion, and the foundation regularly met with Invest Atlanta staff during implementation.[113] The investment initiated by the benefits plan fit into a broader philanthropic strategy advanced by the foundation, which reached $55 million in total spending that the foundation has committed to the Westside.[114]

Throughout, the Blank Foundation's private, philanthropic grantmaking approach left the foundation with the purse strings and the exclusive authority to pursue outcomes from their funding commitment. The benefits plan money was dedicated to neighborhood improvement but was not accountable to the community. The Blank Foundation remained directly accountable only to its handpicked board. While foundation staff reported to the city council, as one local government representative stated, "The city council can't force them to say, you've to spend it this way . . . they're a private entity. All we can do is make sure they can commit to it."[115] And that much proved true—ensured after the community was denied an enforceable agreement that would have bound the city and the Blank Foundation to the outcomes that residents sought.

Insufficient Leverage

As implementation proceeded, it became clear that Invest Atlanta and the Blank Foundation retained sole control over benefits delivery. Early in the process, some community activists attempted to control implementation and how the money was spent. However, their efforts were deliberately limited, and their resource-intensive effort did not significantly determine how Invest Atlanta and the Blank Foundation approached community investment. Invest Atlanta and the Blank Foundation followed the general guidance of the community benefits plan, which outlined priorities but did not specify projects due to the city's successful avoidance of binding promises during the plan's deliberation. How the money would get spent, therefore, was left to the discretion of the government and the philanthropic organization, with no real mechanism to ensure community accountability.

Some residents vowed to remain actively engaged in agreement negotiation after the policy was approved, to keep pressure on the Blank Foundation and Invest Atlanta so that they would remain accountable and responsive to existing residents. In an attempt to establish formal oversight as the final plan was approved, community participants motioned to keep the Community Benefits Plan Committee active throughout implementation—to attempt to keep local government and the Blank Foundation figuratively at the negotiating table. Community members sought to use the body to ensure public reporting, monitor outcomes, and promote community responsiveness.[116]

However, even with the committee intact, its influence and participation declined dramatically after plan approval. It quickly became apparent that the committee lacked leverage during implementation, since it was created for the "specific purpose" of plan negotiation. Therefore, the committee had no empowered oversight capacity.[117] One local government official said that this realization about the committee's narrow role "was an education for some people. I think that when they thought of the committee that they had a tool that they could go out and conquer the world with. . . . No. If you read the resolution, you're empowered to do a specific thing. . . . Of course, you can request, you can ask, cajole, whatever, and advocate for something else. But your [limited power is] plain in the resolution."[118] Because of these limitations, some residents concluded that the committee was just "a formality in the process," intended to expedite development by delivering marginal benefits, rather than a means to generate meaningful community influence over the project and neighborhood investment.[119] While residents sought to increase the scope and power of the committee, they faced significant resistance from those wary of empowering residents, including local government representatives. Rather, the committee could "make suggestions" to Invest Atlanta and the Blank Foundation, "but there's no requirement that residents be told about plans in advance."[120]

As more time passed after plan approval, the committee became "kind of dormant, [and] not really active" with few people attending meetings, and few meetings held after mid-2014. Most local government members soon stopped showing up altogether, including city councilman and committee chair Michael Julian Bond. An article published by the *Atlanta Journal-Constitution* focused on a March 2015 meeting, arguing that the committee "may be one of the loneliest bodies in city government." It noted that city staff had not even set up sound equipment for the meeting, forcing members to yell across the room to hear each other, until they moved closer together. The article ran with a picture of the empty meeting with the caption, "lots of room, if anyone would bother to show up" besides the mostly "unpaid community volunteers."[121]

At this particular meeting, residents discovered that Invest Atlanta had allocated $1.2 million to police cameras in the neighborhoods without community consultation. Community members questioned this strategy, raising issues related to the previous installation of cameras, the ability of cameras to proactively deter crime, and the way in which spending allocations had bypassed community input. However, the article noted that "[n]o officials who could answer committee questions were in attendance." While Councilman Ivory Lee Young, Jr. was present, community representatives complained that committee chairman Michael Julian Bond had not attended for months. Further, no Blank Foundation representative attended. The *Atlanta Journal-Constitution* article was later updated to note that City Councilman Bond and the Blank Foundation representative reached out to the newspaper to say that they were ill, and the city representative was traveling for work. In response to the spending on police cameras, committee members "focused on a motion requesting that Invest Atlanta inform neighborhood groups about spending proposals that would impact them before a development authority vote."[122]

These events around the community benefits committee and the grantmaking approach illustrate how residents stayed at the table to demand and strategize for accountability, quite literally in this March 2015 meeting, to attempt to influence how their promised benefits would be spent. However, it became clear that local government and the Blank Foundation got what they wanted from the negotiation process once the project was approved and moved on afterward. After plan approval, Invest Atlanta and the Blank Foundation awarded grants according to the plan terms, decided by a contested process, but largely avoided calls for accountability to community priorities.

By all accounts, committee participants became extremely fatigued as implementation proceeded. As one local government official put it, everyone had "mild PTSD" after the plan negotiation process. Another participant said that everyone involved was "really worn out" from plan negotiations. Many cited this exhaustion as a barrier to their continued participation in implementation after the contentious plan deliberation process. But, as community participants pushed back, local government participants were tasked with exactly this role and appeared to use excuses to avoid their community obligations. As one resident stated, "This is [their] job."[123]

However, community participants could not just move on without jeopardizing their goals, noting that they had dedicated years of their lives to this organizing effort. Even though some residents had become "quite down," they expressed no choice but to remain vigilant, or risk implementation happening without their input, and potentially creating harm. Therefore, residents must "remain focused, to stay at the table and to call people into accountability. Because if there is nobody at the table holding people accountable, then community benefit will never materialize. What they'll do is they'll wait out another generation." The community worked to generate leverage, remain vigilant, and expose what they perceive as agreement noncompliance during implementation. While their strategy proved inherently reactive, exhausting, and inefficient, one respondent said, "What can I do, what else can we do?"[124]

Residents used the Blank Foundation grantmaking conflict as evidence that the community generated some leverage in implementation, rooted in Arthur Blank's and the city's concern for their reputations. This public relations concern produced some accountability. As one community leader stated, media attention [is] "the way people are held accountable, particularly in this town ... the city is not going to come out with a press release and say, we're not meeting our targets. It's going to take community grassroots, people to bring that to [light]." With vigilance and community organizing, the community can create some degree of accountability. A different resident summed it up by saying that, "The only thing that keeps them at the table is the same thing they keeps anybody: [they're] in the public eye."[125]

However, community responsiveness through public exposure is a fragile and limited oversight form, particularly without dedicated resources. As one resident said, community vigilance "is a tremendous burden, and I feel that every day. And we have to fight to be in a position to drive [implementation]. And everybody might not be up for that fight.... It's a vicious game. I was telling somebody the other day. I said this is like playing chess. Every time you think [you're] over something, something else pops up."[126] Thus, the burden of plan monitoring and enforcement—as a means to achieve community priorities—fell to residents with limited resources, facing extreme exhaustion, but who expressed no choice but to persist.

Despite their work, community residents remained doubtful about the extent to which they could fundamentally alter the way in which local investment occurs—including and beyond the stadium project—and even after plan approval. While residents expressed the ability to go to the media and expose noncompliance, this reactive tactic was a fundamentally limited mechanism to change the philanthropic foundation's overall strategy. One resident said, "I think the Blank Foundation and Arthur Blank and the City will make some significant investments, but they are going to do it in a way that they control investments.... People have tended to give money to people who they know and like. So, they're going to pick the people they know and like ... at a certain point you realize that you don't have any real control now. Do I think that there are some things that we can do? Yes. So, I try to do those things and continue to talk and keep the pressure on, keep communicating."[127] Despite their vested interest in the outcomes produced, residents lacked direct influence over financial disbursements. Community stakeholders held little faith that local government representatives, including those who had stopped showing up to committee meetings, would adequately represent their interests.

Through their nonparticipation, local government representatives placed the burden of oversight and enforcement onto the same community that they argued lacked the capacity to appropriately decide how the money should be directed. This perspective underscores how powerholders, including government officials, have acted to reinforce existing power distributions, favoring pro-development, resourced interests, rather than altering the status quo to empower affected residents. They did so by passing responsibility for vigilance onto overburdened residents, likely knowing that, without direct control, resources, and technical expertise, community residents lacked the ability to enforce their goals alone. According to many, the Georgia Dome benefits effort failed for this very reason.[128]

Local government representatives offered a contradictory position: they claimed that residents lacked the capacity to direct spending, yet residents were supposed to have the ability and resources to monitor and enforce the agreement terms. Throughout, their dominant perception, rooted in the failed Georgia Dome investment, remained that the community could not be trusted to effectively direct resources. As a result, local government and private investors claimed that they had to serve as "stewards of their funds" and direct their money to see it "well spent." Through this process, "You don't have the waste of the money, you don't have the waste of the effort, the waste of the time, because there is enough of that already." Thus, the legacy of failed past investment—despite shared blame—reinforced negative perceptions about the community and relegated residents to an outside role in the investment taking place in their own neighborhoods, which was very publicly intended to benefit them. At the same time, local government and private investors have sought to multiply this investment and foster broader change. Residents expressed concern that Atlanta elites just wanted to encourage neighborhood change without protecting existing residents, which may create displacement.[129]

Responsiveness from Invest Atlanta and the Blank Foundation to the community hinged, in large part, on whether the community could mount and sustain active, effective oversight. This reactive strategy posed inherent challenges. People became less involved over time, leaving a significant burden to fewer individuals. Further, the entire process, and particularly the Blank Foundation efforts, lacked transparency, making it difficult for community members to participate in implementation. As some actors who advocated for the original benefits package moved on, a larger burden rested on those who stayed, leaving the Blank Foundation and Invest Atlanta with even less external oversight. This departure included Georgia STAND-UP, an organization that was deeply involved in pushing for the agreement but was absent during implementation. Rather, the initial community coalition that pushed for the agreement seemingly fell apart during implementation, demonstrating the difficulty inherent to pursuing sustained community pressure, particularly after policy approval and without dedicated resources.[130]

Local government officials did not actively direct oversight, which many community members viewed as evidence of failed leadership and inadequate representation. The Community Benefits Plan Committee lacked direct oversight over Invest Atlanta and the Blank Foundation. Residents sought to create influence, by building and leveraging relationships with local officials and the Blank Foundation, as well as exposing noncompliance through media reporting. However, their influence proved only indirect and largely reactive. While residents influenced how community investment occurred in some ways, including some grants allocations, the city and foundation largely avoided directly responding to community organizing efforts to force investment to address local priorities and community concerns about neighborhood change pressures. Throughout, residents maintained that they could not walk away from implementation without risking the benefits they fought so hard for. They expressed fear that the project would only add to the legacy of local investment failures in Atlanta.[131]

The city and the Blank Foundation have not faced this same risk. Rather, in multiple instances, they revealed that they could walk away from community priorities unless forced to deliver on the community's original vision. The Blank Foundation largely appeared to benefit from avoiding community inclusion, since their efforts expedited the stadium project and enabled them to largely control neighborhood investment to instigate neighborhood change—change that only increases the value of Arthur Blank's and the Falcons' assets. Arthur Blank has publicly espoused his broader commitment to neighborhood change, proclaiming that "if we are not successful in transforming the Westside communities around the stadium, this project will be a failure"—while advocating for the stadium as "a force for good" in the community.[132] Meanwhile, the work that residents have attempted, to ensure that the investment produces local benefits and advances their goals, largely proceeded without their input, sometimes in direct opposition to their expressed wishes. Activists became burnt out. Rather, they expressed feeling like they have been left at the negotiating table, trying to find ways to keep the city and the Blank Foundation accountable to the promises they made: to bring lasting, positive change for the residents next door to the stadium. Without levers of influence to promote accountability, however, their battles continued after policy approval.

The next chapter moves from Atlanta to Seattle, building on the lessons of the Atlanta Falcons stadium and benefits plan. The cases involve striking similarities, despite the vastly different context. The Yesler Terrace community workforce agreement in Seattle concerns the $1 billion redevelopment of Yesler Terrace, a historic public housing community. The redevelopment was a priority for the Seattle Housing Authority and the city. Political concerns motivated the agency and the labor unions to establish a project labor agreement with provisions to hire Yesler Terrace residents on the construction project. Both agreement negotiation and implementation became characterized by *community bypass*, where the Seattle Housing Authority and unions pursued the agreement to advance their own goals with minimal community involvement. During implementation, parties found ways to meet the agreement goals while bypassing these intended community benefits. Similar to Atlanta, the flawed negotiations process shaped implementation, producing a result where residents expressed that the larger redevelopment in question was not fundamentally intended for them. Instead, like in Atlanta, the Seattle project and associated benefits agreement demonstrate the potential for benefits agreements to be used as a tokenistic gesture to expedite development, where community residents are not engaged in an influential capacity and do not experience anticipated benefits.

CHAPTER 2

Community Bypass: The Yesler Terrace Community Workforce Agreement

In July 2002, with initial discussions underway for the redevelopment of Seattle's Yesler Terrace, a public housing community operated by the Seattle Housing Authority (SHA), a coalition of affordable housing advocates, community representatives, and housing community residents sued SHA, the City of Seattle, and the U.S. Department of Housing and Urban Development (HUD). At issue was the $125 million Rainier Vista public housing redevelopment, which SHA had undertaken just before the Yesler Terrace project. SHA was in the process of redeveloping its housing communities. Residents and advocates were outraged by how SHA and the city had bypassed community inclusion and preferences in the planning and redevelopment process.[1]

Similar to the Atlanta development context, Seattle public housing redevelopment projects enter into a tense history of public housing in the region. Previous Seattle redevelopment projects had already eliminated one thousand public housing units since the mid-1990s. Redevelopment processes had been repeatedly criticized for lacking meaningful resident input and for promoting mixed-use, denser development projects that failed to replace all units on-site. This history contributed to ongoing institutional distrust of SHA. The Rainier Vista redevelopment threatened to continue that harmful trend in the city, proposing to reduce the number of public housing units on-site from 481 to 310 units, and failing to define affordability levels for other units.[2]

In response to the lawsuit, a judge issued an injunction to halt the Rainier Vista redevelopment. Among other grievances, the lawsuit argued that the housing authority and the city failed to conduct an adequate environmental review, that it did not sufficiently consider potential displacement and its effects, that the city overlooked important environmental issues and project controversy, and that redevelopers lacked a suitable plan to ensure affordable replacement housing. The community coalition behind the lawsuit sought to change the way that redevelopment would occur on the Rainier Vista project. They also saw an opportunity to avoid the same harmful pattern for the upcoming Yesler Terrace redevelopment. Advocates expanded their attention to pursue deliberate community inclusion in the emerging redevelopment planning process for the Yesler Terrace project, particularly after an effort to secure a provision for "no net loss" of on-site units at Yesler Terrace stalled.[3]

In December, the community coalition and SHA settled the lawsuit over Rainier Vista by specifying terms to govern the rest of the Rainier Vista redevelopment, as well as the upcoming Yesler Terrace redevelopment. Specifically, the settlement stipulated that residents have a right to return to Rainier Vista and priority for low-income residents. It spelled out design and traffic requirements, including limiting the maximum number of housing units. Furthermore, the legal settlement established a citizen review committee for both projects, which formalized a community body to advocate for Yesler Terrace residents *before* planning took place.[4]

In so doing, the Rainier Vista settlement provided several clear entitlements to the future Yesler Terrace committee. The agreement mandated that the committee would

1. "Participate in and comment on development of any redevelopment and renovation plans for Yesler Terrace by the City and SHA,"
2. "Make recommendations to SHA and the City on all land use proposals and housing redevelopment/reconfiguration proposals for Yesler Terrace,"
3. "Make recommendations/comments to SHA and the City that assist in the protection of resident rights," and
4. "Make recommendations to SHA and the City on any variances, rezones, or proposals regarding preservation of low-income housing."

Finally, the agreement included a bold declaration: the committee would have "Full involvement with the city and SHA in any and all planning efforts involving Yesler Terrace." The Seattle Displacement Coalition, a party to the Rainier Vista lawsuit, and the Yesler Terrace community council would each have at least one representative on the Yesler Terrace Citizen Review Committee.[5]

The settlement seemed a clear victory for Seattle housing advocates and community organizations seeking to ensure that Yesler Terrace redevelopment did not follow the path of previous redevelopments and effectively advanced the interests of existing residents. Unlike the committee in Atlanta, which had no legal standing to control the new stadium development, the legal settlement over Rainier Vista ensured that the Yesler Terrace Citizen Review Committee received formal recognition and established pathways of influence over the development project. Due to these organizing efforts, the Rainier Vista settlement provided community activists and Yesler Terrace residents with opportunities to ensure that the Yesler Terrace redevelopment produced less-harmful processes and better outcomes for residents than previous public housing redevelopments.

Beyond the legal settlement, other mechanisms emerged to require community inclusion on the Yesler Terrace redevelopment. In 2011, SHA received a $10.27 million grant from HUD under the Choice Neighborhoods program to catalyze the project's first redevelopment phase. In late 2012, SHA received another grant to support the second phase, for $19.73 million, creating a $30 million total federal investment under Choice Neighborhoods in Yesler Terrace. As part of the program, HUD mandated a mixed-use redevelopment designed to deconcentrate poverty. It required SHA to consider larger community characteristics beyond housing, including "neighborhood" and "people" aspects such as safety, amenities, and economic opportunity. In accordance with the guiding principles and HUD's Choice Neighborhoods conditions, therefore, SHA was directed to focus on connecting residents to major employers and job training programs.[6]

Taken together, funding requirements, a court order, and public pressure aligned to motivate SHA to demonstrate—though not necessarily achieve—community inclusion in the Yesler Terrace redevelopment. The stage seemed set for redevelopment that would advance the goals and address the concerns of local residents. Seattle seemed a prime location to realize the possibility of community responsiveness.

The process that followed in Seattle, however, failed to deliver on the expressed goals of existing Yesler Terrace residents. The Yesler Terrace redevelopment project produced outcomes similar to those in Atlanta, but the road away from community benefits was distinct. In Seattle, the twist was labor and the absence of residents themselves at the table regarding the established community workforce agreement (CWA). Like in Atlanta, the Seattle agreement was flawed from the beginning. In both cases, influential urban actors—in this case SHA and local construction unions—saw an opportunity to deliver community benefits that they thought the community should have, and which would enable a controversial project to move forward. SHA and construction unions put together a project labor agreement with community workforce provisions on the project. For SHA, the agreement would demonstrate inclusiveness and economic opportunity on a contested project; for construction unions, the agreement would ensure that the estimated $1 billion project produced union jobs.

As in Atlanta, pro-growth interests—in this case, SHA and the Seattle construction unions—used the promise of community benefits to marginalize development opposition. Negotiations were dominated by these development proponents, avoiding community influence. As the project unfolded, community benefits did not materialize consistent with the original promises. However, unlike in Atlanta, Yesler Terrace residents were not actively involved in the agreement negotiations or its implementation. Rather, Yesler Terrace residents were more focused on how the redevelopment project would disrupt their homes, community, and quality of life, and how to mitigate these effects.

Therefore, this chapter illustrates the risk of *community bypass* in both agreement formulation and implementation. The pro-development interests shaping the redevelopment project, that is, SHA and the regional construction unions, circumvented the goals and potential contributions of affected community residents. Community bypass occurred even as the housing authority and unions enacted a benefits-sharing agreement, a tool originally designed for community inclusion. This context led to minimal community representation, allowing SHA and unions to center their own needs and priorities in the redevelopment process, even as agreement proponents intended to represent community interests. These deficits shaped agreement implementation, leaving no one working to produce the community outcomes originally envisioned in the CWA. Similarly to the new Atlanta stadium, the resulting project missed the original vision for these agreements, to achieve broad community benefits, consistent with community goals.

The Place

Completed in 1941, Yesler Terrace was the first racially integrated housing project in the nation and the first public housing development in Washington. Once the home of Jimi Hendrix and former Washington governor Gary Locke, Yesler Terrace remains SHA's "most urban family community." The public housing community began as a forty-three-acre site with 863 units, intended to last sixty years. In 1962, eleven acres and 266 housing units were eliminated to make way for Interstate 5 (I-5), which now acts as the housing community's western boundary.[7]

Yesler Terrace houses a diverse population: at the beginning of redevelopment, roughly 30 percent of residents were non–U.S. citizens, including large Somali and Vietnamese immigrant groups. As SHA described, at the time of redevelopment, Yesler Terrace was "part of the most concentrated African-American community in the entire Pacific Northwest, one that is both long-established and dynamic."[8] Yesler Terrace also had a large portion of nonnative English speakers and non–English speakers, and residents spoke twenty-three languages.[9] Only about one-third of residents relied on employment as their primary source of income; others primarily depended on public assistance.[10] In total, in 2008, before redevelopment, 1,190 people lived in the 515 housing units; approximately 35 percent of residents were children, and 15 percent were elderly. Almost one-fifth of residents had a disability.[11]

Yesler Terrace enjoys a central location on prime Seattle real estate. Perched on a hill above I-5, Yesler Terrace is within easy walking of downtown Seattle, with stunning views of downtown, Puget Sound, and Mount Rainier. The community lies close to important local institutions and employers, including Seattle University and the Harborview Medical Center. It is also proximate to public transportation, jobs, and entertainment venues such as the Seattle Seahawks and Mariners stadiums. Before redevelopment commenced in 2008, the community was relatively low-density given its proximity to downtown: Yesler Terrace had mostly two-story buildings, and most residents had their own yards (see Figure 5). The low-income housing community was sitting on valuable and, according to many, underutilized real estate, located within an increasingly competitive Seattle real estate market.[12]

Figure 5. Old Yesler Terrace residences (photo by author).

Redevelopment Plans

SHA had attempted to redevelop Yesler Terrace several times since the 1960s, when the community was roughly two decades old. In the 1960s and 1970s, redevelopment plans proposing to increase density through mixed-use development progressed, but they eventually stalled. In the 2000s, SHA began preparing a new proposal to redevelop the site. The agency argued that the aging Yesler Terrace infrastructure desperately needed significant repairs, including housing upgrades and sewer system replacement. SHA saw the necessary extensive repairs as an opportunity to redevelop the whole site "for the benefit of the entire city," even though Yesler Terrace's existing row housing was already a "reasonably compact form of urban development" for Seattle. Given that the city of Seattle faces significant development pressure, with a growing population, a hot real estate market, and large tech employers like Amazon and Microsoft attracting young, high-income residents, a relatively low-density site near downtown like Yesler Terrace was viewed as a prime location for creating additional density close to jobs and transit.[13]

However, like housing authorities across the nation, SHA needed additional funds for the agency to undertake periodic redevelopment, maintain property, and cover general agency costs. The agency argued that the necessary redevelopment was possible only through land sale, a controversial move that would significantly reshape Yesler Terrace. The agency sought a private developer for the market-rate side of the development. Vulcan Real Estate, owned by late Microsoft cofounder Paul Allen, emerged as a leading contender. SHA sold three Yesler Terrace parcels, comprising 3.7 acres, for $22 million to Vulcan to fund the housing community redevelopment, including infrastructure and unit replacement, plus other agency expenses. The decision drew objections from Seattle activists and Yesler Terrace residents. Many local activists, including residents on the agency's citizen review committee, did not want to see SHA sell land to a private developer. The now-private land is being transformed into a dense development, with roughly 650 total residential units. At least 20 percent of the privately constructed units were committed to workforce housing, to be made available to people making up to 80 percent of the area median income. Leveraging the city's multifamily tax exemption program, Vulcan extended affordability to the 65 percent AMI threshold. While the provision of affordable units is important in a city with a growing housing affordability and homelessness crisis, the high affordability threshold makes these units inaccessible for the very low-income families housed by communities such as Yesler Terrace.[14]

The land sale meant that redevelopment would necessarily create a much-higher-density Yesler Terrace housing community, in order to maintain the same number of units on a fraction of the land.[15] In total, the public part of the redevelopment project was expected to create 561 "replacement units targeted to people with incomes under thirty percent (30%) of the Area Median Income (AMI), two hundred and ninety (290) additional low-income units serving people with incomes from thirty to sixty percent (30 – 60%) AMI and up to eight hundred and fifty (850) workforce housing units serving people with incomes below eighty percent (80%) AMI."[16] The redevelopment was expected to take between ten and fifteen years. Many buildings have already been completed.[17]

Altogether, Yesler Terrace redevelopment will help create the densest neighborhood in the city. Neighborhood density was expected to increase as much as sixfold, to between 110,000 and 132,800 residents per square mile—from its estimated predevelopment density of 19,200 people per square mile. The redesigned area would be more than twice as dense as Capitol Hill, which was the densest Seattle neighborhood before Yesler Terrace's redevelopment,

Figure 6. New Yesler Terrace construction (photo by author).

with about 50,000 residents per square mile. The sale of valuable public housing land and increased density, anticipated to drastically remake the neighborhood, emerged as central issues for community activists. They expressed larger concerns about neighborhood change in a uniquely diverse part of the city. Activists also worried about the future of public housing and the welfare of low-income renters in an increasingly unaffordable region.[18]

Regardless, developers and local government came to view the neighborhood around Yesler Terrace and housing community land as a prime location for new, denser development. Before redevelopment, the city council upzoned the international district next to Yesler Terrace, known as Little Saigon, to create opportunities to concentrate regional growth near downtown. At the time, like Yesler Terrace before redevelopment, the neighborhood had mostly two-story buildings. The upzoning raised concerns that, combined with a denser, redeveloped Yesler Terrace, developers would speculate in the area, displace existing small businesses, and gentrify the surrounding community. SHA staff correctly noted that they can do little to stop the neighborhood change surrounding Yesler Terrace. However, Yesler Terrace redevelopment created new opportunities to amplify real estate speculation and development in the area, which the housing authority saw as an opportunity to generate interest in the land.[19]

SHA land designated for private development was slow to sell at first, viewed as a risky investment in an unsafe neighborhood. However, developers moved in after Vulcan committed to investing $200 million in its initial parcel purchase. The neighborhood started to transform—creating a flood of interest from other developers who saw the potential profits from neighborhood change.[20] Vulcan was a primary catalyst behind the redevelopment of the South Lake Union neighborhood of Seattle, which now houses the headquarters of Amazon. The developer's early investment signaled to other investors that the area was positioned at the brink of a major transformation. Indeed, in 2017, the real estate company Redfin predicted that the nearby First Hill neighborhood, between Capitol Hill and Yesler Terrace, would be the hottest neighborhood for real estate in the nation, with more than 70 percent of houses selling above the listing price. The article quoted a Redfin agent in Seattle: "First Hill is sandwiched between the ever-popular Capitol Hill and the Yesler Terrace redevelopment, with easy access to downtown.... All we need is more inventory."[21]

Vulcan's leadership expressed an opportunity to transform Yesler Terrace and the surrounding area from what developers deemed a "pass-through" neighborhood—for outsiders, at least, and certainly not many longtime residents—to a new South Lake Union, building on the neighborhood's "great bones" of location, views, and transportation access.[22] In total, the entire site redevelopment is expected to last twenty years and cost $1.7 billion, creating as much as 5,000 housing units and 900,000 square feet of office space.[23] Local arts activists organized to demand local benefits from Vulcan, including affordable housing, with some designated specifically for artists, as well as subsidized community and arts commercial space. To date, their efforts have not yielded a dedicated community benefits agreement.[24]

Community Action

As redevelopment planning began, many community advocates argued that this redevelopment was simply a "façade for gentrification" and that, before redevelopment, Yesler Terrace was a functioning, successful public housing community.[25] As one resident said, "Yesler Terrace is no Cabrini-Green."[26] A local academic maintained that "there really isn't a good reason to displace all those people. They were doing just fine. There wasn't a serious crime problem. Their children were safe and in a great location. To justify the redevelopment, SHA had to create and amplify a discourse about the condition of the buildings."[27]

Residents spoke fondly about the community's diversity and the openness, which they argued created a tight-knit community. One resident noted that Yesler Terrace was a place "where you more than waved hello to your neighbors, you said, 'Hey, that smells good, what are you cooking?'"[28] Kristin O'Donnell, a Yesler Terrace resident since 1973 and a member of the Yesler Terrace Community Council and the citizen review committee, spoke frequently in public about the vitality of Yesler Terrace. She contended that Yesler Terrace, before development, was a "community that works, that gives people easy access to the outdoors, gardens, views—and is walking distance to downtown." She said that with redevelopment, however, "You're replacing a community that was designed to be a really good place for people to live, and a real neighborhood, with something that very probably will not be."[29]

While residents advocated against redevelopment, producing documentaries[30] and speaking out at public meetings,[31] SHA maintained that redevelopment was imperative and pushed forward. Residents and community activists lacked the power to stop the redevelopment altogether. However, with the Rainier Vista settlement establishing the citizen review committee, community participation was mandated on the project. The citizen review committee became the mechanism for community input on the project. Even with this role, the committee was a far cry from community control over project outcomes since the project's inevitability was already ensured.

During planning, the citizen review committee began with twenty members, including residents and representatives from local organizations and agencies. The committee participated in the planning process through meetings, beginning with a series of ten meetings to gather resident input, and established key guiding principles for governing redevelopment: social equity, environmental stewardship and sustainability, economic opportunity, and one-for-one replacement housing. Among other facets, the economic opportunity principle sought to "[s]upport training, apprenticeship and living wage job opportunities for residents and those in adjacent communities wherever possible in all phases of Yesler Terrace redevelopment from planning through construction." However, many residents were primarily concerned with displacement and neighborhood change. They focused on, and organized around, ensuring that SHA maintained one-for-one replacement housing, with at least the same number of affordable units on-site. They sought to ensure that all existing residents could stay in Yesler Terrace.[32]

Therefore, the Yesler Terrace redevelopment project included participation from community residents, though their influence was limited in important ways. The agency did consider the guiding principles in the redevelopment's physical design. Further, the agency responded to displacement concerns by granting each resident a guaranteed right to return to Yesler Terrace, if they continued to meet the program requirements; however, many had to relocate in the meantime. The agency used a phased development to maximize the number of residents that could relocate directly into new housing and worked with households individually to ensure optimal placement. SHA provided 18 months notice for relocation, including two summers, so that residents could move at the most convenient time for them. In this way, from the agency's perspective, the citizen review committee "has been a really important group to hold us accountable to the promises we made," with SHA reporting quarterly to the committee.[33]

However, some residents pushed back against the agency's claim that their participation translated into actual influence. As one resident stated, "we've had meetings and meetings and meetings and they still do the same thing."[34] Another said that "they left a lot of what people wanted out of the redevelopment."[35] Kristin O'Donnell commented about the CRC that "I think we made a difference. I really do. . . . We did not get what we wanted, which was another round of-fix up. . . . But realistically, the resources and the federal funding to do that aren't there."[36] Throughout, it is clear that many residents never wanted the redevelopment project in the form it eventually took, as a complete redesign that would remove many cherished elements of the housing community. Furthermore, many residents consistently expressed that they felt they held only slight influence over the plan and had no power to stop the redevelopment altogether.

The Agreement

The political context, project controversy, and concerns about project impacts drove SHA to seek a CWA on the project. The agreement was intended to create opportunities for Yesler Terrace residents to access the construction jobs produced by the redevelopment of their public housing community. According to union and community representatives, SHA was politically motivated to undertake a CWA to undermine opposition to the controversial project, demonstrate community inclusion, and show that SHA was interested in the project's larger effects. Moreover, since SHA had to seek city council approval for components of the redevelopment, including rezoning and a cooperative agreement, SHA did not retain sole authority to execute the redevelopment. The agency, therefore, was particularly focused on public perception and the redevelopment project's viability, viewing a CWA as a means to facilitate the project. However, SHA staff maintained that the agency primarily sought a CWA to both achieve greater project stability and to generate local benefits for Yesler Terrace residents, rather than to address concerns about the agency's public reputation.[37]

Even though they viewed SHA's primary motivations as political, construction union representatives reported that they agreed to a CWA for two main reasons. First, the representatives sought to increase demand for union workers by securing more union projects. Second, the representatives hoped to demonstrate community inclusion in the trades, to improve the public reputation of construction unions in the region. The first goal aligns with the historical role of labor unions as champions of urban growth, part of the "growth machine" advancing urban development, since such activities can create new labor opportunities.[38] Beyond job creation, however, union representatives espoused a commitment to community inclusion and the community workforce provisions, borne largely out of a desire to overcome the long, entrenched, and widely known history of racism and exclusion within the region's building trades. As one individual explained, "Over the years, the building trades kind of lost our way with community groups, there's a lot of distrust, and developing agreements like this, we're bringing that trust back. That actually gives unions a positive role, and some positive feedback in the community; we're not just getting hammered in the community all the time."[39] Union leaders contended that union leadership was changing and turning its back on this legacy of exclusion; particularly given declining union representation nationally, unions could not afford to exclude potential members or fail to build alliances.

To achieve the community inclusion goal, labor representatives viewed lingering community misperceptions as a key challenge to overcome. As one leader noted, regional membership was already sufficiently diverse to meet most community workforce provision targets—as demonstrated by their performance on other ambitious CWAs in the region.[40] Therefore, many Seattle union leaders viewed targeted hire provisions as a way to demonstrate their existing workforce diversity, to offer proof that unions include—and therefore directly benefit—local residents.[41] This narrative illustrates how Seattle unions actively sought to transcend their narrow perception as self-interested growth advocates toward a broader and more strategic position, as advocates for local opportunity, using benefits-sharing agreements as a tool to progress this goal.

To advance the agreement, union leaders sought collaboration from community groups, under recognition that elected officials respond better to labor agreements that include broad community support. Political support is crucial to agreement approval. Since contractors generally want to avoid community workforce provisions, both community and union stakeholders benefit from agreement on the policy terms, despite their often differing interests.[42] Some respondents held that community advocates "drove" the CWA formulation process by formally advocating for the agreement with legislators and with their allies, though others believed that the process lacked sufficient community input. Community stakeholders reported participation, but compared with other CWAs in the region, their input was limited, and the project was not a focus for regional organizing. Some community advocates, however, maintained that unions used the political power of the broader Seattle organizing community to gain agreement approval, to benefit existing union members.[43]

However, unions and community participants similarly agreed that community participation largely did not include the intended beneficiaries: Yesler Terrace residents. Indeed, there appeared to be a widespread lack of knowledge among residents about the existence of this agreement and the job opportunities created. There is no evidence that Yesler Terrace residents actively sought an agreement to access construction job opportunities, specifically. Rather, as redevelopment moved forward, residents expressed far greater interest in the direct impacts of the project, potential changes, displacement, and physical design elements than in capturing the jobs directly produced by project construction.[44] In this way, the agreement bypassed the community, and their expressed priorities, from the beginning. This agreement formulation failure would influence how implementation proceeded.

Regardless, SHA and unions signed on to the Yesler Terrace CWA, entered into by SHA, the Seattle/King County Building and Construction Trades Council, and the Pacific Northwest chapter of the National Construction

Alliance II (referred to as Construction Unions). The agreement took effect January 3, 2013, and ran through December 31, 2017.[45]

The CWA attempted to target jobs to low-income residents and businesses, including public housing residents. The CWA directed hiring to Section 3 workers, defined as, "A public housing resident or an individual who resides in the metropolitan area or non-metropolitan county in which the Section 3 covered assistance is expended and who is considered to be a low- to very low-income person."[46] A Section 3 business is one "a) That is 51 percent or more owned by [a] Section 3 resident; or b) Whose permanent, full-time employees include persons, at least thirty (30) percent of whom are Section 3 residents, or were Section 3 residents within three (3) years of the date of first hire; or c) [that] provides evidence of a commitment to subcontract in excess of twenty-five percent (25%) of the dollar award of all subcontractors to be awarded to business concerns that meet the qualifications set forth."[47] Women-owned or minority-owned business enterprises are "self-identified or certified by the State of Washington Office of Minority and Women's Business Enterprises (OMWBE) to be at least fifty-one percent (51%) owned by women and/or minority group members, including but not limited to African Americans, Native Americans, Asians, Hispanics, and Hasidic Jews."[48]

The CWA set voluntary goals of 14 percent women- or minority-owned business and 10 percent Section 3 business participation, a 15 percent apprenticeship requirement, and voluntary goals of 21 percent minority workers, 20 percent female workers, and 4.5 percent minority female workers.[49] The race-based goals were established as only aspirational because Washington Initiative 200 prevents affirmative action on state-funded projects. Therefore, projects with state funding cannot mandate race-based targeting.[50]

The CWA governed redevelopment of the Yesler Terrace Redevelopment Project but was limited to land that SHA directly redevelops or funds. This restricted scope quickly became a point of contention for building trades representatives.[51] Union representatives argued that they undertook CWA negotiation with the understanding that an agreement would concern the entire $1 billion redevelopment project—later estimated at $1.7 billion. However, during this process, SHA revealed that it was selling off part of the land to fund redevelopment and other SHA expenses. Unions would have to negotiate, separately, a private project labor agreement with the buyer. Therefore, SHA's commitment "turns out to only be about 30 percent of the property," frustrating the union representatives who had sought an agreement on different grounds and to secure work on a larger scale.[52]

The development on the private side was not mandated to be covered by the CWA. SHA expressed concern that a CWA mandate would reduce land sale profits, demonstrating that producing larger community benefits was not the driving priority for the agency. According to SHA, the other parts that were sold off to fund the project were "highly recommended to comply with [the Yesler Terrace CWA], but they don't have the same requirements that [SHA construction contractors] do." Indeed, none of the private projects appear to have adopted the CWA nor met its terms.[53] These events during agreement negotiations contributed to lingering resentment from the building trades, shaping how they approached agreement implementation.

Plan Implementation

Limited public information existed, but all parties acknowledged outreach and recruitment problems.

With project construction ongoing, the Section 3 Advisory Committee oversaw implementation of the Yesler Terrace CWA. Reports produced by SHA and disseminated to the Section 3 Advisory Committee detailed the outcomes produced by the Yesler Terrace CWA. These reports were not publicly available and had to be specifically requested. SHA staff noted that no one had previously requested this information. While SHA responded to requests for information, the lack of public reporting demonstrates the limited public transparency around CWA outcomes. It further illustrates that no one beyond the stakeholders directly engaged in implementation monitored the outcomes produced by this agreement.

Further, the shared reports were broken down by the individual construction contracts for contractors and subcontractors, a practice that makes it difficult to assess the entire redevelopment's cumulative outcomes. Data from the reports revealed varying outcomes across contracts. Moreover, the reporting format obscured important factors such as the share of the total workforce employed on each contract, and whether hired workers were public housing residents. Without comprehensive and detailed reporting, it remains difficult to assess whether the redevelopment comprehensively met the CWA goals or whether contractors hired actual residents on the project—the original agreement intention. While SHA staff noted that the CWA changed their hiring outcomes significantly, this claim is difficult to verify, as hiring reports from previous projects were not digitized nor readily available.[54]

By all accounts, however, the Yesler Terrace agreement proved particularly difficult to implement because of the Section 3 economic targeting requirement. As SHA staff noted, "there is quite a learning curve on this" agreement—the first CWA in the agency, the first agreement administered by a public housing agency in the nation, and the only known agreement in the country to have a primarily economic target in the Section 3 worker classification. Intended to give Yesler Terrace and other public housing residents priority hiring, the Section 3 worker requirement necessitated that unions, contractors, and SHA hire and track workers differently. Geographically targeted-hire initiatives generally screen workers based on their zip codes, data which are easily gathered and identifiable. In contrast, tracking workers by their economic status requires maintaining additional data, which change more frequently than other demographic data, and incorporating these data into the union dispatch process. Unions have historically not tracked their workers by Section 3 status, though some in the Seattle area reported altering their practices to do so, in response. To track and refer workers, unions, contractors, and SHA had to undertake a cumbersome identification and hiring process to be able to identify and target Section 3 workers. Some contractors and unions reportedly chose to ignore the Section 3 requirement altogether. As one individual put it, while the Section 3 requirement makes sense in theory, "in the reality of things, it's kind of hard to [make it] work."[55]

Furthermore, directing Yesler Terrace residents into construction careers proved challenging. SHA, union, and contractor representatives similarly claimed that residents were generally not interested in construction work and lacked any experience with even the most basic construction skills, which made it difficult to hire residents. One individual simply stated, "construction is hard work. [Yesler Terrace residents] don't want to do it." They noted that while SHA "has been doing heavy outreach about these opportunities, supporting apprenticeship programs, things like that . . . there's been a really low interest in sign-up." SHA staff, contractors, and union representatives speculated that Yesler Terrace individuals, many of whom are East African, preferred other types of work to construction for cultural reasons, including hospital work, janitorial work, landscaping, and food service.[56] One Yesler Terrace resident pushed back against this narrative and said, "trust me, anybody is open to a job."[57]

More likely, residents faced significant barriers to entry that could also explain low enrollment, including skills gaps and information asymmetries such as insufficient information about these jobs and their opportunities as they became available. SHA staff members acknowledged a significant outreach problem but passed outreach responsibilities to the construction unions. Union representatives pushed back, maintaining that SHA should have more actively reached out to residents, identifying and screening them for potential applicants.[58] This screening would have helped unions identify more committed and skilled individuals, to reduce their liability as they invested in apprentices.[59]

To cope with recruitment challenges, but still produce CWA outcomes, SHA staff and unions reported that they sought Section 3 workers from beyond Yesler Terrace and, in many cases, from outside of public housing. They were able to do this because the Section 3 classification included nearby individuals who met the income requirements established by HUD.[60] Under pressure to produce outcomes to protect their public reputation and avoid blame for failed community outcomes, some trades found that reclassifying their workers by Section 3 status was a far easier strategy to employ to meet the targeted hire requirement. Because of the deep impact of the recession on the construction industry, many union members fell into the income requirements at this time, since they were out of work for so long.[61] For unions, drawing from existing lists offered a way to meet the agreement goals more easily without the risks associated with recruiting new workers into the trades. Particularly with a narrowed agreement that covered only the public portion of the redevelopment project, union representatives expressed that expending significant resources on CWA implementation was not worth their effort. Many still resented that the community workforce agreement applied only to roughly 30 percent of the total redevelopment, rather than the entire (originally) $1 billion project. Throughout, they argued that the burden and real risk of noncompliance had fallen solely on the unions.[62]

At the same time, however, union respondents reported that their reputational concerns prevented them from just walking away from their commitment to hiring Section 3 workers. They consistently argued that of all the agreement participants, the unions had the greatest need to meet the agreement terms. Their concern with their public perception drove their continued, and sometimes unsupported, efforts. With the ability to reclassify existing workers and hire workers already enrolled in the trades, unions had little incentive to seek out new workers. However, this practice undermined the original agreement spirit, to give public housing residents access to construction careers, not workers already in the trades.[63] When they hired workers already in the trades rather than attracting new workers, unions could technically meet the Section 3 requirements. However, they did not recruit new, targeted workers, including Yesler Terrace residents—as originally envisioned.

Limited Community Oversight

That SHA administered the CWA internally, without an impartial, neutral, and expert third party to check the agency and the contractors, frustrated union leadership. Initially, stakeholders had discussed hiring a third-party administrator to implement this unique agreement, such as a consultant with expertise in CWA implementation. Rather, union leaders contended that they undertook negotiations with the belief that an outside party, not SHA, would administer the CWA. They believed that an impartial agreement administrator would actively hold all parties accountable and have the necessary relationships and expertise to successfully produce results. In general, it can be difficult to motivate internal administrators to enforce an agreement. Internal agreement administrators generally lack external pressure and, often, the expertise necessary to navigate the complex and technical aspects of project labor agreement enforcement. Furthermore, internal agreement administrators may be reluctant to penalize their own contractors or prioritize implementation when it could drive up project costs or harm relationships. Union representatives noted that while SHA agreement administrators are good people and have worked hard, they lacked sufficient expertise and institutional support. In this way, SHA faced lingering concerns during agreement implementation over the agency's capacity, connections, expertise, and incentive to effectively implement this unique and complex policy.[64] These implementation challenges were fundamentally rooted in the way in which both agreement negotiation and implementation unfolded.

The Section 3 Advisory Committee oversaw the agency's internal CWA administration. This committee included representatives from the building trades and community organizations. Community participation in CWA implementation almost exclusively occurred through the Section 3 oversight committee, which governed agency Section 3 HUD requirement activities and was established long before the CWA. The citizen review committee showed little involvement or interest in the CWA. The agreement was barely mentioned at committee meetings: committee minutes show that the agreement was discussed in depth only once, during a ten-minute presentation by the agreement administrator.[65]

SHA representatives attributed resident nonparticipation in the CWA to the more immediate and pressing concerns residents faced during project planning and construction, including potential displacement and upheaval from the redevelopment process. As a staff member put it, residents were "in survival mode." A resident described the disruption facing the community, saying that everything "changed so quickly." Construction on SHA and private land produced jarring impacts on their otherwise "peaceful community."[66] While Yesler Terrace changes drew residents' concerns and attention related to the redevelopment project, community participation in CWA implementation disproportionately occurred only through the formal, ongoing, SHA-created advisory committee. By all accounts, Yesler Terrace residents showed little interest in the CWA or its implementation.

Therefore, the Section 3 Advisory Committee functioned as the only real CWA oversight mechanism, outside of direct agreement administration by SHA staff. According to the CWA terms, the Section 3 Advisory Committee was broadly intended to "monitor" contractor performance along social equity goals and "advise" SHA and contractors on how to better meet these targets.[67] Among the committee members, noncompliance was reportedly a widely acknowledged potential problem. One stakeholder explained the need for proactive oversight: "sometimes, if no one is tracking [contractors], they'll complete the project and hardly anyone will get hired, and they're like *oh* [pauses], or they don't do the outreach they should do in order to get people in." In this way, key actors acknowledged the committee's important role in outcomes production, to ensure that the contractors, unions, and SHA coordinated their activities during implementation to identify and hire targeted workers as construction proceeded.[68]

However, the Section 3 Advisory Committee did not appear to substantially influence contractor behavior to improve community outcomes. Some argued that the Section 3 Advisory Committee drove enforcement through its oversight role, due to reporting requirements by SHA and contractors. Committee members could review reports, ask questions, and generally problem-solve challenges that arose. But a reactive approach is poorly suited to avoiding problems from the outset or even as they arise, to create better outcomes before a contract or policy ends. When CWA outcomes lagged, the committee could only confront contractors about their underperformance during meetings—with no power to assess penalties, to promote enforcement. Without the ability to assess penalties, the committee could only exert minimal pressure on contractors and SHA, lacking any real levers for accountability besides shaming contractors into compliance. Further, SHA only infrequently undertakes redevelopment projects and does not have enough bidders on projects as it is. Therefore, the threat of developing a bad relationship with the agency appeared to provide only slight incentive for contractors to comply with the agreement terms.[69] With little public attention and no real threat to contractors, the CWA offered no substantial mechanisms to motivate compliance.

Therefore, as both project owner and CWA administrator, and with little enforceable oversight, SHA dominated implementation. As one respondent noted, if SHA "isn't willing to hold their feet to the fire, the contractor runs and says, I'm out of here. I'm going to do whatever I want." This same individual argued that the CWA achieved some outcomes because SHA was willing to hold parties accountable, as Yesler Terrace is "a very high-profile project" and, therefore, faced additional scrutiny. This individual further speculated that personal and institutional commitment shaped implementation because SHA "want[s] to do right by the project and by the folks" living in Yesler Terrace. Regardless, however, agreement outcomes remained undisclosed to the public, and neither SHA staff nor contractors expressed a compelling need to meet all the established targets. Rather, they appeared satisfied to give what they perceived as their best effort implementing an agreement that is widely acknowledged to be difficult to implement. Absent significant oversight, they lacked motivation and necessary support to fight to deliver all the promised outcomes, consistent with the original goals.[70] Even as community outcomes on the development became contested, however, SHA received accolades for the agency's work: one of the new Yesler Terrace buildings, Raven Terrace, was named the best public housing redevelopment of 2017 by Affordable Housing Finance.[71]

Throughout, contractors remained primarily concerned with achieving profitable, timely, and effective construction projects. Some expressed a commitment to CWA compliance and a desire to preserve relationships so that their company would be considered for future bids. However, with few bidders for these projects, eligibility for future contracts did not create a significant threat. Rather, contractors appeared largely motivated to maintain business as usual, which was easier and more cost-effective, instead of targeting historically excluded workers and supporting these workers on construction sites, consistent with the agreement governing this development.[72]

The CWA's negotiation shaped agreement implementation, as the community bypass that characterized agreement negotiation extended into implementation. Community stakeholders exerted only weak pressure over the original agreement, with some engagement from activist organizations but without significant participation by the agreement beneficiaries. During implementation, community involvement in oversight occurred only through the Section 3 Advisory Committee, which held no effective levers to motivate the contractors and unions to produce community outcomes and ensure accountability. In this agreement, the community did not drive the process through a watchdog role. Many speculated that community enforcement did not materialize because residents themselves were not that interested in these jobs. With limited community outreach, however, there is little evidence that residents knew critical details about these job opportunities or had the information and abilities to access construction careers absent substantial guidance and preapprenticeship training.

In this way, Yesler Terrace agreement signatories *bypassed* community beneficiaries in important ways during both agreement formulation and implementation. They did not involve Yesler Terrace residents in an influential role from the beginning of the process, a context that produced no significant resident influence over the agreement outcomes. Altogether, residents and activists did not attempt to shape implementation outside of participation on the advisory committee. Rather, SHA, contractors, and unions implemented the agreement largely unchecked, and without outside pressure to focus on Yesler Terrace residents.

Furthermore, the lingering distrust and resentment from CWA negotiations drove unions to pursue the most expedient route to produce Section 3 outcomes, while protecting their own interests: to both secure union jobs and to overcome the perception of persistent discrimination within construction unions. Individuals cited other agreements in the region with high diversity numbers, such as the lauded Elliot Bay Seawall project, as evidence that insufficient diversity within construction unions was not the primary issue undermining Yesler Terrace CWA implementation. Regardless, union stakeholders repeatedly expressed concern that they (a) would be blamed for inadequate worker inclusion and (b) would not meet their secondary goal of demonstrating to the broader public that unions are more diverse than widely understood. Union stakeholders reported that for these reasons, they needed the agreement goals to materialize, which drove them to pursue Section 3 outcomes, even when others provided insufficient support. In this way, the unions' public image offered the most significant demonstrated accountability mechanism during agreement implementation. As a result, union representatives remained the most dedicated to the agreement terms—if not the envisioned community outcomes. Throughout, however, their priorities remained aligned with promoting urban growth. Unions sought to improve union-community relationships to ensure the continued relevance of labor unions, particularly in an era of influential community organizing over local development.[73]

However, unions alone could not direct Yesler Terrace residents into these jobs since they needed outreach and hiring assistance from SHA and the contractors. Even still, unions could control some outcomes if they reclassified and referred their own workers who met Section 3 status. This is exactly what the unions did, taking the most viable path toward meeting the specified agreement outcomes. This approach enabled them to improve outcomes without having to rely on other, potentially less committed stakeholders. Fundamentally, however, the focus on hiring Section 3 workers already employed in construction unions did not advance the original spirit of the CWA, since it did not create new construction careers for residents affected by Yesler Terrace redevelopment. Due to community bypass, community beneficiaries were detached from the agreement process and outcomes, and more focused on potential neighborhood change and displacement. As a result, no one was left to pressure the unions, SHA, and the contractors to fully deliver on their original promises to Yesler Terrace residents—or to check the agency's claims of success.

The Results

Altogether, the Yesler Terrace redevelopment project has produced mixed and complex results, including and beyond the CWA expressly intended to redistribute project benefits. Residents have publicly described a significant sense of loss, but many reported enjoying the new amenities, including views from the apartment towers. Some of those who stayed expressed missing the gardens and the sense of community that existed before the redevelopment. Indeed, the high-rise apartment style, with locked buildings, fundamentally changed the open nature of socializing in the community.[74]

However, a preliminary analysis from a study examining the effects of the Yesler Terrace redevelopment on resident health found some positive results.

From 2012 to 2016, in the middle of Yesler Terrace redevelopment, residents saw higher levels of perceived safety and social cohesion. The scholars who conducted the study attributed the increase in perceived safety to a combination of self-selection, where those with lowest levels of perceived safety or a preference for different housing left, as well as the removal of nearby encampments of people experiencing homelessness.[75]

Throughout, however, evidence suggests that even though residents were primarily focused on avoiding displacement and maintaining their quality of life, many residents did move, and the community demographics have fundamentally changed. In a presentation to the city council in July 2016, SHA executive director Andrew Lofton reported that more than a third of the nearly five hundred families living in Yesler Terrace before redevelopment were no longer living in the public housing community. Of the residents who moved, approximately 90 percent had relocated within the Seattle region. A resident explained the rationale for residents to leave, even if they could stay: "if it's not going to be the way it was, what you loved, what's the point of staying?" The disappointing results at Yesler Terrace parallel events around the preceding Rainier Vista redevelopment, where in 2009, activists had to threaten additional litigation after the housing authority ran out of federal funds to finish the last quarter of the project and proposed walking back its mandated commitments.[76] In 2020, King County Equity Now, a community group affiliated with Black Lives Matter, called for stopping the Yesler Terrace redevelopment project because of the displacement that the project produced and the lack of inclusion of Black residents throughout the process.[77]

Indeed, many foresaw the displacement and gentrification that has unfolded. In 2012, David Bloom, representative for the Seattle Displacement Coalition, testified that Yesler Terrace redevelopment "uses city funds to subsidize a megaproject that will be dominated by luxury condos. It leaves less public housing on-site and a conspicuous loss of trees. It's a blueprint for gentrification in the area."[78] A decade later, Bloom's comment rings true. The neighborhood surrounding Yesler Terrace has transformed into an intensely gentrifying part of a rapidly changing city, dominated by new, market-rate housing. Affordability is no longer the focus. The Yesler Terrace project itself displaced many of its original residents, contributing to this broader neighborhood change pattern. At the same time, as Vulcan has proceeded with the market-rate development, the company leaned into the neighborhood character as a selling point. A residential marketing manager noted the positive design aspects stressing that Batik, one of the new buildings, "felt multicultural" with "a lot of color and texture."[79]

Currently, the neighborhood surrounding Yesler Terrace reflects Seattle's contemporary challenges, with an expensive housing market, rising regional inequality, and a growing homelessness crisis. While a benefits agreement could never forestall the neighborhood change occurring in the area, the Yesler Terrace CWA—in the terms it promised, its implementation, and the outcomes produced—did little to change this trajectory or ensure that existing residents directly benefitted economically from new investment. Rather, the cumulative impact of these changes in the public housing community signal that the land—once entirely dedicated to the nation's first integrated public housing community—is no longer focused on the needs of Seattle's low-income residents. As a *Next City* article described, "While the worst fear of Yesler Terrace residents—that they'd lose their public housing entirely—has not been realized, the redevelopment appears to have accelerated gentrification in the adjacent neighborhoods of Little Saigon and the International District. These enclaves, like Yesler, provide an ethnically, economically inclusive place in an increasingly rich and tech-dominated Seattle."[80] One resident summarized the situation, saying that, "The buildings, the highrise[s], are not for us."[81]

This sentiment—that the redevelopment in question and the benefits agreement that governs the project were not fundamentally intended to benefit existing residents—has defined both the Atlanta and Seattle cases. These concerns also arose in events surrounding the Park East Redevelopment Compact in Milwaukee, which is the focus of the next chapter. However, unlike in Atlanta and Seattle, negotiations around the Milwaukee agreement were widely viewed as successful. Regardless, implementation of the Milwaukee agreement was delayed for nearly a decade because of the economic recession. Over this time, the original stakeholders moved on from the agreement, creating impactful disconnects between the public managers responsible for agreement implementation, the public officials managing oversight, and the community activists once engaged in this process. Developers exploited this *managerial disconnect* to avoid delivering on the agreement's promised benefits.

Therefore, the Milwaukee agreement, like those in Atlanta and Seattle, illustrates how developers look to use benefits-sharing agreements as a tool to expedite development. Without effective agreement oversight and continuing community vigilance, developers can successfully accomplish this goal while avoiding their broader obligations. However, events in Milwaukee illustrate how an effective agreement alone does not accomplish results. Rather, successful deliberations represent a necessary but not sufficient condition to ensure benefits delivery, since issues can arise during implementation to undermine results—regardless of how promising the agreement initially appeared.

CHAPTER 3

Managerial Disconnect: The Park East Redevelopment Compact

Years of opposition from Milwaukee residents led city officials to abandon the Park East Freeway project in the mid-1970s. This action left a one-mile elevated stretch of the freeway that had already been completed. The underused, stranded freeway spur remained intact for decades. It impeded mobility into downtown Milwaukee, decreased the value of neighboring land, and fractured the street grid. For years, the freeway spur disrupted daily life and functionality near downtown. Many viewed the spur as a barrier to downtown redevelopment, with acres of land already cleared for a project that never came to fruition.[1]

The freeway spur was the last remnant of the Park East Freeway project. The larger plan that the project originally advanced promised to encircle downtown Milwaukee with freeways, accommodate anticipated future growth, and ease congestion in the Milwaukee central business district. Unfolding concurrently with the nationwide "freeway revolts" movement that opposed ongoing urban highway construction and related neighborhood harm, the Milwaukee freeway plan raised concerns that the expressway would obstruct the waterfront and harm the local community. Project opponents in the surrounding neighborhoods began organizing in the mid-1960s and eventually secured a court injunction against the project in 1971. After a judge issued a permanent injunction in 1972, proponents abandoned the project. But the freeway spur remained, an enduring concrete symbol of the failed project.[2]

While the freeway was only partially built, the land had already been cleared, severely harming the "thriving Black neighborhood" within which the highway project took place.[3] Despite opposition and protests from residents, the evictions that occurred in the late 1960s cleared land for the anticipated freeway. The Park East Freeway was part of a larger pattern in the city and beyond, where freeways constructed between 1959 and 1971 across Milwaukee County displaced almost 20,000 residents and eliminated more than 6,300 homes. Urban renewal projects undertaken at this time notoriously occurred within and harmed communities of color; events in Milwaukee paralleled this broader pattern. The nearby North-South Expressway, in particular, displaced 600 families when it "cleared a path through sixteen blocks in the city's Black community . . . ultimately intensifying patterns of residential segregation."[4] Displacement represented but one of the harmful outcomes that freeway projects created. By the time the city terminated the Park East Freeway project, the completed one-mile stretch through the Park East corridor had also cut off those who remained from easy access to downtown jobs.[5]

In 1998, Milwaukee mayor John Norquist, an antifreeway advocate who was part of the nationwide freeway teardown movement, led the effort to remove the spur. His efforts faced opposition from locals worried about additional traffic. As part of the freeway demolition movement, advocates sought to repair the neighborhoods that were harmed by the initial projects, to build back toward an urban vision that prioritized walkability and human interaction over car-oriented cities. Mayor Norquist perceived the spur as blight and as a barrier to development. He strongly advocated for removal, which would avoid the estimated $80 million or more needed for freeway repairs and reconstruction. Beyond these considerations, the freeway spur was located in a desirable location adjacent to the Milwaukee River and downtown. For this reason, Norquist viewed demolition as an opportunity to pursue renewed investment in downtown Milwaukee and the surrounding neighborhoods.[6]

Delayed by a lawsuit, it was not until 2002, years before Arthur Blank began publicly advocating for a new stadium in Atlanta, and as planning was beginning on Seattle's Yesler Terrace, that the City of Milwaukee was finally able to begin demolishing the freeway spur. The teardown left twenty-six acres of land near downtown Milwaukee, within a sixty-four–acre redevelopment corridor, available to potential redevelopment.[7] An opportunity stood before the City of Milwaukee: it could pursue development differently, with community benefits attached to the physical transformation of the land. What ultimately occurred, however, was an opportunity only partially realized.

With the freeway spur gone, many saw the redevelopment of the now-cleared Park East land as a potential "catalyst" for up to $250 million in development projects in the area. This vision became a key component of the downtown revitalization that advocates hoped would occur in the early 2000s.[8] The Park East land included sixteen county-owned acres, divided into distinct parcels intended for separate developments. The entire twenty-six acres existed within a newly established tax increment financing district in the City of Milwaukee.[9] The Downtown Milwaukee Plan, the land use document governing the area, encouraged mixed-use development on the Park East land, with open space and a connection to the Milwaukee River and the now trendy Milwaukee RiverWalk.[10]

This chapter describes the attempts to redevelop the Park East land after the remaining spur from the never-completed freeway project was removed. Redevelopment planning began in the early 2000s; development has continued into the 2020s. Local activists saw an opportunity to use the cleared land to create local benefits. They worked with city and county officials to create a benefits agreement to govern redevelopment on the land. After a political battle with then county executive (and later Wisconsin governor) Scott Walker, the Park East Redevelopment Compact (PERC) was approved in 2004. The policy represented a major step forward for the community benefits movement. It was the first community benefits agreement in Milwaukee. As well, the PERC was the first community benefits policy in the nation to govern more than an individual project. Rather, this policy encompasses all development projects across a large tract of urban land: the final policy covers the entire sixteen acres of Park East land once owned by the County of Milwaukee.[11]

While the policy passed in 2004, policy implementation did not begin in earnest until almost a decade later. As this chapter describes, these intervening years critically affected community benefits implementation and outcomes. While initially a committee met to review contracts and enforce the community benefits provisions, involving community advocates, the economic recession of the mid-2000s stalled development in downtown Milwaukee. The land remained dormant while no developers advanced projects, delaying community benefits. Eventually, the committee stopped meeting. Most of the original stakeholders who advocated for the agreement moved on to other projects or jobs and, in some cases, to other cities altogether. The county government leaders who fought for the progressive policy turned their attention to fight new political battles with Scott Walker, who drove a sharp conservative turn in state politics.

As a result, once local development picked up with a strengthened economy, few of the original stakeholders remained to monitor PERC implementation, share institutional and policy knowledge, and ensure that the policy they had fought to pass would deliver on its promises. Therefore, while the Milwaukee agreement began with community advocacy that paralleled the Atlanta agreement, by the time the policy moved to implementation, the absence of community engagement resembled events around Yesler Terrace in Seattle. And while local leaders were once actively engaged and responsive, their attention had also shifted away from the PERC.

Without consistent engagement from the community and local government leaders who had since moved on, PERC implementation was left to county employees. As implementation proceeded, these county staff lacked essential resources, including institutional knowledge, a deep understanding and history of this policy, active oversight from local leaders, and necessary support for policy enforcement. The absence of active top-down oversight to create leverage, and community activists to push for enforcement and share information, left agreement administrators facing a crucial *managerial disconnect*. This managerial disconnect reflected a consequential distance in oversight between the public managers that execute the policy, on the one hand, and, on the other hand, both the oversight body with leverage over implementation and community activists who could otherwise have provided political support for the policy and shared information on the ground—as they did in Atlanta. Similar to the Seattle case, this context left agreement administrators with considerable discretion and insufficient support to ensure policy enforcement.

While these public managers pursued policy enforcement regardless, development interests sometimes exploited this managerial disconnect to minimize their obligations under the PERC. Therefore, while the Milwaukee agreement began very differently than the Atlanta and Seattle agreements, implementation changed this policy's trajectory. Rather, the result in Milwaukee resembles community benefits outcomes in Atlanta and Seattle in an important way: absent pressure from other actors, Milwaukee development interests found ways to avoid delivering community benefits consistent with the original agreement goals.

The Fight for Community Benefits

With the Park East land cleared for redevelopment, local government actors worked with developers and business interests to put forward the Park East redevelopment plan to guide land development. In 2002, as the City of

Milwaukee Common Council[12] reviewed the plan for the sixty-four–acre area, local unions and community organizations noted that the redevelopment plan was proceeding without significant public participation. As a result, the plan had paid little attention to job creation and job quality, despite the large estimated impact of the proposed development.[13]

To address what they saw as an opportunity to leverage future development for local benefits, unions and community organizations representing affordable housing and economic development interests began working together to call for community benefits related to the Park East redevelopment. The groups created the Good Jobs and Livable Neighborhoods Coalition, advocating for a community benefits agreement with the City of Milwaukee related to all the parcels across the twenty-six–acre site. The coalition first met in January 2003, with representatives from roughly twenty-five organizations, including labor, religious institutions, and affected residents. The coalition also involved Citizen Action of Wisconsin, an affiliate organization of the Partnership for Working Families. The Good Jobs and Livable Neighborhoods Coalition did not have any paid staff, but instead involved people from different organizations who similarly sought to advance a policy that could generate local benefits.[14]

The coalition used the Los Angeles Staples Center community benefits agreement as a model for its proposal, a policy similarly driven by a Partnership for Working Families affiliate, the Los Angeles Alliance for a New Economy (LAANE). Based on this work, the coalition submitted a proposal to the mayor and the City of Milwaukee Common Council. This original proposal suggested benefits ranging across environmental justice, economic development, affordable housing, and community services concerns. Among other specifications, the coalition sought to ensure that three of every four jobs created by Park East development paid a living wage and offered health benefits. Developers strongly opposed the proposal on the basis that the additional regulations and associated costs would deter much-needed, broadly beneficial development in a downtown area that was struggling to compete with suburban development.[15]

Despite significant opposition by developers, the Common Council Steering and Rules Committee approved the agreement for developments with public funding, at a time when many council members were up for reelection. This action forwarded the policy to the Common Council. After the election, however, some alderman who had previously expressed public support for the agreement changed their stance. The Common Council voted to approve the redevelopment plan without the benefits agreement. The coalition attributed the policy rejection to insufficient pressure from community residents, who had lost significant leverage over public officials after the election, the desire of council members to support development interests, as well as the absence of an avid champion from the community or within local government.[16]

After the loss in the City of Milwaukee, members of the Milwaukee County Board of Supervisors reportedly contacted the coalition about potential community benefits on the sixteen acres of Park East land owned by the county within the redevelopment area. Developers appeared to exert less influence over the county board of supervisors than the City of Milwaukee Common Council. With political interest and the potential to secure benefits on one-third of the Park East land, the coalition turned its attention to the county parcels. While only covering a fraction of the original land under consideration, momentum built for a benefits agreement with the county. The coalition received support from several county supervisors. Together, they formulated a new version of their original community benefits agreement that became the PERC. The coalition advocated for a broad policy that would cover all projects on the county-owned portion of the Park East land.[17]

The county board of supervisors approved the PERC, which then Milwaukee County executive Scott Walker promptly vetoed. Walker strongly opposed the legislation, contending that the agreement would reduce land value and impede development. He personally lobbied supervisors to oppose the PERC. Both Walker and his supporters and the coalition attempted to mobilize residents to contact their supervisors about the PERC, shaping public sentiment regarding the policy.[18]

Despite Walker's efforts, the legislation held a strong majority. The coalition continued to press for support among the county supervisors. The supervisors were able to overturn the veto in a 15-to-4[19] vote and "didn't lose a single vote" despite the "conservative push" that Walker mounted.[20] After approving the PERC, Supervisor Broderick discussed Walker's opposition and concerns about alienating the development community: "Where we part ways, I guess, is what you see are hurdles and barriers, we see them as opportunities. Profits are still there to be made. It may be that (developers) will achieve a little less and the community a little more."[21]

This comment, and the political battle to achieve the PERC, illustrates the deep political divisions in Milwaukee that came to shape PERC implementation. The battle over policy approval influenced how implementation would unfold, motivating agreement proponents to remain focused on combating political opposition and protecting the policy. Over time, however, agreement proponents came to focus less attention on the specific details of implementation—even though those details would deeply shape policy outcomes.[22]

The approved community benefits package related to the Park East redevelopment was groundbreaking: a county resolution, the first community benefits agreement in Milwaukee, and the first successful attempt in the nation to pass a community benefits–related policy governing development broader than an individual project.[23] As the first policy of its kind, the PERC has received significant attention from scholars, who widely laud the policy as a successful achievement for community development and equity in urban development. However, few followed the policy past implementation, to see what the policy actually produced for the intended community beneficiaries.[24] Therefore, while the PERC is widely understood as an innovative and important policy, its implementation has not been critically examined for what it has delivered and for whom—even though the policy endures, and implementation is ongoing.

This chapter shows that the PERC, a hard-won policy that resulted from political battles, faced challenges to its implementation because of political divisions that persisted after agreement approval. These divisions produced an impactful managerial disconnect, where representatives and public managers responsible for enforcing implementation experienced information and coordination disconnects that sometimes enabled developers to avoid their original commitments. These experiences suggest the need for coordinated and vigilant oversight in benefits-sharing agreement implementation. Beyond managerial disconnects, the efforts by developers to minimize their obligations under the PERC illustrate the ways in which agreements can continue to be contested during implementation.

The Park East Redevelopment Compact

Lasting for the lifetime of the tax incremental district, the PERC is not an agreement between developers and communities in the way that most community benefits agreements function. Rather, the policy specifies that when the county goes to sell each parcel that it owns within the Park East redevelopment, the county must attach community benefits to the development contract with the developer for that project.[25] During the request for proposals (RFP) process, developers put together proposals for individual or multiple land parcels.

Proposal terms include the land sale cost, planned uses and site design, and, ideally, community benefits. The county considers the merits of the various projects, including proposed community benefits, and then negotiates a development agreement with the chosen developer. Thus, the county essentially negotiates the PERC terms into the individual development contracts for each parcel sale, allowing some flexibility across projects. Concerns about potential changes in state laws motivated county supervisors to attempt to codify the PERC terms into individual development agreements to ensure that the benefits could withstand the politicization that characterized policy approval.[26]

To make community benefits possible, the PERC enables Milwaukee County to "seek development proposals which will provide the greatest future benefit in jobs, tax base and image for the communities, as well as, a fair price."[27] With this language, county supervisors sought to promote community development goals by allowing land sale for less than the appraised price, to amortize the developer's risk and provide room for negotiation. As one Milwaukee County representative explained, "Selling land at a discount is really the only thing we have, the real motivator" to generate community benefits.[28]

The adversarial and highly politicized development process in Wisconsin shaped the policy, how it takes effect, and perceptions about the future development climate—creating fragmentation across county government, where representatives held divergent views about the progressive PERC policy. Then county executive Scott Walker, later famous for dismantling much of the state's labor laws, prevailing wage requirements, and public protections as governor, contributed greatly to this disconnect. In his tenure as Milwaukee County executive, Walker sought to undermine much of the economic and community development work across the county by cutting funding and staffing the agency with his allies, arguing that regulation impeded growth. For Walker, the PERC was a key target. However, despite politicization, including many local and state attempts to undermine the PERC terms after its approval, as well as developer and project turnover, the agreement persists because it is negotiated into land development—and therefore county staff have written the terms into Park East development contracts.[29]

Terms of the Park East Redevelopment Compact

The PERC prescribes jobs, housing, and environmental benefits. The policy specifies that construction workers on the project be paid a prevailing wage through the existence of the tax increment district and that developers, contractors, and tenants report these data annually. The PERC mandates that county standards for hiring disadvantaged business enterprises (DBEs) are included in each land sale contract, as well as additional training and apprenticeship opportunities. The PERC also includes provisions to ensure local hiring, defined broadly to target individuals living within Milwaukee County. The policy establishes the goal that hiring should reflect the county's racial diversity.[30] Importantly, this broad geographic definition therefore includes both low-income and affluent areas of the county. However, since construction labor markets are quite large, and workers frequently come from Madison and other areas of the state, prioritizing workers who reside in the county requires contractors to deviate from existing construction industry practices.[31]

The PERC requires that Milwaukee County "sponsor the construction of new affordable housing of not less than 20% of the total housing units built on the County's Park East lands, but they may be built on other infill sites in the City of Milwaukee." However, the PERC also specifies that the county "may require a different percentage of affordable housing or have no requirement at all." The policy establishes that green space and green design be incorporated into proposals for the parcels, to encourage environmentally sustainable development. Altogether, these agreement terms leave significant discretion for county staff to determine affordable housing and green design requirements during individual negotiations with developers.[32]

Finally, the PERC specifies that the county establish a community and economic development (CED) fund with the revenues generated by Park East land sales. According to the PERC, the CED fund is intended to serve as a "catalyst" for "sustainable development" and "would be comprised of a series of programs designed to address 'gap' needs in the marketplace" rather than existing public services, including workforce training, economic development, and environmental mitigation.[33] According to one individual involved in PERC negotiations, the fund "wasn't as much of what the community wanted as something the supervisors thought would be kind of cool to have. Scott Walker was County Executive then. Probably had a pretty tight control on the budget. This was going to be something they couldn't get their hands on."[34] Therefore, the fund reflected the county's concerted effort to create and protect community benefits within a growth-oriented, conservative political climate, particularly after the political battles surrounding agreement formulation. The community coalition's main focus, however, was access to quality jobs, through local hire and prevailing wage provisions.[35]

Therefore, the PERC contains far-ranging provisions that county employees flexibly negotiate into development agreements. County implementation staff, within the County of Milwaukee Economic Development Division, are accountable to the county executive. Beyond Scott Walker, the Milwaukee County executive has often supported business, development, and growth interests. This political stance reflects the more conservative views of the county as a whole, including the conservative Milwaukee suburbs. However, as county employees, they also report to the county board of supervisors, who championed the benefits agreement and have historically included representatives with progressive views. Therefore, these county staff exist within a complicated political space, accountable to public officials who have traditionally held divergent political views and policy stances. Concerning the PERC and other policies, these differing perspectives have sometimes become outwardly antagonistic. These political divisions drove the managerial disconnects that emerged during PERC implementation.[36]

In practice, developers viewed the PERC benefits provisions with varying degrees of resistance. Proponents have long held that the prevailing wage is "the most powerful provision of the Park East Redevelopment Compact" since it offers the largest potential impact for residents, generating economic opportunity—particularly as historically marginalized workers gain access to the jobs produced by local development.[37] By all accounts, the prevailing wage became the most controversial PERC provision in implementation, as well: the prevailing wage is "the one [PERC requirement] that developers argue about the most" since wage requirements unavoidably raise project costs. In contrast, the green design provision reportedly elicited the least resistance from developers. Rather, developers generally viewed green design as contributing to the value of their developments, consistent with their goals.[38]

Many developers reportedly also attempted to reject the affordable housing requirement, though community stakeholders and county agreement administrators similarly attributed their refusal to misunderstanding—the PERC places mandates on the county, not developers, to ensure affordable housing. The county's effort to require affordable housing was an attempt to govern its own future behavior that further demonstrates the fundamental clash between progressive and conservative politics in Milwaukee County, which frequently emerged around land use decision-making. This conflict motivated negotiators to include as many mandates within the policy as possible, to protect community benefits against shifting politics and leadership. Altogether, conflicts over various PERC provisions illustrate how developers used the process of negotiating benefits into development agreements to differentially contest PERC requirements, influencing the outcomes the policy has enacted and achieved.[39]

To promote accountability, the PERC established the Park East Advisory Committee to oversee implementation and to participate in the RFP process. After PERC approval, the advisory committee created the primary means by which community participation in PERC implementation occurred. The PERC structure allowed the committee to influence bid selection during the RFP process to ensure that development projects would advance PERC goals. The advisory committee, including community stakeholders, would review development proposals and "as a separate body, would give a recommendation" to the Milwaukee County Board of Supervisors Economic and Community Development Committee about the project. Original committee participants included members of the Good Jobs and Livable Neighborhoods Coalition, other community groups, and the local realtors association. The PERC policy language tasks the committee with producing an annual report to the county board of supervisors, in coordination with the director of economic and community development. Similar to the PERC, the Park East Advisory Committee extends through the life of the tax incremental district within the PERC area.[40]

Recession to Implementation

Redevelopment of the Park East land stalled during the recession, which halted PERC implementation.

For most of the decade after PERC approval, many projects were proposed, and some moved forward, but little development actually occurred on the Park East land. Initially, the board of supervisors approved multiple projects: Park East Square, a two-phase $65 million project with hotels, apartments, and retail; the roughly $150 million Palomar Hotel and Residences, which also included retail; and the Marcus Theatres project, with a movie theatre and office and retail space. The Palomar Hotel and Residences project fell through in 2009 because of low demand for housing downtown and restricted lending after the financial downturn. The Park East Square project faced lengthy financing delays. The Marcus Theatres project halted when the corporation's option ran out in September 2014; the company was never able to attract tenants to fill the office building.[41]

The timing of the recession proved disastrous and enduring for initial development on the Park East project—though some blame the PERC, faulting the county for attaching additional regulations to the land. By 2009, the county had sold only one parcel, though the project had "been delayed indefinitely."[42] The Park East Square project, renamed Avenir Apartments, began moving forward only in 2012, after a new developer, Wangard Partners, joined the project and was able to secure financing. The project was completed in 2015 and sold in 2018 for $22.3 million. It was only the second project to begin construction on the land. Previously, the Milwaukee School of Engineering, located adjacent to the Park East land, built a parking garage with a soccer field on top on one of the parcels, completed in 2013 (see Figures 7 and 8).[43]

In 2012, Kohl's Corporation attempted to bring its headquarters to the Park East redevelopment area. To move the development project forward, the proposal would have sold the land to the corporation at a low cost and included an estimated $145 million in financial incentives. Community

Figure 7. Milwaukee School of Engineering parking structure and soccer field (photo by author).

Figure 8. Map of Park East parcels (sources: Esri, DigitalGlobe, GeoEye, i-cubed, USDA FSA, USGS, AEX, Getmapping, Aerogrid, IGN, IGP, swisstopo, and the GIS User Community).

advocates hesitated to support the project, despite the pressing need to develop the vacant land, since the corporate relocation would likely not bring new, long-term quality jobs to the area. In the end, however, Kohl's decided against the relocation and the development project never materialized—though local officials cited even the attention from Kohl's as progress past the stalled development situation.[44]

As the Park East land faced low demand for development, the area to the east (and therefore not subject to the PERC) had many successfully completed redevelopment projects over this same period. These projects include construction of the Moderne apartments, a high-rise building, the North End apartments, the Flatiron Condominiums, and the Aloft Hotel. Figure 9 shows the Aloft Hotel, with the vacant Park East parcels in the background. This larger area also exists within the Park East tax increment district.[45] And yet, while other community benefits agreements would have fallen through when developers move on, the PERC persisted because the county attached the policy to the land itself, rather than a specific proposal.

Figure 9. Aloft Hotel with vacant Park East parcels in the background (photo by author).

County and community representatives, who maintained that the PERC is a valuable community development policy, largely attributed delayed development to the economic downturn of the mid-2000s. The recession, which halted demand for real estate development and made it more difficult to finance large development projects, began just after agreement approval. According to a county representative, during the recession, "Many developers tried to present proposals, and there were times when the developers . . . would give us deposits so they could work on doing what needed to be done. But in most cases, the projects fell through, projects weren't completed, projects weren't even initiated, because it was so hard to get the packaging of finances in order to go forward with the project."[46] In her highly cited article on community benefits agreements, Laura Wolf-Powers (2010) reached a similar conclusion, attributing failed projects to the recession. She used the PERC as evidence that community benefits agreements require a strong real estate market, such that project demand exceeds the (real or perceived) additional costs of providing community benefits.[47]

Beyond poor economic conditions, brownfields issues and lingering freeway remnants on the Park East land created additional uncertainty about the land and increased cost projections, which deterred development. The original freeway removal only addressed aboveground construction and did not remove the underground pillars built to stabilize the freeway. Developers would have to address the underground pillars, as well engage in costly brownfields and related environmental remediation work, before building on the land. As one county representative said, "[the land] is such a mess. There's really no way around it, it is such a mess."[48]

However, different parcels had varying degrees of environmental, brownfields, and grading issues, which partially explains why some were particularly slow to generate interest. The eastside of the freeway "never really got completely built. There aren't as many piers there. It's an area where there's a lot more built-up around it, so those were the more attractive pieces." The eastside portion of the PERC land developed more quickly, while the westside was "kind of this barren wasteland" with storm sewers, fuel piers, and brownfield issues from industrial manufacturing use. Because of the combination of industrial issues and the known costs associated with remediation, developers perceived this land as a riskier investment, with land issues that likely would become fully apparent only with construction activity.[49] Figure 10, a photo from late 2015, shows the parcels that laid vacant for more than a decade. Development proceeded on the land that laid PERC did not cover, including the high-rise Moderne luxury apartment building—all while the Park East land remained dormant.

Local government and community participants also attributed early development delays to political and bureaucratic disconnects across jurisdictions and divisions, which slowed the RFP process. Developers reportedly often included city-governed stipulations in their county proposals, such as parking structures and environmental remediation. Without a city representative in the original RFP process, the county would approve a project dedicating city resources, only to have the city refuse to provide the proposed benefits. After many failed attempts, the county worked to bring the city into the RFP process, to streamline development approval and enable all parties to assess project feasibility from the outset. One local developer attributed this improved process, demonstrated in the improved cooperation between the city and county around the Kohl's development proposal, to a "quantum step forward" for Park East.[50] In this way, it took time, and the concerted efforts

Figure 10. Western Park East parcels with brownfield issues (photo by author).

of all parties, for stakeholders to figure out how to effectively implement the complex policy and overcome impactful disconnects.

Further complicating implementation, the Wisconsin Department of Transportation (WisDOT) retained oversight of the freeway spur even after the agency turned jurisdiction over to the County of Milwaukee. Because of the funding involved, the Federal Highway Administration also gained some oversight, with repayment on land sale. Therefore, the County of Milwaukee needed a federal exemption and memorandum of understanding to sell the land for less than fair market value, due to the input that both agencies had over the land sale price. With the most interest in ensuring community outcomes, the county fought hard to sell the land for less than market value and brought these different stakeholders into the RFP process to further streamline the complex development process. Finally, to compound fragmentation issues, Walker let the position of economic development director sit vacant for years, even temporarily abolishing the position, which made it more difficult for county development projects to progress.[51]

Therefore, economic conditions, land issues, and managerial disconnects coincided to frustrate early efforts to develop the Park East land. In defense of the PERC, one county representative said, "the PERC gets a really bad rap. And it's not because it was bad legislation. It just didn't come at a very good time; the market wasn't super strong then, or even if the market was strong initially, the communication between the city and the county wasn't there. So, projects were failing, not because of the PERC, but because the county wasn't cooperating with the city, and you need the intergovernmental cooperation in order to have a successful development."[52] In this way, even though development failed to materialize on much of the Park East land for over a decade after the land became available for development, the benefits policy represented only one factor influencing development activity on the land.

Pro-development interests, however, largely blamed the PERC for stalled development. To them, the PERC added additional, costly regulation, which deterred developers from even proposing projects. For developers, therefore, the PERC requirements necessitated other funds such as government subsidies, otherwise some projects became no longer viable—despite heavy land discounts from the county. To developers, prevailing wage requirements posed a particular disincentive, since the provision unavoidably raised wages, directly increasing project costs. One developer estimated that the prevailing wage requirement could add 8 to 10 percent to the final project cost. In contrast, the requirements for disadvantaged business utilization, for example, could be achieved without necessarily increasing costs, but simply by hiring different subcontractors.[53]

To encourage additional development amid developer reluctance, and after the failed Kohl's Corporation proposal, the county and city teamed with the Commercial Association of Realtors to launch a marketing campaign. The campaign, which began in 2014, was intended to "create badly-needed buzz" around the Park East and "rebrand" the area.[54] At a press conference announcing the marketing plan and streamlined approval process, then mayor Tom Barrett claimed that "we think this area is ready to explode."[55] City Development Commissioner Rocky Marcoux echoed this statement by saying, "I think we can honestly say it's a new day for the Park East."[56]

Development accelerates with the Milwaukee Bucks proposal.
It was not until the latter half of 2015, however, that the PERC land began receiving significant interest after a proposal from the new owners

of the Milwaukee Bucks basketball team. A new stadium had long been the rumored goal of then Milwaukee County executive Chris Abele and local business interests. The existing Bucks arena was located near the Park East land, and the owners began moving forward to build a new arena on a site directly next to the Park East land. The Bucks owners saw an opportunity for a large new development. The Bucks owners are experienced and wealthy hedge fund managers including Marc Lasry, Wes Edens, and Jamie Dinan, who have a combined estimated net worth of roughly $5 billion. As one community representative put it, the owners "don't really know anything about sports per se, but what they do know is how to build retail and develop."[57]

When the new owners bought the team, they included a clause in their offer that the team could be moved from Milwaukee if they did not get a new arena—and the Bucks ownership and the National Basketball Association threatened exactly that. Beyond a new arena, the owners wanted to build an entertainment complex next door, to capture the economic spillover that the team generated, particularly after development picked up with a strengthening economy. The undeveloped Park East land provided sufficient acreage for the project, and the Bucks owners expressed interest in purchasing the westside parcels.[58] Given renewed interest in redevelopment in downtown Milwaukee and the new arena proposal, team owners saw an opportunity. The vacant land next to the new arena was suddenly ripe for development.

In September 2015, the county sold ten acres west of the Milwaukee River to the Milwaukee Bucks majority owners. The land was estimated at $8.8 million but was sold for one dollar, consistent with the PERC terms. Known environmental remediation that the land requires, including removing the freeway footings and altering the existing sewer, was estimated at approximately $8.3 million.[59] The Bucks development on the PERC land was estimated at $400 million and, with the now-completed arena, exceeds $1 billion in development in the area. This includes a new $31 million practice facility for the Milwaukee Bucks, as well as housing, restaurants, and office buildings. The arena development alone cost an estimated at $524 million, drawing $250 million in public funding from various sources, including new bonds and city and state funds.[60] The local economic impact is significant: the Bucks proposal was estimated to generate $5 million in property taxes each year, and more than 3,700 jobs, of which 1,000 were expected to be permanent, including 700 office jobs and 100 grocery store jobs.[61] From the county's perspective, because of the known and potentially additional brownfields issues on the land, the issues with attracting investment, as well as the public benefit that this large-scale development could generate, the significant land discount would pay off. As one county representative said, "rather than get the $10 million that would be a face value estimate that did not include any sort of remediation estimate . . . [county representatives] offered a dollar for the land. And we said, okay, a dollar now for a $400 million development here or just nothing. Let's take the $400 million."[62]

In total, the Bucks ownership paid for only roughly half the cost of the new arena, with state and other public revenue covering $250 million. After including the associated costs, subsidies, materials, and tax exemptions, one local investigative report estimated that the total cost for taxpayers would reach $800 million—directly benefitting the wealthy ownership, who have raised ticket costs since the stadium opened in 2018. Further, the new ownership will keep much of the revenue, including all the naming rights money (up to $120 million) and part of the parking fees.[63] A *New York Times* article highlighted the project's inherent contradiction, given the public funds supporting the project during a time of deep austerity throughout the state, championed by political leadership—most notably, then governor Scott Walker. The state legislature, supported by Walker, cut the University of Wisconsin system budget by $250 million in 2015, yet Walker simultaneously pushed for a similar amount of public subsidies for the Bucks project. The article noted opposition from Black residents, in particular, in a city where the Black population is around 40 percent. The article cited local assemblyman Jonathan Brostoff, who objected that the project represented a significant payoff to "two of the richest people in the U.S.A."[64]

The timing of the new stadium was "completely coincidental" in aligning with the RFP for the land. The proposed Bucks development reportedly temporarily slowed other proposals, as developers waited to see if the Bucks development moved forward. The Bucks development plan, with a practice facility, parking, commercial, retail, and residential uses on the former county-owned and adjacent lands, was immediately expected to transform the Park East area and attract other development around downtown Milwaukee.[65] Since project approval, other developers turned their attention to the Park East land, and the adjacent land experienced renewed interest. About the recent redevelopment projects, developer Stewart Wangard publicly said, "[These projects] are reinforcing the desirability of the neighborhood. . . .

Milwaukee is on a roll. A lot of office users are considering downtown. There is momentum building."[66]

Managerial Disconnect and Park East Redevelopment Compact Implementation

However, as development finally unfolded across the Park East, making the PERC more relevant than ever, the policy has faded into the background. Those who originally fought for the agreement had moved on, and those responsible for oversight became focused on other battles. This context left county staff primarily responsible for writing the agreement terms into development agreements, with little support from others—who otherwise could have encouraged compliance and provided important information.

As a result, a crucial managerial disconnect emerged between agreement administrators and the PERC oversight body, which undermined policy enforcement during a key period of policy implementation. County staff administering the PERC reported a distant relationship with the county board of supervisors; with oversight by the county executive, staff did not actively coordinate with the board because of the persistently adversarial relationship between the county executive and the board. County board oversight became limited to periodic reporting in which board members asked questions—a reactive implementation structure that prevented their intervention to improve results before they fully materialized. Rather, under this structure, when reports revealed issues, the county board could only expose noncompliance afterward. In this way, local politics spilled over to influence PERC implementation, even after policy approval.[67]

Throughout, as with both the Atlanta and Seattle agreements, vigilant oversight proved crucial to ensure PERC benefits delivery. Developers and the business community in Milwaukee continued to oppose the PERC and additional land development regulation, and could shape policy outcomes through development agreement negotiations. As in Atlanta and Seattle, policy approval did not reconcile the core resistance by pro-growth interests to community benefits, giving developers and contractors little incentive to comply with the agreement terms unless so motivated. Therefore, even as the PERC still governed development on the land, the structure of implementation changed from when the policy was initially approved. Throughout, these events underscore that agreement approval does not necessarily ensure that the actors involved will prioritize and seek to deliver agreement outcomes.

As PERC implementation finally moved forward, most of the original participants had already moved on from vigilant oversight.

Because of delayed land redevelopment, PERC implementation has unfolded over the decades since policy approval. The new Bucks arena, now called Fiserv Forum, opened in August 2018. The final tab reached $524 million. The second phase of the Bucks development, including residential, hotels, and office buildings, is in the planning stages. Wangard Partners has pursued multiple projects in the Park East area. The mixed-use Avenir Apartments development, with apartments and retail space, was completed in 2015. Two additional projects were expected to be completed in 2018, creating around 145 new apartments, at a cost of roughly $30 million.[68] However, in late 2018, Milwaukee County announced that Wangard's option to purchase the parcel adjacent to the Avenir development had expired, and the land was listed for sale again in 2019.[69]

Despite ongoing PERC implementation, with outcomes continuing to materialize, many of those who initially participated in the agreement had moved on since the agreement was approved more than a decade before. In the initial years after PERC approval, the Park East Advisory Committee met regularly when there was a proposal to review and, by all accounts, was taken seriously by local government. In one instance where the committee did not review a proposal before it advanced to the Economic and Community Development Committee, stakeholders noted that a county supervisor held up the proposal in committee to make sure it was properly reviewed before it proceeded. Throughout these early implementation stages, some community members expressed concern that the county executive would try to strip PERC provisions through a developer-driven Park East committee, so community activists remained vigilant in the implementation process.[70] Altogether, the community and local government actively participated in initial policy implementation, through the project proposal process and the Park East committee.

However, as development proposals slowed, the committee no longer needed to meet. The committee met "five or six times to review parcels ... maybe it was 10 times," but, with little interest in land development, there was not a lot for the committee to review, and there were rarely competing projects from which to choose. As a result, the committee's role in ranking various proposals was infrequent. It also does not appear that the community ever actively oversaw PERC implementation beyond its participation in RFPs; with few developments underway, there was little opportunity for additional community involvement, since initial projects did not progress.[71]

After development picked up again, a decade later, there were proposals to review, but the committee was no longer active. Since PERC approval, both community and local government stakeholders shifted their attention elsewhere. One key staff member of the county board retired, and local government and community stakeholders attributed lost institutional memory and dedication to that person's departure. This staff member was responsible for convening committee meetings and played a significant role in PERC development and approval. For those remaining, the initial momentum had dissipated. The Park East Advisory Committee did not convene on its own and, while some supervisors expressed strong continued support for the PERC, the board did not take an active leadership role in PERC oversight after the lull in development activity. Even as the Bucks development proceeded through the initial planning stages, the committee had not convened since before the current county executive's tenure, and since far before the surge in development interest on the Park East land.[72]

Therefore, despite the PERC process creating a structure for policy enforcement, the established committee did not meet to review the new Milwaukee Bucks development proposal. According to a community stakeholder, one supervisor "was going to convene [the committee], and then we just weren't convened... [some] members didn't live in Milwaukee anymore. We had had a dialogue about it, and then it didn't happen." Key local government representatives believed that the committee *did* meet to discuss the Bucks development, though committee members maintained otherwise. One community representative attributed this misunderstanding by government officials to the former committee chair testifying to the county board about the project. Indeed, some community advocacy did attempt to shape the Bucks proposal, even though it did not proceed under the Park East Advisory Committee. According to one individual, "people were working on it in different segments, whether it was talking to country supervisors or talking to the people who handled the approvals or talking up at the state legislature.... We just weren't convened under the Park East Committee banner to do it."[73]

Regardless, because of community advocacy and encouragement from the city, the Milwaukee Bucks development approval dedicated some community benefits. Among these, the development included community workforce provisions to require contractors to pay a prevailing wage and to hire 40 percent of its construction workers from the Residents Preference Program, including unemployed or underemployed residents of the city of Milwaukee. The franchise further committed $375,000 to worker training and workforce development, to ensure that residents could access the targeted jobs. The city agreed to match this funding. The Bucks also agreed to a wage floor of $12.50 per hour for service-sector jobs at the new arena, with union representation, after significant negotiation with local labor unions. The wage floor specifies that wages increase in 50-cent increments each year until $15 is reached in 2023.[74] In this way, the Milwaukee Bucks development includes a similar spirit of community benefits, with a focus on high-quality jobs, but established separately from the PERC process.

However, even though the Bucks appeared to have largely met the established hiring requirements, the significant public funding underlying the project triggered outcry that the scale of local benefit did not match the profit that the owners secured. In particular, the naming rights sale proved controversial. Fiserv received $12.5 million in state tax breaks for the company to remain in the state, leading multiple state senators to argue that the state essentially subsidized the purchase of naming rights for a company that made an estimated $1.2 billion in profits in 2017.[75] Altogether, the development has further enriched the Bucks' wealthy owners; estimates from Forbes show that the franchise's value has grown from the $550 million purchase price in 2014 to $1.35 billion in 2019.[76]

Fragmentation and disconnects have undermined PERC implementation.

Therefore, while community representatives demonstrated significant continued interest in local development and community benefits organizing, they were no longer focused on the PERC—even though the hard-fought policy still governs the land and PERC oversight has remained necessary. By all accounts, the formerly influential committee, empowered to oversee the agreement, became dormant during a key implementation stage. Further, the county board became detached from active PERC oversight even as significant development projects proceeded on the Park East land. Instead, county representatives, despite valuing the policy, left PERC implementation to those who negotiate the individual development agreements. In this way, the decade of stalled land development dispelled initial momentum around the agreement and its enforcement, while advocates shifted to organizing along alternate, and sometimes parallel, avenues. Separate, ad hoc negotiations have proceeded for new projects.[77]

With minimal top-down oversight from local leadership on the one hand and external, grassroots oversight from the community on the other hand, PERC administration was left largely to the county staff tasked with issuing RFPs and negotiating development contracts. However, given significant personnel turnover since PERC approval, key individuals deeply involved in policy approval and initial implementation moved on or retired. Reportedly, even as of late 2015, with the Bucks development underway, no member of the Economic Development Division had worked in the agency before 2013. Regardless, staff members expressed a deep commitment to the spirit of the PERC, using their legal backgrounds and experience with community benefits agreements to support implementation. Local government and community stakeholders similarly expressed trust that economic development staff have worked hard to implement the PERC.[78]

Despite their avowed and recognized commitment, however, county staff members overseeing implementation lacked important information related to the policy—including advisory committee membership, since the body had not been active during their entire tenure. County staff also expressed unfamiliarity with PERC provisions such as the CED fund. In fact, by the time development picked up after the recession, no one involved with PERC implementation seemed to remember what happened to the community fund. According to some, the land sales may have contributed to a workforce development program, but they did not know if the CED fund "was ever actually formally established"—even though, according to the agreement terms, the fund should still exist.[79] These events demonstrate the challenges inherent to implementing an agreement over a long time frame, particularly absent institutionalized, resourced oversight mechanisms.

Facing key knowledge gaps, new staff learned how to administer the agreement as development picked up, but these challenges effectively delayed reporting and made it difficult to track PERC outcomes publicly. Detailed implementation knowledge, such as which performance metrics yield the most relevant data, is critical to effective oversight but requires expertise. County employees claimed that most projects were meeting their community benefits outcomes. However, at the time of research, it was not possible to independently verify outcomes. County administrators noted that they lacked the "time to [input data] in real time . . . data entry is always last on the list because it has to be." However, even as late as 2015, far into PERC implementation, staff inputted data manually using Excel spreadsheets and did not publicly report these data. This cumbersome, obscured approach delayed data analysis and reporting and limited transparency.[80]

However, county administrators began instituting improvements to data analysis and reporting, including transitioning to a certified payroll reporting software to produce reports in almost real time, and hiring additional staff to cope with the extra work. This shift was undertaken to enable responsive implementation, by allowing developers, contractors, and the county to address outcomes and challenges as they materialize, before a project ends. County administrators also sought to establish baseline data from which to gauge compliance. While agreement administrators maintained that prior county contracts were "moderately compliant," the county lacked the baseline data to compare to non-DBE and prevailing wage projects, making it impossible to know whether PERC projects yielded better hiring outcomes than previous projects.[81] Altogether, these shifts illustrate how county staff learned from and responded to implementation issues as they arose—though key knowledge gaps and data reporting challenges hindered public reporting and limited transparency.

Beyond the challenges of delayed data and minimal public information, county staff lacked active oversight in many ways, including over PERC outcomes. The PERC specifies only yearly reporting, with vague language that gives little direction for implementation. While supervisors remained generally aware of Park East land development progress because of their role in development approvals, such sporadic oversight did not create an active oversight mechanism to improve outcomes as they materialized. Rather, as one staff member put it, the PERC "doesn't tell you how to implement it and nobody is checking to make sure you're doing it right." As a result, county staff were left with essentially sole oversight responsibility, but with limited authority and little guidance for how to navigate the technicalities of agreement administration. This lack of active oversight from county supervisors over the managers responsible for day-to-day tasks created a managerial disconnect, resulting in insufficient support, with key knowledge and oversight gaps. These conditions suggest that if county staff did not take implementation seriously, developers would have little accountability to PERC outcomes—paralleling events in Seattle.[82]

As a result, county staff members became directly responsible for agreement administration and were largely left to manage implementation on their own. They employed several strategies to promote developer compliance. First, the county began assessing a $50,000 performance deposit on developers before construction, which would be returned when developers complied with the agreement terms. County staff retained discretion over whether developers complied sufficiently to get their money back. As one stakeholder noted, while the deposit "might be a drop in the bucket ... they're always looking for their $50,000 back at the end." The potential for penalty assessment built in some leverage for the county to ensure community benefits delivery even after a development moved forward—leverage that was missing in Seattle. Beyond the financial penalty, for phased developments, the county could also prevent or delay noncompliant developers from exercising future options to develop. However, after a phased development begins, developers gain more leverage, since few developers want to come in to finish what is essentially another developer's planned development. Therefore, the threat of withholding future options could endanger the county's interests, as well.[83]

Beyond penalties, agreement administrators claimed that developers focused on agreement compliance to avoid the "public relations nightmare" that could arise if the public learned about their broken promises. In contrast, PERC compliance could improve a developer's public image since, "it looks good if you [meet the goals]; you can say, oh, look what I've given back to the city, look at what I've done." However, as the Atlanta agreement also shows, the threat of bad publicity hinges on someone monitoring outcomes and exposing failures, to question the sometimes false narratives about what developments achieve. Without regularly updated and publicly reported outcomes, it becomes difficult for community actors to expose noncompliance, even if someone is trying to observe this process. Moreover, with relatively few developers in Milwaukee, county staff need to maintain good relationships with developers, with whom they will likely work in the future. Finally, with a dual responsibility to both the Milwaukee County executive and the county board, county staff have implemented the agreement within a precarious political context, which can discourage controversial political action.[84] Therefore, as the Atlanta and Seattle agreements also show, the ability to expose agreement noncompliance is not always logistically or politically feasible.

PERC outcomes suffered under managerial disconnects.

The limited evidence on PERC implementation suggests that outcomes varied across development projects, as the practice of writing benefits into development agreements produced different terms. Some flexibility is needed to negotiate agreements that work across different parcels and project contexts. For example, county staff reportedly had to permit relatively low local hire numbers as greater demand for construction workers under a strengthening economy left fewer workers in the out-of-work labor pool. However, in some cases, this flexibility during negotiations allowed developers to eschew the objectives set forth in the PERC. In particular, some of the earlier agreements were reportedly "not great" and "said nothing" about crucial provisions such as residential hiring and apprenticeship requirements—undermining the PERC's community benefits outcomes during policy implementation.[85]

Beyond variation across projects, developers sometimes used managerial disconnects to their advantage during negotiations, exploiting key information and oversight gaps. For the Wangard Park East Square project, for example, the PERC prevailing wage requirement was written to govern only on-site work. The county staff at the time were not lawyers, so they relied on county lawyers external to the department, who lacked construction-related knowledge, to write the contract. As one individual put it, county lawyers were not "subject matter experts on [the PERC]; they're not dealing with it every day." The information and coordination disconnects between the lawyers writing the contracts, the county staff dealing with day-to-day implementation, and the board with oversight and approvals authority produced a contract that failed to cover off-site work—a situation that effectively allowed Wangard to create a contractual loophole to minimize their obligations under the PERC.[86]

Wangard acknowledged that it did not pay prevailing wages for the project's off-site work, and that "some" work was undertaken in a modular fashion, with onsite work restricted to mostly project assembly. This strategy enabled Wangard to drive down wages and project costs while remaining in contractual compliance. While Wangard maintained that the off-site, low-wage work governed only a small portion of the total work on the project, others rejected its claim. Without payroll data, it remains difficult to independently assess these claims, to understand the amount of total work completed under the prevailing wage—the project's main community benefits outcomes. County administrators readily acknowledged the weaknesses in this particular contract and expressed that they have worked to close this on-site work loophole in future contracts. Administrators argued that, as a result of this event, they sought to ensure that PERC oversight proceeded with greater vigilance, technical capacity, and strategic oversight.[87]

Throughout, once enacted, the negotiated development agreement created a new, enforceable contractual standard for community benefits. County employees reported that Wangard worked to promote the contract terms by pressuring their subcontractors to meet the performance goals. In one instance, the county discovered that a drywalling subcontractor was not paying his employees prevailing wage and, "Wangard was very good about not paying them when we discovered it." While the district attorney did not press charges, the contractor reportedly did not get paid and the county put the contractor "on a list, so for at least three years, they can't work on any Milwaukee County project." The county did not hold Wangard responsible because it "worked with us when we discovered the prevailing wage issue," although Wangard reportedly did so only after the noncompliance was exposed by the county. However, the county's cooperative approach was likely motivated by the small development community in Milwaukee: the county needs to retain good relationships with local developers, who, in turn, seek to remain eligible for future contracts.[88] Throughout, however, the enforceable nature of the contractual agreement facilitated compliance—though only to explicated contractual terms, rather than the original spirit of the PERC.

The complex way in which Wangard successfully avoided some PERC goals around this project was not publicly known at the time of research. This knowledge gap demonstrates the challenge inherent to monitoring and enforcing these technical agreements, in which terms can be met while obscuring or not delivering community outcomes. At the time of research, members of the Milwaukee County Board of Supervisors appeared unaware of Wangard's means of PERC avoidance. Since the agreement terms were technically largely met, and county staff reported directly to the county executive, rather than the board, these crucial implementation details—which reveal the policy's ultimate, broader outcomes—would only be revealed to them if members asked the right questions during annual reports.[89] Therefore, within a technical implementation effort, this fractured, politicized oversight structure created impactful disconnects between the oversight body and implementation managers—preventing a united, effective enforcement effort.

Echoing project proponents in Atlanta and Seattle, Wangard's actions illustrate how developers generally have little incentive to work to adhere to the agreement spirit. Rather, they are only structurally compelled to achieve the legal minimum necessary to meet contractual terms and avoid public scrutiny and, when relevant, financial penalties and lawsuits. Throughout development contract negotiations, developers reportedly strategized to reduce their obligations for community benefits provisions, to avoid additional costs and barriers to development. In Milwaukee, pro-development interests demonstrated a resistance to community benefits provisions from the outset. Rather, developers agreed to benefits provisions because local government policies and staff adherence to those policies made it the only option for developers to build on the Park East land. Throughout, developers repeatedly focused on project profitability, which motivated them to negotiate to include fewer benefits in development agreements, as well as to deliver the bare minimum in community benefits. Altogether, these events illustrate how agreements require strong oversight and accountability mechanisms, including penalties and strict contractual terms, to ensure that developers produce the promised community benefits after project approval.

Even though the PERC had an effective formulation process, and the policy was widely lauded, managerial disconnects fractured oversight during implementation, influencing policy outcomes.

County staff members largely drove and controlled PERC implementation but faced a crucial managerial disconnect with the Milwaukee County Board of Supervisors that limited the county staff's enforcement capacity. County staff tasked with implementation were widely acknowledged to particularly care about community benefits provisions because of both personal and professional commitments, possessing unique skills to improve implementation. However, these staff members began working in this capacity during a critical time in implementation, as development was picking up after the recession. They faced a significant learning curve to PERC administration at a key moment, while struggling to implement flawed contracts written before their tenure.

At the same time, community advocates could have played a driving role to additionally motivate compliance, such as in Atlanta. However, the original community participants turned their attention elsewhere in the decade following PERC approval, despite their once-active participation. While some community representatives focused on parallel community organizing work to influence local development, they moved on from the PERC specifically, rather than vigilantly tracking the community outcomes actually produced by the PERC. While county supervisors could have taken a strong oversight role, leveraging their formal oversight capacity, they did not oversee PERC implementation at a critical time, instead only requiring periodic reporting. In this way, elected officials entrusted implementation to county staff, who lacked support to help them pursue vigilant oversight and encourage accountability.

Altogether, PERC implementation demonstrates that many barriers can frustrate community enforcement, even if the original agreement negotiations produced a valued policy. Almost a decade passed before significant development proceeded on the land and triggered community oversight, and community stakeholders had moved on from the policy. The work of the initial active, influential advisory committee suggests that the policy could have been vigorously and more effectively enforced if development had begun in 2004 and proceeded continuously thereafter. However, with the development downturn, by the early 2010s, the work of the original community participants had shifted elsewhere. While many remain committed to community development in Milwaukee, as evidenced by their advocacy efforts around the new Bucks arena, the established, potentially influential community enforcement mechanisms became dormant—even as oversight remained as relevant as ever.

Also, the county board did not maintain a vigilant role in agreement implementation. Rather, driven by the highly politicized Wisconsin development process, members of the county board of supervisors proved more focused on protecting community benefits by issuing additional legislation than tracking policy outcomes. At the same time, ongoing political efforts have continually sought to erode the policy goals of these elected officials, motivating their focus on enacting new policy. County and community stakeholders expressed ongoing concern that the Wisconsin legislature would eliminate the prevailing wage in public works, after legislation to eliminate prevailing wage requirements on local projects was approved in 2015. In response, county officials attempted to protect prevailing wage laws by writing these standards into PERC contracts and development agreements, to improve the likelihood that the policy would continue to apply even if prevailing wage laws were eliminated on state projects. Indeed, in 2017, the Wisconsin legislature eliminated prevailing wages for state construction projects. A study by the Midwest Economic Policy Institute shows that this change was associated with a 5 percent drop in construction wages and a lower likelihood of those workers having employer-sponsored health insurance—even as earnings for construction industry CEOs in the state rose 54 percent.[90]

Further revealing the ongoing political opposition as PERC implementation unfolded, then governor Scott Walker, the state legislature, and county executives worked together to pass Act 14 to reduce county costs in 2013. The legislation cut the salaries of the full-time county supervisors to a part-time wage, while reducing terms from four years to two and transferring some powers from the board to the county executive—even though, as one supervisor noted, the work was "the same."[91] Furthermore, one of Walker's final acts as governor was to restrict the power of the future governor—the Democrat who ousted him from office.[92] In this way, Walker continued to exert enormous influence in local land development and county-level affairs, demonstrating the highly politicized context in Milwaukee and throughout Wisconsin at a critical time in PERC implementation. As a result, the county board of supervisors faced a persistent onslaught of political events that threatened their authority and goals. For this reason, county board members focused their attention on political battles and issuing protecting legislation, at the expense of PERC oversight.

The county board of supervisors extended the PERC requirements beyond the Park East land in response to Act 55, even as PERC outcomes remained largely undetermined. Approved by the Wisconsin State Legislature in 2015, Act 55 reduced the influence of the county board of supervisors by enabling the Milwaukee county executive, in concurrence with the county comptroller, to sell land without oversight or approval from the Milwaukee County Board of Supervisors. This action enabled the county executive to bypass the county board of supervisors and act unilaterally, greatly reducing the influence of the county board over land development in the county.[93] In response to Act 55, the board passed an ordinance to "essentially codify the PERC" and extend its terms throughout the county. In 2015, County Supervisor John Weishan introduced this bill, requiring local hire, prevailing wages, and environmentally sustainable design, as the PERC mandates, on projects with more than $1 million in county financial support.[94]

In this way, the county board of supervisors prioritized approving broad policies to foster community development rather than overseeing agreement administration, even as it may have improved results by actively overseeing enforcement. However, the unresolved challenges of PERC implementation arose with this new policy, as well. County staff noted that Act 55 eliminated their obligations to follow the ordinance, but "for the most part, we're going to. But there are certain things in here that are just not necessarily feasible or well done. They're not flexible enough." In one example, the new legislation raised the green design requirements in the PERC to call for new developments to be LEED certified or have another national environmental certification, which developers and county staff alike claimed is "just bonkers" for development—further illustrating the continued managerial disconnect shaping policies and their outcomes. Other provisions, such as one that development agreements include a community safety plan requirement, were vague and therefore difficult to effectively implement.[95]

Throughout, county staff members maintained that they would follow the ordinance as best as they could, stewarding implementation to ensure community benefits delivery. Indeed, they demonstrated a commitment to PERC implementation, so there is reason to believe that they would continue to work to ensure that policies deliver, when possible. And as with the PERC, county employees anticipated that the work of implementation and outcomes delivery would fall to them.[96]

The PERC was approved as a nationally groundbreaking community benefits policy, and was a major win for both local advocates and the community benefits movement. However, the process that followed illustrates the complexities of delivering on the promises made in the initial policy. Because of the economic recession, and the challenges and costs associated with environmental remediation and building on the Park East land, in particular, more than a decade passed before development on the land began in earnest. As a result, and within a context of political battles between Scott Walker and his allies on one side and progressive advocates and policy makers on the other side, county administrators were largely left to deal with the complexities and technicalities of agreement administration when it came time to implement the PERC. The managerial disconnect that this context created, even with strong political support for the policy that was absent in both Atlanta and Seattle, left oversight gaps and limited authority in ways that undermined outcomes delivery. While benefits proponents continued to focus on protecting and securing additional benefits, their inattention to implementation limited the ultimate outcomes produced by the policy. As in Seattle, beneficiaries were missing from the conversation, creating an organizing void, and leaving few stakeholders focused on outcomes delivery.

Therefore, as in the Atlanta and Seattle cases, events in Milwaukee illustrate how equitable and inclusive agreement negotiations are a necessary but not sufficient condition to achieve results. Unlike the Atlanta and Seattle agreements, community and local government stakeholders worked together to approve a widely lauded agreement with active oversight. At first, this enforcement structure worked. However, as time passed, the economic downturn dispelled momentum and people moved on. As a result, a once-functioning oversight structure fell apart. When oversight became necessary once again, it was left to county staff, who were loosely overseen by county supervisors. Therefore, events in Milwaukee show how even equitable and inclusive agreement negotiations can produce partial results if issues arise to undermine implementation. Rather, inadequate implementation can undo even exemplary benefits-sharing agreements.

The Los Angeles case in the next chapter shows what can happen when all elements align to create a supportive structure: top-down, active enforcement by oversight bodies that have enforcement capabilities, and bottom-up vigilance from community actors that put pressure on other stakeholders to delivery on their community commitments. Together, these factors force all stakeholders to be focused on implementation and on the material delivery of community benefits. However, even with this successful structure, the Los Angeles case suggests that community benefits policies can achieve only a *fragile but persistent accountability*, hinging community benefits outcomes on the careful, continued alignment of stakeholder interests and policy enforcement structures.

CHAPTER 4

Fragile Accountability:
The Metro Project Labor Agreement

Los Angeles County voters approved Measure R in 2008, which promised to reshape transportation across the Los Angeles region. Measure R instituted a half-cent sales tax increase to raise $40 billion for transportation infrastructure projects over thirty years. The Los Angeles County Metropolitan Transportation Authority (Metro) championed Measure R to fund a wide range of projects, including the construction of new light-rail lines. The measure was part of a regional effort to dramatically expand public transit provision across the Los Angeles region, with a deliberate focus on building new light-rail infrastructure.[1]

As in Atlanta, Seattle, and Milwaukee, the new investment and improved urban infrastructure created by the proposed projects—in this case, from decades of future Metro projects—offered potential opportunities for residents. However, as in the other cases, the proposed projects enter into legacies of institutional disinvestment and harm. Future projects threaten to worsen inequality and amplify ongoing neighborhood change across Los Angeles at the same time as they bring new investment. One new proposed light-rail line, the Crenshaw Line, exemplified this tension. The controversial Crenshaw Line project would cut across a historically disinvested, predominantly Black South Los Angeles neighborhood sometimes called the "heart of Black Los Angeles." As the first major Measure R project, the Crenshaw Line became an immediate focus of local organizers seeking to create new opportunities and to avoid the harmful patterns of past investment by public agencies such as Metro.[2]

Metro touted Measure R as a means to bring significant economic opportunity for local residents by creating new construction jobs and generating additional local spending. At the outset, Metro estimated that Measure R would produce 210,000 new construction jobs and $32 million in regional economic spillovers.[3] These construction jobs offer a valuable local opportunity because they pay relatively high salaries, involve workforce training and growth potential, and do not require college degrees. Many historically marginalized groups, including Black workers and women, continue to face discrimination in the construction industry. Discrepancies in representation are especially true for higher-wage technical jobs. At the time, the recent recession had halted many development projects and produced high unemployment in the construction industry.[4] For these reasons, many local residents and activists quickly raised an important question: who would gain access to these high-paying jobs? Would the local community—including Black workers from the Crenshaw and surrounding neighborhoods—benefit from this substantial, and locally impactful, public investment?[5] This question paralleled the concerns that community activists raised in Atlanta, Seattle, and Milwaukee.

This question about the costs and benefits distribution produced by Metro projects was particularly important given the conflictual history between Metro and South Los Angeles. Residents and community activists have repeatedly claimed that Metro has neglected the urban poor, particularly communities of color, in part by favoring light-rail over bus transit. Low-income residents disproportionately rely on public transit, bus service in particular. In what would prove to be a landmark event, a community coalition, including the Bus Riders Union, sued Metro in 1996. The coalition won, successfully proving that the agency discriminated against low-income riders in its transit provision. The Bus Riders Union is still active in regional organizing and continues to attempt to force Metro to better serve low-income residents.[6]

Even after the lawsuit, Metro's poor reputation for serving low-income riders has persisted, and disparate treatment continues.[7] In one lingering point of contention, Metro frequently builds light-rail at street level (at-grade) in low-income communities, rather than above or below ground, as it generally does in wealthier communities. Building transit at-grade creates potential hazards for pedestrians and drivers. Consistent with this pattern, the Exposition Line (or Expo Line, since renamed the E Line), under construction at the time through the Crenshaw neighborhood, was built at-grade.[8]

Beyond issues related to the physical safety dangers from building light rail at-grade in low-income communities, early Crenshaw Line proposals did not include a station in Leimert Park, a historically Black neighborhood next to Crenshaw having the most Black-owned businesses in Los Angeles. Residents had to fight for a station there, which Metro originally opposed because of cost. The initial decision to forgo a stop in Leimert Park clearly signaled to residents that the new light-rail line was not created for them: the line would disrupt their lives and exclude residents from the investment's direct benefits.[9] Subsequent agency plans received similar critiques for fast-tracking and favoring projects that benefit wealthier residents, including light-rail projects and freeway projects. These agency decisions added tension to the already fraught relationship between Metro and low-income residents, extending Metro's history of disinvestment in low-income communities of color across Los Angeles.[10]

At this moment of opportunity and peril, a variety of factors and forces coincided to support the development and approval of an ambitious project labor agreement (PLA). A determined new supervisor, tenacious community representatives, and local development advocates saw an opportunity to pursue development differently, through a bold benefits-sharing agreement. The PLA advanced ambitious provisions to secure jobs for historically marginalized groups within the building trades. The PLA has largely met its goals on the Crenshaw project—though producing, observing, and maintaining results has not come without conflict. The relationships forged between local government and community representatives, and their continued dependence on each other to achieve their individual goals even after agreement approval, created the basis for a *fragile but persistent accountability* surrounding this unique PLA. This fragile accountability implementation structure drove agreement outcomes—and represents a dramatic difference from the Atlanta, Seattle, and Milwaukee policies.

Approving a PLA on Measure R Projects

As voters approved Measure R in 2008, change was already underway among Metro leadership. County Supervisor Mark Ridley-Thomas took office in that year and became a member of the Metro board of directors. From 2008 to 2020, Ridley-Thomas represented the Second District, which includes South Los Angeles and the Crenshaw neighborhood that the light-rail line would soon transverse.[11] Ridley-Thomas campaigned on his reputation as a strong community advocate, particularly for Black residents, and won the election by a wide margin. Before assuming office, Ridley-Thomas was executive director of the regional branch of the Southern Christian Leadership Conference, a prominent Black civil rights organization. He also served as a Los Angeles city councilman, a California state assemblyman, and a California state senator.[12]

As a new supervisor, Ridley-Thomas sought to respond to resident calls for greater diversity on Metro construction projects and greater agency responsiveness to the needs of low-income residents. At this time, community stakeholders were "making their voices heard" to demand change from Metro's board of directors.[13] Since large-scale development projects often contribute to neighborhood change, gentrification, and displacement, and the Crenshaw Line represented a massive public investment that threatened to disrupt their community, residents expressed concern that the new line would exacerbate neighborhood change but produce few local benefits. For this reason, regional activists, Crenshaw residents, business owners, and organizations maintained that residents should receive targeted benefits.[14]

Community activists saw a PLA as one way to direct public benefits from this investment to the affected community, particularly as labor unions worked to advance a labor agreement. Los Angeles has a history of innovative PLAs, including within the Los Angeles Unified School District and at the port. The community sought targeted hire, a workforce development strategy by which certain groups of workers gain priority in the hiring process. In this case, they wanted the agreement to target jobs to local and marginalized residents. With targeted hire, advocates hoped to ensure that Crenshaw residents, specifically Black residents, would capture the jobs produced by development projects taking place in their communities. Throughout, their goal was to create long-term construction career opportunities for these workers, to open the construction trades to historically underrepresented workers, not just produce temporary, one-off jobs.[15]

Supervisor Ridley-Thomas championed the PLA, working with community representatives and organizations, including the Los Angeles Alliance for a New Economy (LAANE) and the Los Angeles Black Worker Center (LABWC), to advocate for the policy to govern Measure R projects. LAANE is a regional advocacy organization focused on organizing and policy advocacy. LAANE was instrumental in crafting and enacting the first community benefits agreements. As a member organization of the Partnership for Working Families, LAANE had important expertise in negotiating benefits-sharing agreements. The LABWC, then directly affiliated with the UCLA Labor Center, is a community organization based in South Los Angeles that focuses on addressing employment discrimination and improving job quality and access for Black workers. These entities constituted key players in an informal coalition that pushed for the ambitious PLA.[16]

Supervisor Ridley-Thomas and the organizations knew that the Crenshaw project was "coming down the pipeline" and would represent a massive investment in Ridley-Thomas's district and surrounding area.[17] At the time, Metro was nearing completion of the brand-new E Line, which crossed through Crenshaw as it connected Santa Monica (in a later, now completed phase) to Downtown Los Angeles. Since the second phase of the E Line was completed with local money, it included targeted hiring goals. However, the agreement on the E Line lacked strong enforcement powers and faced criticism for producing few of the community outcomes it originally promised. Therefore, Ridley-Thomas, LAANE, and the LABWC wanted to create a broader, agencywide policy with strong enforcement language to govern the wave of projects that Measure R would bring. In particular, they sought to ensure that local residents in the Crenshaw area received at least some of the construction jobs produced by the Crenshaw Line project.[18]

Paralleling the work of other community advocates, the LABWC took specific interest in targeting new work opportunities to Black residents, who remain underrepresented in construction unions. Through its affiliation with the UCLA Labor Center, the LABWC had a strong connection to academic expertise around labor and organizing. Further, the LABWC mistrusted Metro, rooted in the agency's poor history with the local community and Black residents in particular. Both LAANE and the LABWC similarly sought to ensure that the Metro PLA produced construction careers, not just one-off job opportunities, but sustained employment for local workers in construction unions. The LABWC sought construction careers for Black workers in particular.[19]

Beyond Supervisor Ridley-Thomas, other Metro board members were open to a PLA to ensure timely progress on agency megaprojects, as Metro had received criticism in the past about project delays. Access to the unions' trained workforce for skill-intensive light-rail construction work would expedite construction, consistent with one of the main rationales generally advanced by management for pursuing PLAs. Simultaneously, unions pursued a PLA to capture the jobs produced by these large-scale, regional construction projects, working with Ridley-Thomas, Metro staff, other elected officials, and the community organizations to craft the agreement terms.[20] Therefore, the Metro board, unions, and community stakeholders played a key role in advocating for a PLA and in specifying its terms, as each had a vested interest in securing a PLA on Metro projects.

The PLA had to be carefully written in order to adhere to legal requirements associated with state and federal funding, which make it difficult to enact targeted hire initiatives. The PLA deviated from traditional agency policy and required approval from the Federal Transit Administration (FTA) to allow the agency to target hire while maintaining federal funding.[21] As the agency was writing the policy, legal challenges arose with the targeted hire language. Many Metro board members reportedly lacked motivation to find a way to overcome legal barriers and to make this new policy work. However, key pressure from Supervisor Ridley-Thomas and his office, in collaboration with LAANE and the LABWC, drove negotiators to find alternatives. In this way, Metro staff and leadership maintained that community pressure gave the agency crucial political support and additional expertise to pursue a policy that deviated from agency practices and the status quo. While Supervisor Ridley-Thomas drove the policy, community organizations used their political influence to indirectly shape the agreement terms, by working with construction unions, the agency, and the Metro board.[22] This political advocacy paralleled the important role played by local officials in Atlanta, Seattle, and Milwaukee in championing agreement approval—support that similarly moved the policies toward approval.

Their efforts created a PLA approved by Metro and the Los Angeles/Orange Counties Building and Construction Trades Council. Metro enacted the agreement on January 26, 2012. This PLA was the first master PLA approved by a regional transportation agency in the nation, meaning that the agreement applies to all agency projects with Measure R funding.[23] The Metro PLA was designed to ensure that the jobs and career opportunities created by Measure R's public funds would extend to historically marginalized workers and create local economic spillovers to benefit broader communities. In sum, the PLA was intended as a community development strategy to build human capital, create local economic development, and address structural workforce discrimination.[24] Agreement formulation involved both grassroots mobilization by community organizations seeking to enhance access to construction careers and lobbying from union representatives, as well as leadership from the Metro board of directors, particularly Supervisor Ridley-Thomas.[25] This top-down and bottom-up advocacy structure would, uniquely, continue through a key period of agreement implementation.

Metro has been implementing its PLA since it was approved in January 2012.[26] While early agreement versions contained more specific local hire provisions, Metro faced limitations in enacting local hire in the final agreement. Rather, jobs needed to be available at a national scale in accordance with FTA policy.[27] For this reason, Metro had to secure approval to pursue the policy, which the agency was granted because of the substantial amount of local funding that Measure R included.[28] Further, since Measure R projects involve state funds, California's Proposition 209 affirmative action prohibition extends to the PLA. This prevented the agency from advancing an agreement mandating race-based or gender-based preferences. Therefore, the Metro PLA targets hiring to "disadvantaged workers," a classification that broadens the beneficiary pool.[29] That these projects are largely funded by local, public funds was an important reason why Metro could push the FTA to allow this ambitious PLA with worker targeting provisions.[30]

Thus, for many at Metro and in the community, the Metro PLA was originally envisioned and specifically designed to address historical and contemporary injustice by ensuring that members of historically excluded groups such as Black workers were hired for these construction projects, particularly on the Crenshaw Line.[31] To this end, the agreement mandates that "Local Targeted Workers, with priority given to Community Area Residents" undertake 40 percent of total work hours for projects governed by the PLA. Agreement participants noted that this target is high relative to other PLAs.[32] Ten percent of total work hours would be undertaken by "Disadvantaged Workers whose primary place of residence is within Los Angeles County."[33] Further, the PLA specifies that apprentices must undertake at least 20 percent of project hours.[34]

Through the apprenticeship provision, the PLA was crafted to achieve two ends: first, to ensure that the targeted workforce had the necessary skills to gain access to jobs, and second, to create career opportunities. Apprenticeships provide a means for residents to gain entry into construction careers and the building trades by enabling them to receive training while working. This is particularly important, since workers need to continue to develop skills in order to advance from entry-level apprentice positions to higher-paying journeyman positions.[35] To oversee progress toward these hiring targets, the general contractor would be required to hire a Metro-approved "jobs coordinator" who would be given the responsibility to support contractors to implement the PLA.[36]

The disadvantaged worker classification represents a zip code proxy for targeting hire to local historically excluded groups. In creating this proxy, however, the targeted worker classification broadens the pool of eligible workers, a consequential difference that could produce different hiring outcomes from the narrower geographic and race-based hiring goals.[37] The disadvantaged worker classification creates ambiguity within the agreement that permits the PLA terms to be met in ways that may not achieve the goals that inspired community participants to advocate for the agreement. Specifically, local Black workers do not have to be hired to meet the disadvantaged worker agreement goal, even though some community activists sought a PLA for exactly that reason. This vagueness, combined with the lack of transparent data and limited community control over producing outcomes, led stakeholders to challenge agreement outcomes during implementation.

As the agency moved forward with this policy, it continued to pursue local tax dollars to fund future projects—a strategy that makes the agency dependent on public support. Metro, like many public agencies, faces declining federal investment and an uncertain fiscal outlook. The agency has turned to ballot measures to secure funding for future projects.[38] In November 2012, four years after Measure R approval and less than a year after PLA approval, Metro sought voter approval for a new ballot measure. Measure J proposed to extend the sales tax increase that Measure R initiated for an additional 30 years. Consistent with Metro's history and priorities, Measure J prioritized light-rail transit. Community groups, including the Bus Riders Union, strongly opposed and actively organized against Measure J, which failed to receive the necessary two-thirds majority by a slim margin. Metro staff understood that failure to secure the funds proposed by Measure J imperiled future regional transit construction and the agency's goals. The agency would need to gain community approval—or at least marginalize community opposition—to win future ballot campaigns.[39]

When Metro put forward another, similar ballot measure in 2016, it cited the PLA as evidence that Metro has included low-income residents in projects, not just through public transportation provision.[40] The ballot measure passed, so the agency secured significant local tax dollars to fund its ambitious agenda to transform regional public transportation, primarily through significant light-rail investment. However, to accomplish this goal, the agency remains dependent on strong community relationships to gain voter approval for future agency funding and to justify current public investment.

As a result, the agency now finds itself in an era in which future project funding hinges on community support. For this reason, Metro has an interest in at least *appearing* to deliver community benefits from agency projects.[41]

Indeed, immediately after the agreement was approved in 2012, and even before PLA implementation had begun, Metro received substantial public accolades for the policy. Many saw the policy as proof that local residents would benefit from the projects—even before a single construction worker was hired on PLA-related projects. Just after the PLA was approved, then Los Angeles mayor and Metro board chairman Antonio Villaraigosa declared, "I am proud that the MTA board voted unanimously to become the first transit agency in the nation to use federal and local dollars to create jobs targeted at economically disadvantaged communities and individuals. This landmark program is part of a strategy to deliver public transit projects while creating jobs that will lift people out of poverty and into the middle class."[42] Since then, public reporting has continued to portray this PLA as an overwhelming success, with the agency and local public officials supporting this narrative. The high-profile *Los Angeles Times* and local news outlets ran thirty-three articles referencing the PLA in just the three years after PLA approval, thirteen of which primarily focused on the Metro PLA as a major victory for the community, through local job creation and infrastructure investment.[43]

Further, the secretary of labor and the secretary of transportation both visited the Crenshaw project in its early stages. These high-profile public officials visibly promoted the Metro PLA as a national model to enhance access to construction careers for local, low-income residents that should be replicated across the country—lending the appearance of PLA success, even as implementation was just beginning.[44] Indeed, the Metro PLA served as the basis for a one-year local hire pilot by the FTA, which allowed future projects to pursue similar objectives that Metro accomplished through its waiver.[45]

As a result of this positive attention, Metro effectively promoted a narrative in which the agency had already produced community outcomes even with ongoing Crenshaw Line implementation—and even as many Measure R projects remained in the early stages. In some ways, this public narrative meant that Metro, as an agency, largely achieved its original objective of improving its community image from PLA *approval*, before it produced any of the outcomes required for communities to experience material benefit. And yet, despite the agency's successful public relations campaign, project construction on the Crenshaw Line was only just beginning.[46]

Metro PLA Implementation on the Crenshaw Line

The Crenshaw/LAX Transit Corridor project, the first megaproject under Measure R funding, will produce the Crenshaw Line: a brand-new, 8.5-mile light-rail line through the neighborhoods of Crenshaw, Leimert Park, Baldwin Hills, Hyde Park, Inglewood, and Westchester, in South Los Angeles. Project construction began on January 21, 2014. The line was anticipated to open in 2019, but opening is now slated for late 2022, with construction issues delaying timely progress.[47] The Crenshaw Line (since renamed the K Line) will connect the E Line and the C (formerly Green) Line and end close to Los Angeles International Airport. In total, the Crenshaw Line will cost an estimated roughly $2.1 billion, largely funded through Measure R sales tax funding, but also including state and federal grants.[48] PLA implementation on the Crenshaw Line illustrates the conflicts that can arise during implementation of a benefits-sharing agreement, even after policy consensus has been reached.

The Crenshaw neighborhood is a predominantly low-income, Black community. As one of the few remaining (relatively) affordable, centrally located Los Angeles neighborhoods, it faces rising housing costs, gentrification, and displacement pressures.[49] At the beginning of the Crenshaw Line project, 62.5 percent of residents were African American or Black, in contrast with 8.2 percent across Los Angeles County. At 29.7 percent, the Crenshaw area had roughly twice the share of households with an annual income of less than $20,000 than at the county (17.2 percent), state (15.1 percent), and federal levels (17.6 percent). Further, roughly half (51.5 percent) of all households in this area had a total income of less than $40,000, compared with 36.3 percent across the county and 32.9 percent across the state.[50]

At the beginning of the Crenshaw Line project, Crenshaw residents had attained relatively less education and earned lower incomes compared with county and state levels. In Crenshaw, 25.4 percent of adults aged twenty-five or older held a high school diploma or equivalency but no college, compared with 20.5 percent across Los Angeles County and 20.7 percent across the state. A slightly greater proportion of residents (13.4 percent) were above retirement age than in Los Angeles County (11 percent). A greater share of residents older than sixteen were not employed (15.7 percent) or not in the labor force (39.9 percent) than at the county (10.8 percent unemployment and 34.8 percent not in the labor force), state (11.0 percent and 35.5 percent), and federal (9.3 percent and 35.3 percent) levels. Unemployment levels among African American or Black residents in the Crenshaw area (15.9 percent)

Fragile Accountability 121

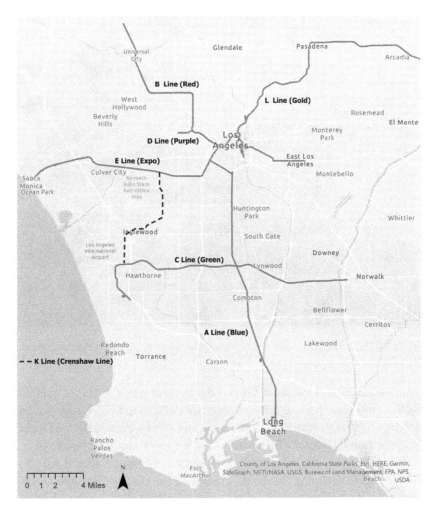

Figure 11. Map of Crenshaw Line (sources: Metro, n.d.a.; Metro, n.d.h.; Esri, DeLorme, HERE, MapmyIndia).

corresponded with levels across the county (16.0 percent), state (17.0 percent), and federal scales (15.9 percent). Finally, Crenshaw residents were underrepresented in the construction industry. Rather, 3.5 percent of Crenshaw residents held construction industry jobs, compared with 5.8 percent of county residents and 6.2 percent of state residents.[51]

The Crenshaw area began to feel the neighborhood impacts of the Crenshaw Line early in the construction process. Business owners quickly

Figure 12. Disruptions from construction along Crenshaw Boulevard (photo by author).

witnessed changes, such as landowners declining to renew leases. As a result, business owners expressed concern about their ability to benefit from nearby development early into the process. As one business owner stated, "We fought so hard to get the station. Then I wondered if we would still be here to enjoy it."[52] Road closures and interrupted foot traffic (sees Figures 12 and 13) also contributed to declining profits and business closure in the Crenshaw neighborhood. One business owner described how, "little by little, [her regular customers] are going. That's big trouble. Christmas is usually busy, but we don't know this year."[53]

Metro responded to local business concerns by creating an "Eat, Shop, Play Crenshaw" initiative, intended to encourage people to support local businesses during the construction disruption. This initiative was undertaken in recognition of the negative impact of Metro construction on local businesses, by covering storefronts, removing parking, and restricting pedestrian access. Metro also designated $10 million to a business interruption fund to "provide eligible businesses up to $50,000 annually, not to

Figure 13. Disrupted businesses along Crenshaw Boulevard (photo by author).

exceed 60 percent of business revenue loss to address construction impacts along on the project alignment."[54] Metro dedicated space on its website to advertising, with discounts for Metro users. However, many business owners reported worrying about qualifying for the business interruption fund. The program mandated that businesses needed to be located directly on the rail corridor, be either a for-profit business or a nonreligious nonprofit, be solvent and in good standing with taxing and licensing authorities, have been in continuous operation for more than two years, and employ twenty-five or fewer full-time workers.[55]

Regardless of these efforts, the Crenshaw neighborhood, and South Los Angeles generally, continues to experience significant gentrification and displacement pressures, not just from the Crenshaw Line construction, but also from other major development projects in the area and broader housing pressures across Los Angeles. The new SoFi stadium is one such project. The stadium now houses the Los Angeles Rams and Los Angeles Chargers NFL teams. As Crenshaw Line construction proceeded, the stadium project was in the planning stages and under construction in nearby Inglewood. This area of South Los Angeles has become one of the hottest real estate markets in the region. Residents continue to raise legitimate concerns about whether they will be able to stay in the neighborhood. Indeed, the community has already witnessed significant changes since the Metro PLA was approved in 2012, including skyrocketing rents and housing prices.[56] According to the real estate website Redfin, the median home sale price in South Los Angeles was $640,000 in March 2021, up 10.3 percent compared to the previous year. Housing sale prices nearly doubled in the five-year period since March 2016, when the median house sold for $369,000. As of March 2021, the median sale price in the Crenshaw neighborhood was $810,000.[57]

As the Crenshaw Line project initially moved forward and contributed to ongoing neighborhood changes, conflict quickly emerged between the community and Metro. At first, reports suggested that the Crenshaw Line would create 18,000 new jobs. Elected officials highly touted this figure to demonstrate the project's community benefits. The estimate gained traction with the media.[58] As a result, many community residents believed that this work could produce jobs for everyone in the community and expressed excitement about the investment.[59]

However, the figure was misleading. The project would generate closer to a few hundred new jobs, since most work would benefit individuals already employed in construction. This difference occurred partially because PLAs allow some jobs to be directly routed to "core workers" who permanently work with particular contractors or subcontractors across job sites, to enable contractors to rely on trusted employees.[60] The initial estimate also included spillover jobs beyond the construction industry, as well as work performed by workers already in the industry. Metro staff expressed frustration at how elected officials characterized job creation, claiming political overpromise. Staff members noted that they continued to work to overcome the suspicion that this action generated in the community about these jobs. For many in the Crenshaw community, the disputed number exacerbated institutional mistrust. This incident contributed to lingering contention between the community and Metro.[61]

Community enforcement on the Crenshaw Line encouraged accountability.

As Metro PLA implementation proceeded, stakeholders created a fragile accountability to community outcomes, in large part because of the influence that community residents gained over the agency and local leaders. After the Metro board of directors approved the PLA, the agency hired additional staff members tasked with implementing the agreement internally to the agency. With implementation underway, these staff members worked to ensure that the agreement would meet its goal: that targeted workers gain jobs as they emerge, by coordinating with contractors, community organizations, and local unions. They also sought to troubleshoot problems as they arose so that barriers to implementation did not undermine ongoing progress toward the agreement goals in the project's critical early years.[62]

Metro implementation staff were hired after PLA approval and, as Metro employees, gained a stake in the agency's ability to successfully fund future projects through ballot measures. Since the Bus Riders Union and other community organizations successfully opposed the ballot measure following Measure R, agency staff appreciated the need to change the agency's public reputation. These factors motivated implementation staff members to build a better reputation with communities of color and the broader public in their work, at least to promote agreement implementation and agency support. Therefore, implementation staff worked to cultivate strong relationships with the community after PLA approval, both to improve PLA implementation and to generate support for future funding measures.[63]

Similar to the Milwaukee agreement, public managers with control over implementation demonstrated a vested interest in upholding community benefits. Metro implementation staff expressed serious personal commitments to producing outcomes, rooted in their individual beliefs in promoting economic justice and existing community relationships.[64] As in the other cases, these public agency employees claimed personal motivations that inspired their dedication to the agreement terms, which motivated them to work to overcome the hiring and other implementation challenges that arose after the policy was approved—even beyond what their job would require. However, unlike in the other cases, vigilant oversight of the agreement outcomes further motivated and supported Metro staff to produce outcomes, deriving from both community monitoring efforts and proactive oversight from the Metro board of directors.

Early conflicts generated additional suspicion and further inspired community vigilance. The LABWC quickly emerged as a watchdog of PLA implementation and the Crenshaw project as implementation proceeded. Driven by agency mistrust, rooted in past relationships between low-income Black communities and regional institutions such as Metro, the LABWC began organizing to pressure Metro to vigorously enforce the PLA even *before* it was approved. Through its vigilance, the LABWC came to play an important, albeit indirect role in Metro PLA implementation. Initially, the organization sought an authority role in implementation, such as participation on an oversight committee with enforcement capabilities. However, Metro did not extend direct oversight capacity to the community in this way, and thus official enforcement remained limited to the agency and the Metro board of directors.[65] This represented an important decision in which Metro leadership prevented a potential mechanism to create community power during implementation—paralleling the decision of the Atlanta leadership to maintain their representative capacity, rather than enabling direct community influence.

Regardless, the LABWC organized to influence PLA implementation on the Crenshaw Line in multiple ways. Its efforts began with the initial step toward worker hiring on Metro projects: the Metro board's general contractor hiring on the Crenshaw Line, a process that began shortly after PLA approval. Motivated by concern that other PLA proponents would move on and community benefits would not materialize, the LABWC developed a strategy to maintain vigilance and ensure that the Metro board, the agency, and now the construction contractors would remain focused on community outcomes delivery. The organization graded prospective general contractors on their past behavior, including transparency, discrimination, and community relations, both to reveal concerns about contractors who had previously engaged in harmful hiring and worker treatment practices and to pressure contractors to pay attention to community priorities. The organization presented the report card findings to the Metro board of directors and the contractors that bid on the project.[66]

The report card organizing tactic proved influential. Metro considered the findings in their final decision, sought to meet with the LABWC and to gain access to the data and findings to use for future bidding processes. Further, contractors expressed interest in the report card methods and their low scores. Some reportedly attempted to work with the organization to ensure that they scored higher on future projects. Stakeholders expressed that when contractors were confronted with their performance, with their reputations and future contracts on the line, contractors were suddenly interested in their community impacts and the organization's enforcement goals.[67] In this way, the LABWC began outside organizing efforts immediately after PLA approval. Its monitoring and enforcement activities drew attention and response to generate *accountability*—even though the organization was excluded from a more direct, resourced, and empowered role in agreement oversight.

Afterward, the LABWC shifted its attention to influencing the hiring of the jobs coordinator, a role unique to the Metro PLA. The jobs coordinator is an outside organization contracted to facilitate implementation and coordination between community groups, construction unions, contractors, and Metro, to reduce barriers to implementation as they arise. Therefore, the jobs coordinator was tasked with a vital role in implementation; the chosen organization would greatly determine whether and how the PLA would meet its goals. Originally, the selected jobs coordinator came from outside the Crenshaw area. However, after community stakeholders, including the LABWC, expressed concern to Metro and its board of directors that this jobs coordinator lacked the local knowledge to work effectively and immediately with community groups to direct workers, the contractor selected a jobs coordinator, PV Jobs, located in South Los Angeles.[68] This incident further demonstrated Metro's growing community responsiveness.

Like in the other cases, the community was denied a direct role in overseeing the Metro PLA. However, through continued organizing, the LABWC was able to continue to influence events around the Metro PLA, even after the agreement was approved. These continued efforts paralleled the persistent vigilance of community activists in Atlanta and the early work of activists in Milwaukee, contrasting with the role of community actors in Seattle. Unlike in Atlanta, however, the efforts of community activists successfully shaped key decisions around policy implementation. Importantly, in Los Angeles, these efforts occurred within a respected and established community organization, which effectively caught the ear of responsive leaders with authority over outcomes.

Metro PLA outcomes on the Crenshaw Line have exceeded expectations—but data transparency became contested.

As of March 2021, with 96.23 percent of the project complete, the PLA had exceeded its established goals as set forth in the agreement terms.[69] Significant work for the Crenshaw Line began in Summer 2014. Table 3 shows data from reports based on certified payroll data and made public on the Metro website. While early reports indicated that the project was not meeting apprenticeship goals, these numbers improved as the project progressed.[70] However, when examining the breakdown by race and ethnicity, it becomes apparent that worker characteristics quickly differed from Crenshaw area demographics, which community representatives sought to change.

Table 3. Metro PLA Outcomes

	Percentage Cumulative Reported Craft Hours (as of March 2021)	Percentage Cumulative Reported Craft Hours (December 2017 Report)	Percentage Cumulative Reported Craft Hours (October 2015 Report)	PLA Goals for Percentage Total Craft Hours
Total Completed Work Hours	96.23%	80.80%	36.75%	**N/A**
Economically Disadvantaged Area Hours	59.71%	59.71%	59.33%	**40%**
Disadvantaged Workers Hours	10.39%	12.41%	10.31%	**10%**
Apprenticeship Hours	23.80%	22.80%	17.76%	**20%**
Caucasian Workers	21.08%	22.24%	22.81%	
Hispanic Workers	62.78%	60.71%	55.11%	
African American Workers	11.30%	12.36%	16.24%	
Asian Workers	1.47%	1.21%	1.23%	
Native American	.80%	1.28%	1.17%	
Other	2.56%	2.35%[71]	3.01%	
Not Specified			0.42%	
Female Workers	3.62%	3.42%	2.60%	

Source: Los Angeles County Metropolitan Transportation Authority, 2021; Los Angeles County Metropolitan Transportation Authority, 2017; Los Angeles County Metropolitan Transportation Authority, 2015c.

Note: Percentages refer to cumulative craft hours completed on the project by the end of the reporting period.

Furthermore, the number of African American workers on the project have declined over time.[72]

As PLA implementation on the Crenshaw project got underway, Metro staff reported progress on the PLA monthly to the Metro board of directors for the Crenshaw project. The Metro board required additional reporting for Measure R–funded megaprojects, including the Crenshaw Line. Representatives from Walsh Shea, the prime contractor for the Crenshaw project, were required to attend those meetings, in case a board member wanted to question contractors directly. According to one Metro employee, this demonstrated "the level of attention that [the PLA is] getting" by the powerful Metro board of directors and "how important [the PLA] is not just to staff, but the governing board. This is to be taken seriously." Therefore, in meetings, the board showed its commitment to the PLA and pushed Walsh Shea to prioritize project labor outcomes delivery. This attention gave staff the institutional support to enforce the agreement with contractors.[73]

However, because of the reporting format, it remained difficult for outsiders to track important local workforce outcomes as implementation proceeded—even if data was reported in a timely fashion. Data reporting obscured necessary details, including information about race and gender representation across different job categories. Data such as the percentage of total payroll, rather than project hours completed, would reveal this information. Rather, jobs have been aggregated by "craft hours," or the number of work hours completed in a given trade. This categorization prevented outsiders from tracking individual workers across the project as construction on the Crenshaw Line picked up—critical information to understand whether projects produce construction careers or one-off job opportunities. This information was particularly important in light of early anecdotal reports from residents that they observed women and Black workers holding signs— relatively unskilled work that limits a worker's ability to advance through the trades. Therefore, the manner of reporting data publicly limited the ability of outsiders to observe long-term job creation, by obscuring information related to the number of workers hired, how long each individual worked, and whether they gained skills that would allow them to promote within the construction trades.[74] And yet, these data were essential to understanding whether the PLA was meeting the community's original goal of creating long-term construction career access for local workers from historically excluded groups, including Black workers.

Even after reporting ambiguity became apparent, Metro staff described their disinclination to aggregate data by total workers. Since many construction jobs are temporary, reporting total worker numbers obscures how long a worker is employed on a project—which may be only a few days. This tracking system could also motivate contractors to hire and fire workers more frequently, to increase worker totals. However, community groups continued to seek these data, to observe the number of jobs the project generated, and who gained access to this work. They emphasized that these data represented vital information for assessing the ultimate community outcomes of the PLA: what jobs are created, who gets them, and the extent to which workers can translate jobs into long-term careers through skill development and work experience. The types of jobs produced by this project and who gets these jobs shape the community development outcomes produced, since construction jobs vary significantly in the current and future opportunities they offer. Construction of a light-rail line requires various labor types, including electricians, sheet metal workers, laborers, and painters. These jobs differ in pay, educational and training requirements, health hazards, and potential for career mobility.[75]

As implementation proceeded, Metro indicated openness to giving these data, but only after "educating" the public about the ways in which tracking individual workers can mislead about worker duration. They cited the issues around the project's initial jobs estimated as a reason for their reluctance.[76] It is understandable that the agency would hesitate to release data that could be misunderstood, wanting recipients to understand the nuances involved with this technical information. Regardless, by preventing community members access to the fullest possible hiring information, Metro forestalled efforts to demand transparency. Rather, Metro avoided releasing hiring information vital to tracking community benefits outcomes.

At the same time, however, Metro also altered reporting to require more data, including a female worker participation scorecard. This effort was motivated by agency need, as well as the Metro board's request for additional data, in part driven by community advocacy. Furthermore, the agency created an oversight table to enable the community to directly share and access information about agreement implementation.[77] In this way, community advocates continued to use their political relationships to demand transparency and accountability. They lobbied their elected officials on the Metro board of directors and built relationships with Metro staff, the general contractor, and labor unions to increase community influence over the implementation process toward greater accountability. These stakeholders proved responsive to community pressure. Even still, the community gained only indirect control over the delivery of the promised benefits since community activists could not directly hire workers nor directly assess penalties. Rather, the community's role was mediated through other actors, who retained potentially differing interests regarding PLA goals.[78]

Regardless, community advocates continued to pressure Metro to produce outcomes, with Metro's public reputation and future funding at stake. In one example, community residents reported that they did not see Black residents working on the Crenshaw project, which led them to distrust the hiring numbers that Metro was reporting. Metro pushed back against these claims and contended that many local workers were hired on the project but working underground. Their assertion was potentially beneficial: underground work is generally higher-paying work that offers additional skills training. However, this observation was difficult to independently observe without jobsite access.[79]

In response to visibility concerns, Metro installed large posters of hired workers meeting the disadvantaged worker categorization at light-rail construction sites along a major intersection in the Crenshaw neighborhood in late 2014 (Figure 14). The posters remained up for years. The posters amplified Metro's successes at hiring and training underrepresented local workers—even if only for the three featured workers. Metro staff members argued that the agency displayed the posters at one of its largest construction sites on the project to meet this community concern and increase worker visibility on Metro projects, particularly for Black workers. According to Metro staff, this action further allowed them to "multiply the effect" of worker hiring. The female worker in the photo, LeDaya Epps, was widely promoted as an example of hiring success on the project after meeting the secretary of labor on the project. She was invited as a special guest to the 2015 State of the Union address by First Lady Michelle Obama. The secretary of transportation publicly shared her story.[80]

Figure 14. Metro construction site billboards (photo by author).

The cumulative impact of these posters and visibility efforts is difficult to assess. There is an obvious performative aspect to these posters, which implicitly signal that the project, and Metro's work generally, provides only benefits to the neighborhood and community—rather than costs. These posters therefore obscure the real conflicts that have characterized this agreement, its implementation, and the outcomes that continue to materialize, since the community lacks a similar platform through which to dispute this public narrative. At the same time, these posters further demonstrate the power that the community generated to shape Metro's behavior. The agency responded to community outcry by taking substantial, public action to address their concerns. Metro's actions underscore how the community influenced Metro's behavior and the implementation process. In this way, like in Atlanta, and in contrast to the events in Milwaukee and Seattle, the community successfully maintained vigilance during key implementation stages. However, community vigilance in Los Angeles transformed the actions of institutions with influence over implementation, in multiple ways and far beyond what occurred in the other cities. This response resulted, in large part, from the agency's and public officials' responsiveness to community pressure.[81]

Beyond lingering questions about whether Metro has met the goals it claimed to achieve, worker visibility also matters. Rather, it is an important outcome that this historically underserved neighborhood, where many residents have mistrusted Metro because of the institution's harmful activities, "sees itself" in this local, large-scale, public project.[82] As one community respondent explained, community residents need to be able to share local problems with their representatives and witness change from their efforts:

> We're taxpayers just like everybody else, but our voice gets drowned out by the Westside and the Valley and folks who have had institutional access to power at City Hall for a lot longer than we have. Metro and any department, any agency is not going to [implement an agreement] perfectly. It's just impossible. So really for me, success ... comes down to: this is *our* community, you're literally tearing up *our* streets where *we* drive every day, where *we* walk every day. We need to see *our* workers—who have been historically pushed out of the trades for many, many reasons, some of them have to do with Metro, a lot of them don't—we need to see *our* workers on these jobs. And we need to see community benefit because we, just us,

we are going to struggle through this five-year project. You know? We need to be able to have enough power at these places to say this is what we need, and to see response. We all have enough power to walk into a public meeting and say what we want to say, but *are people paying attention*? Are people actually taking our voices to be important enough to actually evaluate how they're doing and to say: we can make a change here.[83]

The agreement was intended to mitigate historical inequality in South Los Angeles, which has been perpetuated and exacerbated by local institutions such as Metro. However, this goal could not be met without genuine community influence over Metro's and the contractor's behavior, to ensure real accountability in the development process—a power that, as this individual described, more privileged communities across Los Angeles already enjoy.

The persistent conflict over implementation and enduring institutional distrust motivated the LABWC to maintain its community enforcement efforts, to assess whether Metro actually achieved the inclusive hiring it claimed and to push for Black workers to be hired. The LABWC began conducting community monitoring of worker characteristics and treatment on the Crenshaw Line. In this effort, individuals watched workers enter jobsites early in the morning. They recorded whether they observed Black workers and women on the project, what roles they performed, and whether obvious health and safety violations occurred. Without access to construction sites, however, the organization faced challenges in collecting accurate observations, including poor visibility into jobsites (see Figure 15), particularly as the project shifted into underground drilling phases. The organization used the gathered information to produce and circulate public reports, including to the Metro board of directors, to monitor Metro's data and outcomes related to this PLA. In so doing, the LABWC produced its own data, despite obvious barriers limiting data reliability and validity, to question the agency's account, push for greater transparency, and remind contractors and Metro that the community is watching.[84]

The pressure that this effort successfully created and maintained—which was absent in Seattle and Milwaukee, and rendered ineffective in Atlanta by nonresponsive local leaders—proved impactful in Los Angeles. The general contractor, Walsh Shea, and the Metro board of directors, including Supervisor Ridley-Thomas, took these reports seriously, if only to dispel community concerns. To prove their hiring numbers, and encouraged by Metro, Walsh

Figure 15. Jobsite visibility issues facing community monitors (photo by author).

Shea allowed LABWC staff to enter jobsites on the Crenshaw Line, observe working conditions, and more easily track hiring outcomes. This action was quite significant and rare on construction sites, demonstrating the extent to which community pressure increased transparency and altered the behavior of both Metro and development interests. From the contractor's perspective, this action was really about "controlling the message" and letting the community get a better sense of construction work and these jobs sites. From Metro's perspective, it reflected an opportunity to increase transparency and improve community relationships. Regardless of the motivation, this action signals the extent to which the community effectively altered the behavior of those parties with direct control over the desired community workforce outcomes: Metro and its contractors.[85] By calling the contractor's message into question, the community gained a major concession in transparency and promoted a continued focus on community outcomes delivery.

In this way, Metro representatives reported that the LABWC came to play a fundamental role in PLA implementation on the Crenshaw Line project: sharing on-the-ground reports to improve agency information, creating preapprenticeship programs to bridge local skills gaps and direct Black workers into construction careers, and pushing Metro to produce additional outcomes, increase transparency, and be held accountable to the local community. By pressuring the Metro board, Metro staff members noted that the community gave the agency the support necessary to demand results from contractors.[86] Expending vital resources, the LABWC kept its somewhat adversarial enforcement position during key moments in implementation, yet acknowledged the gains made by the agreement's community workforce provisions, and the work undertaken by Metro, the jobs coordinator, and the contractors. However, the organization maintained pressure on Metro to fully comply with the agreement and, in particular, to hire Black workers, women, and apprentices. It acted out of concern that the agency would neglect community outcomes without persistent vigilance.[87] With leadership from the Metro board and agency staff, LABWC's advocacy was strategically directed to create community influence over actors with control over community outcomes.

Metro PLA implementation produced a persistent, albeit fragile, accountability to community outcomes on the Crenshaw project—though lacking dedicated community resources and direct control.

As with the other agreements described in this book, community stakeholders in Los Angeles gained little direct and formalized power over public and private developers, contractors, and pro-development interests during implementation—for example, participation in an enforcement body authorized to make hiring or penalty assessment decisions. Rather, under PLAs, contractors, subcontractors, and construction unions largely control community outcomes during implementation because they directly refer and hire workers, even though contractors and subcontractors are hired after agreement approval and are not agreement signatories. Thus, the general contractor operates "like a third party" to the agreement, meaning that, as a Metro staff member stated, "the contractor taking ownership over the PLA, just like they do any other provision of the contract, is key." Metro's prioritization of the PLA proved crucial to motivate contractors to produce outcomes since Metro has oversight responsibility and the ability to assess penalties. As one Metro respondent stated, "if Metro was lax, if Metro was not enforcing, if Metro was not reporting, on a monthly basis, if it's not being transparent, no one is going to take this program seriously"—particularly the contractors who hire workers.[88]

However, the LABWC, with a strong focus on the Crenshaw neighborhood and Black worker employment, worked to secure influence during implementation. As a result, even though the agreement itself afforded community stakeholders no direct control nor an empowered role in agreement implementation—and therefore, over community outcomes delivery—the LABWC secured demonstrable influence over Metro PLA implementation on the Crenshaw Line project. Even still, community stakeholders remained unable to directly control worker hiring.[89] As a result, some community activists publicly critiqued PLA implementation, questioning the extent to which this policy would benefit local residents at the same time that covered projects threaten residential and commercial displacement.[90]

In this way, different stakeholders came to contest the Metro PLA implementation process to promote their respective constituencies or interests, but retained differential ability to influence which workers got hired onto these job sites. Without direct participation in implementation and outcomes delivery, but with high-level political support and cultivated relationships with PLA administrators, community stakeholders gained indirect, though not inconsequential, influence in this process. This influence largely derived from their relationships with Metro board members and staff—a product of the inclusive PLA formulation process, which evidenced community influence. Among others, Supervisor Ridley-Thomas's leadership in championing the PLA gave the agency the authority and motivation to focus on PLA outcomes and to work with the community to address resident concerns.[91]

This implementation structure motivated the general contractor on the Crenshaw Line, Walsh Shea, to hire local workers. Beyond monthly reporting to the Metro board of directors, the prime contractor faced financial penalties if PLA goals were not met. Given that Metro assessed penalties on a previous contract, penalties represented a legitimate threat. If Metro was unwilling to assess penalties for noncompliance to the community benefits provisions, or any other part of the PLA, contractors would lack a key structural incentive to adhere to the policy. As one Metro staff noted, penalties gave the prime contractor "skin in the game" so that it gained an incentive to implement the agreement, forcing subcontractors to similarly work to achieve outcomes. Further, as Metro is the major transportation provider in the greater Southern California region—the second largest metropolitan area in the country, with many billions of dollars in contracts at stake—contractors interested in working on transportation construction in Southern California cannot afford to gain a bad reputation with the agency or its board. With so many large-scale transportation projects coming down the pipeline in Los Angeles at the time that project planning began, future contracts additionally motivated contractor compliance—but likely only because Metro prioritized community outcomes delivery.[92]

This incentive drove contractors to work closely with unions and the jobs coordinator to refer targeted workers onto job sites. The union referral process is a critical component of ensuring that contractors have a pool of eligible workers from which to hire. Unions are primarily concerned with ensuring that "good folks" enter the construction trades, through "high standards," to safeguard their investment and ensure that unions produce quality work. As one union representative stated, "We don't want to take somebody in [and] a year later, after we spend an initial amount of money, find out that they really didn't know they had to have a shovel, use the shovel, or climb on ladders. It's a waste of money because there is somebody behind them that is really wanting that job."[93] Since construction unions invest so heavily in training during the apprenticeship process, they want to ensure that those individuals pursue construction as a long-term career. One way in which unions have come to additionally screen workers is through preapprenticeship programs, often administered by community groups, which put candidates through classes to teach them workforce skills and assess the worker's commitment before they enter an apprenticeship program.[94]

In response to barriers within the union referral process, the LABWC further sought to bridge critical local skills gaps that could otherwise prevent local worker hiring by creating preapprenticeship programs to screen local residents, direct them into construction union hiring processes, train basic workforce and technical skills necessary for workers to succeed in union apprenticeship programs, and support them on job sites. Metro also partnered with Los Angeles Trade Technical College to create boot camps that have served as preapprenticeship programs, to ensure that a sufficiently prepared local labor pool would exist for Metro to meet the PLA targeted hiring goals. Furthermore, with the Metro PLA, the jobs coordinator played a crucial role in coordinating between the contractors, unions, the community, apprenticeship programs, and Metro to identify and vet community members and direct them into these projects.[95]

Despite lacking a formal role in implementation, the LABWC sought to keep all parties focused on community interests, playing an important role in implementation. The LABWC successfully maintained pressure on elected officials and Metro, giving agency staff necessary support and an additional mandate to enforce the agreement with contractors, while providing crucial information and directing potential workers into targeted hire jobs. As one Metro employee stated, "the community partners have insights that we can't have, just because we work here, and we work in this building. We're out there, we try to go out there, but they're out there every day . . . you won't be successful, you won't be, if you don't engage your stakeholders." In this way, Metro staff repeatedly emphasized, both publicly and privately, that the community came to play an instrumental role in implementation, bringing essential resources to improve PLA outcomes, including information and local relationships.[96]

However, LAANE did not maintain a similar role in agreement implementation. Some speculated that this difference may reflect the organization's lack of funding for implementation work. In addition, as a regional organization, LAANE focuses on organizing around broader policy advocacy rather than on neighborhood-specific outcomes and advocacy for Black workers, in particular. Regardless, the organization's shifted role during agreement implementation—when the promises in the agreement could become real opportunities for residents—is an important reminder of the barriers, challenges, and costs inherent to agreement monitoring efforts.[97] While the presence of a community watchdog may have emerged in Los Angeles, communities face real barriers to mounting and maintaining these efforts.

Altogether, community activism and responsiveness from other actors created a fragile but persistent accountability to community benefits around the Crenshaw Line: those with control during implementation were repeatedly held accountable—indirectly but demonstrably—to the community. Throughout, however, the achieved accountability remained fragile. Rather, the enforcement structure was always vulnerable to falling apart if circumstances changed, including any one participant no longer needing to meet community outcomes to achieve their individual goals.

Fragile accountability does not mean that implementation will proceed smoothly and without effort, or that all individuals involved will be satisfied throughout this process. Rather, it suggests that all stakeholders have their incentives aligned to work to produce community outcomes even after policy approval and are held to community outcomes delivery as an ultimate policy objective. The foundation for this structure was laid during agreement negotiations, with enforceable agreement provisions and vested participants who built relationships. The structure persisted throughout a key period in agreement implementation on this important project. For this reason, Metro PLA participants remained committed to successful community benefits delivery during the Crenshaw Line project implementation, and in a manner consistent with the community's original goals: construction career jobs for targeted community members.

In this way, when each stakeholder has a vested interest in community benefits outcomes, either because they genuinely want to achieve benefits or they could face harm if outcomes do not materialize, stakeholders can work together to promote implementation by identifying, referring, and supporting targeted workers. Unlike in Milwaukee, the Metro PLA avoided managerial disconnects through the strong, active, and *proactive* relationship between all stakeholders, which was motivated and informed by influential community participation. While largely successful, accountability has remained a remarkably fragile process, vulnerable to shifting priorities, personnel turnover, and external changes.[98]

Therefore, pressure from the Metro board to remain focused on delivering community outcomes, encouraged by community vigilance, motivated agency staff, the contractors, and unions, even after the agreement was signed and the project moved forward. Community advocates continued to monitor and enforce the PLA, to question the agency and challenge its reputation within the community. This effort motivated Metro's changing practices. The LABWC was invited to enter jobsites on the Crenshaw Line, observe working conditions, and more easily track hiring outcomes through participation in implementation. Metro also altered reporting in response to community concern, though conflict over reporting persisted. Further, informed by the community, the Metro board actively pursued enforcement, regularly questioning the prime contractor during its monthly meetings. Finally, Metro extended its efforts to create an ambitious new goal for hiring female construction workers on its projects, producing a score card grading its activities. In this way, Metro staff members faced pressure from both top-down and bottom-up enforcement during implementation, driving them to focus on community outcomes.[99] The Atlanta, Seattle, and Milwaukee agreements did not produce this top-down and bottom-up enforcement structure; the processes and outcomes that these policies produced reflect their fractured accountability to community benefits.

Metro PLA implementation on the Crenshaw Line demonstrates that when all parties engaged in implementation are motivated to produce community outcomes, before *and after* agreement approval, benefits-sharing agreements can produce the community outcomes they promise and promote community goals. The dedication of the Metro board, the agency, contractors, unions, and community activists directly resulted from the relationships built during PLA formulation, and the commitments made to community benefits delivery. As a result, all parties remained motivated to stay at the table, working together to deliver community benefits, rather than walking away from the commitments made during negotiations.

Regardless, even in the most ideal scenarios, such as the Metro PLA, implementation remains fragile and difficult. It is difficult to ensure that all parties with influence over community outcomes retain a vested interest in community outcomes during implementation. Many factors could disrupt this structure, from changes among the Metro board of directors, to the community lacking the resources or wherewithal to persist in community enforcement, to economic or political fluctuations that affect construction labor markets and project progress. Such changes can cause accountability structures to fall apart, leaving the remaining parties without external motivation or necessary resources to produce community outcomes. In the Metro PLA case, the community emerged in a watchdog role, to indirectly pressure agreement administrators and the oversight agency to motivate all parties to stay focused on the promised community outcomes, achieved via their influence over the elected officials on the Metro board of directors. However, their influence was effective at inducing compliance only because the other actors involved, particularly Metro and contractors, remained vulnerable to community pressure. As the project nears completion, some of these transitions have already occurred: Supervisor Ridley-Thomas left the Los Angeles County Board of Supervisors in 2020.[100]

In the Crenshaw Line case, while community stakeholders lacked the ability to directly produce outcomes, they gained considerable, albeit indirect, influence during implementation. Community enforcement proved effective: community organizations in Los Angeles leveraged their political influence and developed relationships with Metro staff and the county supervisors on the Metro board of directors. They used these relationships to increase their influence over PLA implementation. As a result, community actors gained access to work sites for observations, influenced PLA reporting, extended and inspired new policies, and motivated stakeholders with direct power to produce desired outcomes. Moreover, the Metro PLA—once a controversial, novel workforce development policy that many believed was beyond the scope of a regional transportation agency—has become a core agency policy.

As a result of their efforts, the Crenshaw project under the Metro PLA included far more work conducted by Black workers than other projects and met established goals. Through their efforts, community stakeholders created a productive, though sometimes adversarial, relationship with other stakeholders, including Metro staff and board members. Indeed, all stakeholders recognized the community as an influential and beneficial participant in implementation—one that has enhanced outcomes. As a result of their combined effort, the project has achieved unprecedented outcomes for Black construction workers in Los Angeles. As one respondent summarized, "There is nowhere in L.A.—*on no project in Los Angeles*—where there is that percentage of African Americans working on a project."[101]

The next chapter builds on the lessons from Atlanta, Seattle, Milwaukee, and Los Angeles to explain why benefits-sharing agreements systematically risk falling short of their community benefits promises and often fail to significantly shift existing power distributions in urban development. Regardless of these fundamental limitations, the cases described here show how benefits-sharing agreements can generate meaningful benefits for affected residents if these policies are effectively developed and implemented. Therefore, the final chapter identifies strategies for creating agreements that deliver on their promises.

CHAPTER 5

Limits Learned: The Challenges and Opportunities of Benefits-Sharing Agreements

Driven by economic growth and renewed investment, American cities have experienced significant urban growth in the twenty-first century so far. Growth interests, including landowners, developers, and labor unions, have pursued new and marquee projects. They have hoped to capture massive profits and advance their development goals, often assisted by local government support and public subsidies. These locally and regionally impactful projects include those discussed in this book: the Mercedes-Benz stadium in Atlanta, the Park East redevelopment in Milwaukee, the Yesler Terrace redevelopment project in Seattle, and the Crenshaw/LAX transit project in Los Angeles. As in the past, urban elites with a growth agenda, money, and influence have largely advanced these projects, supported by local government, disproportionately controlling which projects get built and how development takes place. In the process, elites have continued to attempt to organize urban areas and governance processes to their benefit.[1]

These projects enter into a consequential, ongoing history in which urban development projects have produced considerable harm for adjacent communities and afforded minimal or limited chances for local participation. These patterns occurred before and during urban renewal, and have continued since, in different forms. New projects pose similar issues for low-income communities—disproportionately communities of color, and often the same communities that endured past harm. New urban development projects threaten to follow older patterns: to gentrify communities, displace existing residents, reshape cities, and exclude many residents from the prosperity they promise. However, many of these projects also offer unique opportunities. They supply needed investments for historically underserved communities and neighborhoods that have long grappled with the immediate and cumulative effects of decades of disinvestment. If future development promotes equity and inclusion, low-income residents could capture important benefits from local investment, including jobs. How can we maximize these possibilities? Examples from the past provide some lessons for the future.

Community activists began using benefits-sharing agreements as a tool to shift the historical distribution of the harms and benefits associated with large-scale urban development projects. They sought to ensure that impacted communities faced less harm and experienced greater benefits. They intended to accomplish this goal by leveraging urban growth to foster change through two related pathways: (1) altered benefits distributions, toward greater community benefits, and (2) more equitable power distributions in urban development decision-making, accomplished through influential community participation in project approval and agreement negotiations. The advocates that originally designed these agreements held high hopes that this new strategy would deliver lasting benefits to communities. They hoped to establish an equitable development paradigm, using agreements as a tool to enhance community power. This shift was intended to enable community advocates to generate sufficient leverage over developers that historically underserved communities could gain some degree of control over local development—not just token participation or minor input, but the ability to fundamentally direct how local development occurs and who benefits. Due to their potential to transform urban development, these agreements have since spread across the nation.

With opportunities to build equity-focused coalitions with allied interests, communities have sometimes partnered with labor unions looking to advance projects and secure more union jobs amid lower unionization rates. Consistent with prior research, the Seattle and Los Angeles cases show the enormous potential for using community-labor coalitions to enact progressive labor-related policy. These agreements demonstrate how some unions are attempting to strategically move beyond exclusive and often discriminatory hiring practices, toward a more inclusive, intersectional organizing model where unions and communities pursue equity-focused policies together.[2]

These cases show that while labor remains a clear urban growth ally in many ways, community benefits organizing and related equity-oriented labor policies such as living wage campaigns have produced important urban organizing shifts. These policies reflect that community and union interests now commonly pursue broad political support for benefits agreements, local labor opportunities, and equity-oriented labor policy.[3] Because they have potential for delivering important opportunities, benefits-sharing agreement negotiations have become a new and highly consequential organizing arena. Communities contest development projects, sometimes aligned with labor unions, to draw developers and local governments to the negotiating table, to determine how development projects proceed.

However, the agreements detailed here illustrate how benefits-sharing agreements can fall far short of the ideal that early advocates held for significant power redistributions in urban development. Rather, as urban and planning theory would suggest, growth and capital interests still dominate local development. Communities alone often lack the power to reject unwanted development entirely or to fundamentally alter projects to their advantage unless growth interests support their goals. Therefore, benefits-sharing agreements generally fit within, and do not fundamentally threaten, the existing neoliberal paradigm, in which those with money and power disproportionately control urban development processes, largely determining the final and cumulative outcomes produced. While these agreements represent an important land use innovation to potentially redistribute project benefits, they have not significantly altered *who* controls development, and *to what end*.

Since benefits-sharing agreements do not reconcile the fundamental power asymmetries in urban development, which bias toward growth, these agreements inherently risk delivering little to the communities that organize for benefits. Even if negotiations reach an agreement acceptable to all parties, pro-development interests generally get what they want when the agreement is signed. After this happens, these actors can walk away from their community commitments, finding ways to minimize or avoid benefits delivery. Even union allies may find that when the rubber hits the road of implementation, their goals motivate them to pursue implementation in different ways than residents would. When this happens, communities and their interests can become figuratively *left at the negotiating table,* with few alternatives to hold others accountable to their commitments.

Even still, while benefits-sharing agreements deliver disparate and often limited outcomes for communities, they can produce meaningful benefits to the communities negotiating them. Therefore, it is important to understand how stakeholders can undertake these agreements in ways that advance community goals during both agreement formulation and implementation—to shape the final outcomes produced. This chapter responds to that question by describing the systemic challenges that benefits-sharing agreements face, as a tool to promote equitable processes and outcomes in urban development. This discussion helps explain why some agreements deliver on their community promises while others do not. The final chapter builds on this analysis, identifying key ways for communities to ensure benefits delivery. Throughout, the lessons from Atlanta, Milwaukee, Seattle, and Los Angeles are crucial to understanding both the perils and the possibilities for future benefits-sharing agreements.

Why Communities Get Left at the Table

The Challenge of Negotiation

Theories of consensus building, referring to settings that range from negotiation[4] to collaboration,[5] help explain why residents, developers, unions, and other participants enter into benefits-sharing agreements.[6] In contemporary urban development, the relationships among communities, developers, unions, and local governments are frequently characterized by *mutual interdependence*, where these actors depend on others to achieve their desired goals, whether it be project approval, promoting local investment, or delivering local benefits from such investment.[7] Each party holds some leverage over others: residents can publicly oppose and delay projects through the public approvals and environmental review processes; unions can withhold support and their skilled labor pools; developers greatly determine how and where investment occurs, project specifics, and who benefits; and local governments can promise or withhold support, public approvals, and subsidies.[8] From Atlanta, to Seattle, to Milwaukee, to Los Angeles and beyond, this interdependence can effectively afford communities some leverage to demand new benefits from developers, local governments, unions, and other pro-growth interests—even if communities generally lack the structural and policy power to stop unwanted development altogether.[9] This context represents the underlying rationale that drives parties to the negotiating table to pursue benefits-sharing agreements.

Flawed negotiations can explain some of the contestation and limited outcomes produced in Atlanta and Seattle, as well as other benefits-sharing agreements that govern projects throughout the nation. Research on consensus building suggests that when deliberations[10] fail to meet certain conditions, they cannot be expected to deliver mutually beneficial outcomes.[11] Among these necessary conditions, the key stakeholders must be at the table, must be able to engage in a productive and honest dialogue, and must mutually depend on each other to achieve their individual goals.[12] In Atlanta, local government and community representatives entered into negotiations over a community benefits agreement. However, core dimensions of a benefits-sharing agreement were never genuinely on the table, including active negotiation with the Blank Foundation in community deliberations, the amount of money at stake, and whether the final policy would be legally binding. These restrictions limited community influence from the outset.

Flawed negotiations also characterized the Seattle agreement. In Seattle, community residents did not actively participate in negotiations. Labor union representatives repeatedly expressed that they lacked key information about the project, including how much of the total redevelopment project the agreement would govern. As a result, when it became more difficult to hire Yesler Terrace residents on the project than originally envisioned, the agreement parties lacked a key stakeholder in benefits delivery—community residents—and unions held lingering resentment over negotiations. Therefore, unions pursued the most viable route: bypassing community outcomes to meet the agreement terms, if not the original spirit of community benefits. These cases, therefore, illustrate how problematic agreement formulation contexts can undermine the policy terms, while also creating issues that extend into implementation.

Beyond flawed negotiations, however, critiques of consensus building and deliberative governance suggest that urban development negotiations create a forum that is poorly suited to generate transformative community development outcomes. Rather, deliberation can reinforce the existing dominance of urban elites over the development process and neutralize development opposition. Urban studies research has long demonstrated that urban elites—including developers, labor unions, and local governments—frequently coordinate their efforts to dominate local decision-making and outcomes. What Logan and Molotch (1987) call the "growth machine" reflects the ongoing search by urban elites to promote urban growth in order to generate profit, seeking more intensified land uses and less regulation in development. The growth machine's control is not complete; rather, the ongoing, resultant conflict between pro-growth and slow- or anti-growth interests shapes urban development outcomes in important and varying ways.[13] Those local residents and communities affected by development proposals often fall in the latter, anti-growth category, as they generally experience concentrated harm but minimal benefits from new development projects. Through their continuing interactions and developed relationships with local governments, growth interests generally enjoy disproportionate influence and institutional access in the development process, affording them more power to effectively advance their goals than underserved residents and communities. Because of the potential to secure additional work, labor unions have historically acted to support the growth machine.[14]

Deliberation over urban development outcomes, including benefits negotiations, can further concentrate the influence of urban elites over urban development outcomes. Deliberation is inherently exclusive and resource intensive, which frequently prevents open participation through selective engagement. As a result, deliberation offers a limited form of democratic participation, *at best*. Rather, deliberation tends to systematically overrepresent elites, their interests, and procedures where outcomes accrue to their benefit. At the same time, deliberation often excludes marginalized groups, their interests, and procedures that would sway processes to their advantage, including public accountability measures.[15] Throughout, deliberation participants exert disproportionate control over the final agreement produced, even as their interests may not reflect or represent broader public interests.[16]

Therefore, even optimal benefits-sharing agreement negotiations are not fully open or democratic: negotiation participants largely shape the agreement terms, a process that tends to exclude nonparticipants and their goals. Power differentials between stakeholders cannot be easily removed from deliberation, but rather intrinsically shape relationships between stakeholders, and therefore transcend deliberations. In this way, consensus-building deliberations are inextricably situated within, and therefore at least partially reproduce, the existing power structures in which they occur.[17] This suggests that negotiation for community benefits is an inherently political and power-laden endeavor: nondemocratically selected parties represent and negotiate benefits for a broader community that cannot be entirely included in deliberations, a format that already favors urban elites. These settings, therefore, privilege elite interests and empowered voices—namely, urban growth priorities.

Furthermore, the decision to pursue negotiations can co-opt or neutralize opposition to development that might otherwise occur, operating as a tool to promote order. Simply through their participation in negotiation, participants are motivated to reach agreement and not undertake strategies that produce conflict or call for larger transformations than deliberations generally allow. Rather, the process of seeking consensus can obscure relevant conflicts, gloss over material forms of difference, and perpetuate the status quo by preventing some conflicts that may otherwise occur—*such as whether the development should take place at all.* Instead, conflict shifts toward a less adversarial and more incremental benefits negotiation process. In this way, deliberation enables elites to "legitimate their policies while bypassing electoral responsibility" through the appearance of consensus, while also rendering the public even more passive.[18] This is what happened in Los Angeles, Atlanta, and Seattle, where the benefits agreements were strategically used (in differing ways, and to varying degrees of success) as a tool to legitimize controversial, high-profile development and avoid additional public conflict.

Within a context where much of the pressure for urban development and growth reflects regional, national, and global political-economic forces, local deliberations over development projects represent a poorly suited forum to neutralize negative project effects. Rather, project harms are shaped by, and in turn can amplify, larger, impactful neighborhood change processes beyond the scope of any individual project. In pursuing a strategy often used to depoliticize controversial activities and obscure conflict, through ad hoc negotiations over individual development projects, such local deliberations cannot counter broader urban development forces that transcend the local scale. For this reason, many equity scholars and practitioners have called for urban organizing to "scale up" to broader regional, statewide, and even national campaigns. This position reflects the challenging reality that while the local scale deeply shapes how people experience inequality and governs important land use outcomes, moving political organizing and policy creation to broader scales than the local level can generate critical political leverage, link to larger social movements, build coalitions, minimize urban political opposition, and enhance organizing flexibility.[19]

Therefore, taken together with the avoidance of other, more conflict-driven strategies, the pursuit of ad hoc benefits negotiations can reinforce the status quo, offering an inherently limited strategy for enabling relatively less powerful participants to create more transformative outcomes.[20] In this way, collaboration "denies disempowered groups their most promising political tool" by prioritizing agreement and preventing conflicts that could possibly enact larger transformations.[21] Planners, public administrators, and public sector actors more generally are similarly co-opted from a potentially more transformative role. Rather than working to counter the broader political and economic processes that drive urban inequality, their work often addresses marginal concerns such as project design elements, not calling into question the projects themselves or linking to broader movements. Therefore, the work of planners and public administrators shifts from seeking to promote the long-term public interest to facilitators between stakeholders, with an emphasis on communication and consensus. In practice, these efforts operate to mitigate concerns about capital dominance, rather than tackle these issues outright.[22]

Benefits-sharing agreements ultimately represent such a concession, where communities may accept new projects that they might otherwise not support (such as the Mercedes-Benz stadium), leveraging projects for local benefits, rather than opposing new development altogether. While this tactic may co-opt opposition that could otherwise occur, this discussion is not intended to blame those community members who choose to negotiate. Within a legacy of community disinvestment and institutional neglect, many underserved communities face a difficult decision when forced to choose between accepting or rejecting local investment that could bring jobs, new amenities, or services—even if they fear the project may offer more harm than direct benefit.[23] In Los Angeles, for example, many leaders believed that it was a better long-term strategy to ensure that the new Metro line, with local stops, included the Crenshaw community, even if it threatened gentrification. The alternative, to be excluded from the regional transportation network, also posed extensive long-term harm.

Beyond the challenges associated with rejecting potential investment, many residents in these cases—like many communities across the nation—recognized, at the project outset, the strong likelihood that these projects would happen regardless of their opposition. As in the past, the preferences of urban elites and pro-growth interests frequently win out, potentially leaving residents with no direct project benefits, and no input into how the project unfolds. When viewed in this light, the pursuit of benefits negotiations can represent a bold and consequential demand—and sometimes the most viable community organizing option. When this is the case, the question then becomes, How can advocates work to ensure that these agreements deliver results for communities? The next section describes the particular challenges of benefits-sharing agreement implementation.

The Challenge of Implementing Benefits-Sharing Agreements

Taken together, therefore, deliberation, consensus building, and urban regime theories offer explanations as to why benefits-sharing agreements do not produce transformative processes, in which community participants gain control over how development occurs. Negotiations afford developers additional influence in the development process to advance growth interests. At the same time, the consensus building process creates ways for participants to avoid reconciling core conflicts over growth and profit. Since deliberation can act as a tool to undermine or co-opt resistance to development, rather than substantially altering the distribution of power or resources, even ideal deliberations can fail to motivate developers and development proponents to deliver on their promises if they have already met their original goals.

These interest and power asymmetries suggest that elites may not be motivated to deliver even the incremental benefits promised to communities during negotiation. Rather, we should expect that urban elites often seek to maintain as much control as possible over development, to promote growth and maximize their gain. Therefore, agreement implementation becomes critically important, explaining why some agreements do not deliver the outcomes promised.

Research on implementation—when the results of policies and plans are made real through the "carrying out of a basic policy decision"—reveals how the power asymmetries and conflicts not reconciled during consensus can manifest during implementation.[24] The structure of policy implementation can create unequal control for participants over what benefits-sharing agreements deliver, and for whom. Implementation research recognizes how, regardless of how agreements are formulated, actors have different levels and means of influence over the final outcomes produced based on their particular roles, ability to exert discretion, and actions. While both top-down policy enforcement and bottom-up community organizing and advocacy influence how implementation unfolds, those actors with direct control *during implementation* hold enormous influence over the outcomes that policies produce.[25]

Therefore, implementation research implies that when pro-development interests control implementation, they can disproportionately determine what gets delivered to communities and how—and potentially walk away from their community benefits commitments. From Atlanta, to Seattle, to Milwaukee, to Los Angeles, the agreements reviewed in this book illustrate how urban elites retain outsized influence over both creating and observing outcomes after the agreement gets signed. Afterward, these same actors may lack motivation to deliver promised community benefits. Furthermore, since pro-development interests generally get what they want early in the process— to promote development through project approvals, to publicly claim benefits delivery, and/or to secure public resources and subsidies—they may have little incentive afterward, *unless explicitly motivated*, to produce (often costly and cumbersome) community outcomes. At the same time, community leverage over pro-growth actors declines when the project moves forward after agreement approval. This structural pattern systematically leaves communities the most vulnerable to not getting what they originally sought from agreement negotiations. This inherent temporal and power asymmetry, combined with the tendency to deny community oversight during agreement implementation, means communities may fail to receive promised benefits—even after a benefits-sharing agreement gets signed.

Therefore, community interests may become marginalized during implementation when they lack direct influence over agreement provisions, such as worker hiring and grant allocations. Rather, pro-development interests frequently control these important outcomes during implementation. At the same time, those parties that negotiate benefits alongside communities, such as labor unions, may control benefits delivery during implementation in ways that community interests cannot, unless explicitly given authority during implementation—splitting these once-allied interests. The Seattle case, in particular, illustrates how even though labor unions might have been motivated to commit to community workforce provisions in order to improve their community reputation and secure additional union jobs, they retained different goals from community interests that shaped their implementation approach. For this reason, when it came to implementing the agreement and pursuing the challenging Section 3 hiring goals, unions avoided adhering to the spirit of the agreement—to draw new Yesler Terrace residents and Section 3 workers into unions—and instead reclassified and hired their own workers to produce results. Since they directly controlled worker referral, unions could protect their own interests during implementation, but did so at the expense of community outcomes.

These events illustrate the fundamental conflict that even a successful deliberation cannot overcome: the interests of community residents, local government, developers, and labor, and potentially other allies, likely differ in important ways—even if they align in advancing community benefits provisions during negotiations. It should be expected that these differences produce conflicts during implementation in ways that jeopardize community benefits delivery.[26] The Seattle agreement outcomes reflect the differing bottom lines of labor and community interests. In this way, while community-labor coalitions represent a powerful tool for equity organizing, this research suggests that the work of uniting disparate groups must continue even after a successful policy campaign or political victory.

Altogether, the agreements described in this book show how uncommitted or disinterested developers and elected officials, unions that are not held to their community commitments, agreement administrators constrained by resources or institutional commitment, and community activists who lack the time, resources, or ability to monitor implementation, can—and often do—move on after the agreement gets signed. Their departure jeopardizes community benefits delivery. Even for committed parties, the process of distributing benefits and monitoring outcomes, such as observing the intricacies involved with targeted worker hiring, can prove difficult to achieve. Indeed, in Atlanta, Milwaukee, and Seattle, some participants walked away from the process before community benefits fully materialized, endangering the promised benefits. Furthermore, developers, local governments, and unions sometimes exploited their inherent advantage in the timing of benefits delivery to their own benefit after the project moved forward. Their actions enabled them to secure their own goals first. Afterward, they could sometimes avoid or reduce their obligations and obscure outcomes, often in direct opposition to the community's original goals.

When pro-growth interests move on without delivering community outcomes, communities can organize to force developers, project owners, and other powerholders to deliver on their promises. Indeed, community organizing offers an important means to generate leverage and secure wins. However, community organizing for enforcement hinges on the structure of the implementation process—as in, who controls enforcement mechanisms, and their responsiveness to community pressure—as well as whether communities can create leverage through advocacy and outside enforcement strategies. The Los Angeles Black Worker Center's efforts around the Crenshaw/LAX transit project exemplify the potential for community organizing to effectively promote policy enforcement.

Research on community enforcement and co-enforcement implementation models, in which community groups promote implementation through advocacy and organizing, shows how communities can enhance and encourage implementation. Community actors can introduce new information, act as a watchdog, put pressure on other, more empowered actors, and highlight instances of noncompliance or insufficient transparency.[27] Scholars are careful to note, however, that these efforts must complement, rather than replace, more formalized and top-down implementation mechanisms. Rather, community activists often lack the information, resources, regulatory mechanisms, and direct control over outcomes to replace institutions as enforcement agents. Furthermore, while community enforcement enables community stakeholders to promote outcomes when other actors do not prioritize implementation, this strategy has proven most effective when it targets parties vulnerable to political pressure, such as elected officials. Interests not subject to public accountability mechanisms—such as the developers, contractors, and unions involved in benefits-sharing agreements, or elected officials unconcerned with accountability—can prove more impervious to community organizing.[28]

Potential Agreement Pitfalls: Nonresponsive Community Investment, Managerial Disconnections, and Community Bypass

This chapter has described how power systematically shifts away from communities as benefits-sharing agreements move into implementation, which can undermine community benefits delivery. The cases described in this book reveal three specific ways in which agreements can minimize accountability, related to this power shift: nonresponsive community investment, managerial disconnects, and community bypass. These patterns emerged from agreement structures and contexts that favored pro-development interests, creating barriers to implementation and undermining community outcomes.

The Atlanta Falcons Community Benefits Plan shows how, absent accountability mechanisms, philanthropic and local government participants can endanger community outcomes through *nonresponsive community investment*: community investment that does not carry out or accommodate community priorities and pressures. The Blank Foundation and local government officials and agencies in Atlanta pursued the Mercedes-Benz stadium development and the associated benefits plan with little concern for community goals, power sharing, and meaningful participation. As a result, legitimate questions persist about the extent to which this development project perpetuated the harmful legacy of stadium development in Atlanta—despite the best efforts of community activists to pressure the Blank Foundation and the city to deliver on their original commitments, consistent with community goals. This top-down, nonresponsive community investment approach, extending beyond the stadium benefits package as growth interests attract further investment into the Atlanta Westside, risks investing in neighborhoods in a way that will not meet the needs and priorities of existing residents. Rather, despite the best efforts of local organizers, the agreement did little to protect residents from the gentrification and displacement pressures that have already begun to take place.

The Yesler Terrace community workforce agreement shows the perils of benefits-sharing agreements that engage in *community bypass*, whereby agreements neglect to involve residents in meaningful ways. In addition to the challenges inherent to implementing this agreement, the intended beneficiaries—Yesler Terrace residents, public housing residents, and economically eligible Seattle residents—never pursued this agreement. Indeed, there is little evidence that the targeted community beneficiaries ever knew key information about these job opportunities. Rather, Yesler Terrace residents consistently focused on how the disruptive, controversial redevelopment project would impact their community, not on the construction jobs produced. In contrast to the Atlanta and Los Angeles agreements, where community residents and representatives fought for the agreement, remained vested in its outcomes, and maintained motivation to fight for community outcomes during implementation—that never occurred around the Yesler Terrace agreement. Absent community participation in the original agreement, no actor engaged in implementation focused on community benefits delivery, consistent with the original spirit of the agreement.

The PERC in Milwaukee illustrates the perils of *managerial disconnects*, where insufficient alignment and communication across public agencies tasked with implementation can reduce oversight effectiveness and create openings in agreement implementation for developers to potentially exploit. In Milwaukee, the county board of supervisors fought for the PERC and have continued to tout its benefits. However, in the decade that passed between when the policy was first approved and when development began, the board of supervisors and original participants moved on to fight new battles. Without vigorous oversight, and with key turnover in institutional personnel, county staff members strived to overcome implementation barriers and produce outcomes. Evidence indicates that developers exploited this disconnect between implementation staff and the board of supervisors to minimize their obligations under the PERC. Altogether, this context of managerial disconnect created a fractured accountability structure that limited agreement enforcement.

The Potential for Fragile but Persistent Accountability

These cases demonstrate that agreements must be carefully structured to ensure that all parties remain focused on community outcomes delivery. This structure requires vigorous and transparent enforcement, consistent with the community's original goals—even after participants meet their individual goals that originally drew them to the negotiating table. The Los Angeles Metro PLA produced this structure on the Crenshaw Line project through key moments in agreement implementation, with top-down administrative oversight from the Metro board of directors and bottom-up community enforcement from community activists. Leadership from elected officials motivated agency staff to prioritize community outcomes during implementation. Their top-down, active enforcement gave staff the authority and responsibility to hold contractors and unions accountable to referring and hiring targeted workers. While the Metro Board took a leadership role in driving the PLA, active community enforcement held Metro leadership accountable. As a result, the Metro board and staff remained engaged in vigilant oversight after the agreement transitioned to implementation, informed by community knowledge and supported by dedicated resources. This structure forced the agency to implement the agreement at least in dialogue, if not in accordance, with community priorities.

The Metro PLA was predisposed to strong top-down enforcement because of its status as a prominent agencywide, multiproject policy that captured media attention, rather than a small-scale, ad hoc agreement. This agency policy has governed transportation construction across the region, making it difficult for contractors to avoid working with the agency and through this policy. In contrast with Seattle, where the policy governed only one development project in an agency that infrequently undertakes new construction, the Metro PLA has already covered many billions of dollars in transportation projects. This scale, combined with the seriousness with which the Metro board and agency staff have taken the policy from the very beginning, helped ensure that all parties continued to work to deliver community outcomes. The scale also ensured that parties had key resources to promote enforcement, including a jobs coordinator. These conditions suggest that broader policies that increase the governance scale, combined with a strong role for the public sector in shaping the policy and promoting enforcement, can improve community benefits outcomes.[29] Throughout, however, previous research warns that public actors must not dominate negotiations and implementation in ways that undermine community power.[30]

Altogether, this combined top-down and bottom-up Metro PLA enforcement structure on the Crenshaw Line project afforded the community some influence over outcomes, however indirect. Further, it motivated all participants to remain focused on community outcomes delivery: the contractor faced penalties or ineligibility for future contracts, encouraging them to coordinate with the unions to hire targeted workers. This process was overseen by agency staff directly reporting to a highly vested oversight body actively monitoring outcomes, informed by community activists and supported by the jobs coordinator. However, this accountability structure remained remarkably fragile even during implementation, vulnerable to shifts in participation by elected officials and residents.

In Atlanta, Milwaukee, and Seattle, all or parts of this accountability structure were missing. In Atlanta, elected officials prioritized growth interests over community representation. Biased, stigmatized perceptions about community capacity motivated elected officials, Invest Atlanta, and the Blank Foundation to dismiss community concerns and priorities as they pursued local investment. Community advocacy in Atlanta did not generate community control or significant influence, as elected officials, Invest Atlanta, and the Blank Foundation proved largely nonresponsive to community pressure. In Seattle, community bypass produced an agreement where no outside party monitored agreement progress. In theory, the Section 3 hiring committee pressured contractors and unions to enforce the agreement terms, but this committee existed within the Seattle Housing Authority and had few tools to generate leverage. Therefore, contractors and unions exhibited little incentive to produce outcomes consistent with the original agreement spirit. Finally, in Milwaukee, a managerial disconnect emerged between the oversight body, the county board of supervisors, and county staff. While the county board and staff proved vested in the agreement and its outcomes, the board of supervisors shifted its attention to other issues, and staff were directly accountable to the county executive. Without pressure and information from community participants, who moved on from the agreement, the board of supervisors did not take a proactive oversight role or closely monitor community outcomes.

In this way, the Los Angeles agreement and context created an accountability structure that did not exist in the other cases. How can communities follow this model for successfully implementing a benefits-sharing agreement? The next chapter tackles this question by offering strategies to create accountability, to ensure that benefits-sharing agreements deliver on their community promises.

CHAPTER 6

Toward an Accountable Future: Strategies for Community Benefits Delivery

While some benefits-sharing agreements have provided important opportunities for communities, many have fallen short of their promises. How can future agreements follow a different path? This chapter prescribes necessary conditions for benefits-sharing agreements to deliver on their community benefits promises.

As this book illustrates, both agreement formulation (the events before the agreement gets signed) and implementation (what happens afterward, as actors work to carry out the agreement) critically shape what these policies actually deliver to communities. While implementation processes often remain overlooked, the agreements described in this book underscore how implementation represents a critical stage to determine agreement success. Indeed, those with control during implementation significantly influence the final outcomes produced by these agreements. Therefore, to achieve community benefits delivery consistent with community goals, agreements must be designed to promote accountability and ensure community influence until the final outcomes materialize. In particular, when agreements experience active top-down and bottom-up enforcement, they can create accountability and results—as occurred in Los Angeles.

This chapter outlines strategies to achieve accountability and foster the necessary conditions to deliver community benefits. Without carefully structured agreements, which promote enforcement and accountability even after the agreement gets signed, key challenges can arise to undermine community outcomes. Among these issues are those that emerged in Atlanta, Seattle, and Milwaukee: nonresponsive community investment, community bypass, and managerial disconnect. This chapter offers suggestions to avoid these paths.

To this end, the following strategies can build accountability to community outcomes and promote community goals. These provisions are necessary to improve benefits-sharing agreement outcomes:

1. Agreements should include penalties for noncompliance that hinge the interests of all stakeholders on community outcomes delivery.
2. Agreements require established and influential oversight bodies.
3. Both agreement negotiations and oversight need a resourced, impartial, and expert third party to promote transparency and outcomes and to protect community interests.
4. Agreements must enable communities to stay at the table, by sharing power and resources with community beneficiaries, to ensure that they have an influential and resourced role in agreement oversight.
5. Agreement implementation, like negotiations, should be transparent, inclusive, and responsive.
6. Agreements need provisions to protect these policies during leadership, staff, and community transitions.
7. While agreement terms necessarily differ based on the local context, communities should consider prioritizing benefits that promote long-term stability, to help residents avoid displacement or other harm.
8. Planners, public administrators, and other relevant public actors should cultivate and use their expertise to inform and improve, but not dominate, agreement negotiations and implementation.
9. Communities and local government actors should work together to scale up agreements to broader policies where it is possible to do so without sacrificing community benefits.

Recommendations

1. Agreements should include penalties for noncompliance that hinge the interests of all stakeholders on community outcomes delivery.

As the agreements reviewed in this book reveal, benefits-sharing agreements create a consequential asymmetry that, left unchecked, can undermine community outcomes: after the agreement gets signed and the project moves forward, pro-growth stakeholders can often walk back from their community promises. However, agreements can be designed to create penalties for such noncompliance, to promote accountability. As prior agreements and comparable policies demonstrate, effective penalties could include required deposits that are returned only on compliance, clawbacks (provisions where developers must pay a financial penalty if they do not meet certain provisions), delayed payments or repayments of public money such as bonds, and nonfinancial provisions such as ineligibility for future contracts. These tools similarly help ensure that developers remain vested in community outcomes even after the project moves forward. Since many of the projects that benefits-sharing agreements govern at least partially hinge on public funding, local governments can work with developers and communities to sequence funding in ways that enable projects to move forward while retaining levers to keep developers accountable to their original commitments. With potential noncompliance penalties at stake, stakeholders should also work together to determine clear and fair success criteria, to democratize expectations and enforcement.

In this way, rather than project approval and public funds issuance (if applicable) representing a free pass to move forward, agreements can structure implementation to create real penalties if developers avoid their commitments—or alternatively, material benefit from developer follow-through. Even in Milwaukee, where county administrators required a $50,000 deposit—a relatively low amount for a multimillion-dollar project—evidence suggests that the threat of penalties effectively motivated developers to deliver on their contractual obligations. In turn, this deposit encouraged developers and prime contractors to pressure subcontractors to comply with the terms. In Los Angeles, the threat of withholding access to future, lucrative Metro contracts further inspired contractors to work with the agency to meet goals that they might not otherwise have prioritized.

Events in the Atlanta and Seattle cases may have proceeded very differently with the potential to assess penalties, clawbacks, or sanctions—particularly if communities had a vote over this decision. In Atlanta, hinging at least some project subsidies on community benefits delivery, consistent with the objectives of community advocates, may have motivated the Blank Foundation and Invest Atlanta to pursue community goals more directly. In Seattle, the Section 3 Advisory Committee lacked a compelling lever to motivate contractors to produce community outcomes or undertake additional outreach. Furthermore, with few bidders and only occasional redevelopment by the

Seattle Housing Authority, the threat of eligibility for future contracts did not significantly jeopardize future contractor profits. Absent other incentives, the unions and contractors lacked a structural motivation to deliver on the agreement's original community benefits vision.

2. *Agreements require established and influential oversight bodies.*

Agreements should establish an influential oversight body in the agreement terms, to hold accountable developers, contractors, unions, local governments, and others with control over community outcomes. This oversight body needs transparent access to wide-ranging, relevant data to observe the nuances of agreement outcomes, produced in a timely manner. Timeliness is critically important: some agreement provisions are complex and challenging to achieve, requiring time for participants to figure out how to deliver results. Early delays or failures in establishing worker pipelines or dedicating grants, even despite stakeholders' best efforts, can undermine cumulative possibilities for success. Oversight bodies should be able to deploy both carrots (incentives, resources, and expertise to support agreement implementation) and sticks (the penalties for noncompliance mentioned previously, including clawbacks that allow for revoking subsidies or payments on noncompliance, and ineligibility for future contracts). The combination of carrots and sticks can promote compliance in ways that enable participants to flexibly create effective incentive structures across contexts.

The agreements presented here illustrate how, even with vigilant oversight, community benefits may not materialize because of the inherent challenges of implementation; the competing, frequently opposing interests of developers and communities; and insufficient information or clarity about agreement outcomes. However, evidence from Milwaukee and Los Angeles illustrates how, when an influential oversight body oversees agreement implementation, this body can promote community benefits delivery. In Milwaukee, the original Park East Advisory Committee met to review and rate development proposals. While the committee stopped meeting during the economic recession, it originally shaped how development occurred on the Park East land. If properly resourced and authorized, this influence could have continued throughout implementation.

Similarly, in Los Angeles, Metro PLA outcomes on the Crenshaw Line have been widely attributed to vigilant oversight by the Metro board. While the Metro board has not granted direct community control over agreement enforcement, it holds public meetings with active public participation and involves democratically elected leaders. The agency demonstrated responsiveness to resident concerns, therefore remaining broadly accountable to residents in this case. To this end, the Metro board worked with contractors to improve outcomes over time, troubleshooting issues that arose with the agreement's complex hiring goals and processes, and supporting contractors to overcome the intricacies of implementation. In contrast, influential oversight was explicitly denied in Atlanta. Rather, the Community Benefits Plan Committee in Atlanta was limited by local government to acting only as a review committee with no oversight control, despite residents' best efforts to use the body to act in this capacity.

3. Both agreement negotiations and oversight need a resourced, impartial, and expert third party to promote transparency and outcomes and to protect community interests.

Both agreement negotiations and oversight should include expert third parties, to promote impartial and effective oversight. The ad hoc nature of benefits-sharing agreements and their implementation poses significant problems for community beneficiaries. Rather, independently negotiated agreements risk multiple issues because they often lack the scale to warrant significant resource investment in negotiation and implementation. As a result, negotiations may not effectively represent community interests and ensure that community negotiators can achieve a fair deal. Further, ad hoc agreements may suffer from structural implementation failures that undermine compliance, such as insufficient levers that ensure broad stakeholder participation in implementation and penalties for noncompliance.

Benefits-sharing agreements are often extremely technical. This is particularly true for targeted hire provisions, which require effective management; established relationships and expertise related to worker referral; ongoing troubleshooting; coordination with government agencies, unions, community groups, and construction firms; and active monitoring and enforcement. As many cautioned, there is a significant learning curve to implementation. Even parties with the best intentions may struggle with implementation if they lack sufficient resources and experience.[1]

For these reasons, many labor and community representatives cited the need for impartial, expert third parties to lend their expertise to overseeing agreement negotiation and implementation, to effectively promote transparent and inclusive processes. In this way, impartial, expert third parties can ensure that benefits-sharing agreements achieve fair negotiation processes and terms for community beneficiaries, to help equalize (however partially) the power and expertise imbalances inherent to negotiations. Third-party negotiators are frequently involved in PLA deliberations to bring critical expertise to these highly technical agreements, including agreements across the Los Angeles and Seattle regions.

Furthermore, impartial third-party agreement administrators can improve agreement implementation if they are insulated from political and other pressures. This separation can allow them to promote accountability more readily than internal administrators (agency staff who oversee implementation). Since they are not bound by institutional obligations or conflicts, and are not as vulnerable to political conflicts, third-party administrators may be more likely to assess noncompliance penalties. However, this is true only if third-party administrators are funded through agencies in a way that enables independent enforcement. If so, impartial experts can be used to oversee implementation with the sole task of ensuring accountability, just as professional consultants are frequently brought in to negotiate PLAs in the first place.[2] Thus, third-party administration can help ensure that community interests remain a priority during implementation, treated as a necessary deliverable just like any other contractual provision. Furthermore, this role can give parties to the agreement the resources and technical expertise to effectively troubleshoot problems as they arise.

4. Agreements must enable communities to stay at the table, by sharing power and resources with community beneficiaries, to ensure that they have an influential and resourced role in agreement oversight.

Agreements should include provisions to ensure that communities can remain engaged in implementation oversight, including with empowered roles on oversight bodies. Community participation in oversight not only helps build accountability to community outcomes but can help move development processes toward more inclusive decision-making. While local governments and developers alike widely avoided direct community control over agreement oversight, participation by community stakeholders in established oversight bodies could help ensure that agreement outcomes are protected and accepted.

Not only can community participation build trust and improve implementation dynamics, but research on community enforcement and co-enforcement models[3] shows how community participation in policy enforcement can improve outcomes by yielding new and important information. The role of community participants in the Los Angeles Metro PLA illustrates this dynamic, where the LABWC improved information and further motivated other stakeholders to pursue top-down enforcement. In Los Angeles, representatives from Metro, contractors, and the community reported that community enforcement improved implementation, including by providing on-the-ground reports and unique information. Further, community engagement gave agency staff the political backing to push for outcomes to materialize, while fostering connections between other stakeholders and the community, including agreement beneficiaries. Community groups won major concessions, including access to work sites for monitoring, and additional and altered reporting. Importantly, outcomes improved over time in many ways.

While residents in Atlanta similarly organized to enforce implementation, their efforts produced different results since they lacked sufficient leverage to compel local government and philanthropic responsiveness. In this way, community organizing to enforce implementation of benefits-sharing agreements requires developers and local governments—and through them, unions and contractors—to remain vulnerable to community pressure, even after the agreement gets signed. The agreements show that, beyond strong leadership from public officials who seek to represent their constituents, and unless authorized by an oversight role, the community's real, persistent source of leverage after the agreement gets signed is its ability to publicly endanger the reputations of other stakeholders by exposing noncompliance. Yet, even where parties are sensitive to their public reputations, the threat of public exposure by residents may not necessarily generate sufficient incentive to induce public and private stakeholders to produce community outcomes. Therefore, even motivated community participants face persistent and significant barriers to maintaining sufficient leverage after the agreement gets signed.

Unless ensured a seat at the table during agreement implementation, community stakeholders have only indirect control over whether their outcomes will materialize. Without direct influence, they must rely on other stakeholders to comply with the agreement. Therefore, unless the agreement mandates such a protected implementation oversight role, no real guarantee exists that stakeholders will voluntarily adhere to the agreement terms and that community outcomes will materialize. Even with organization, motivation, and sufficient resources, community stakeholders approach implementation from an inherently weak position if the agreement does not afford them influence during implementation.

Furthermore, community vigilance comes at a cost, including significant time, money, technical expertise, and effort. Community watchdog efforts place a significant burden on residents and organizations. Community monitoring and enforcement requires the resources to be vigilant and effective, to gain the necessary information to track implementation, and to make their voices heard in an environment where media reporting favors resourced, prominent actors and storytelling about larger geographies than neighborhoods.[4] By leaving underresourced residents and organizations to monitor and enforce agreements, the burden of compliance falls to communities that generally lack essential resources for this work. Therefore, agreements must provide financial compensation and other resources for community participation in oversight throughout implementation, to give community residents and organizations the ability to remain vigilant until promised outcomes materialize. Unless resources are dedicated to support community participation, agreements effectively deny many community advocates the ability to participate in benefits delivery, while often simultaneously burdening them with this task.

Without institutional support and formalized participation, residents face significant barriers to information access, particularly for outcomes that are not readily or reliably observable. Community stakeholders also face significant turnover; the PERC shows the difficulties involved in sustaining community vigilance for more than a decade—which is what some agreements require. Though far less time passed in Atlanta, residents became exhausted and struggled, because of the cumbersome negotiations process and their nonresponsive counterparts, to mount the oversight effort needed. As some residents experienced burnout and moved on, this unsustainable, unfunded burden fell to a smaller number of residents.

Therefore, it remains problematic to leave agreement oversight to nonresourced community enforcement efforts, since community organizations and residents act from an inherent resource disadvantage. However, residents are uniquely positioned to improve implementation, because of their local knowledge, different information, local embeddedness, and deeply vested interest in the outcome. It is also right and important to ensure that residents can participate in implementation, to build inclusive participation throughout the process, generate trust, and create more equitable planning processes. For these reasons, agreements should include provisions to resource community participation. Without such efforts, community participation and outcomes cannot be ensured, leaving community benefits dependent on the actions of other stakeholders, who often maintain different priorities.

Altogether, benefits-sharing agreements—if they are to be a tool to promote equity and inclusion in urban development—must share power with community beneficiaries, accomplished through empowered and resourced roles in agreement oversight. Indeed, power sharing, with inclusive and equitable processes throughout deliberation and implementation can build community influence, capacity, and trust, largely through transparency and accountability. To accomplish this, however, agreements must allow communities real control over development outcomes—not just in agreement deliberation, but also in implementation. This distinction enables community stakeholders to call into question the moments when agreements depart from the original goals, and to hold all parties accountable to their original commitments.

5. Agreement implementation, like negotiations, should be transparent, inclusive, and responsive.

As the events described in this book underscore, implementation is a critical but often overlooked stage of the community benefits process. Rather, for benefits-sharing agreements to improve equity and inclusion in urban development, transparency, inclusivity, and responsiveness must exist in agreement implementation, as well as negotiation. These processes are inextricably linked.

Each agreement described here demonstrates the importance of being able to observe the fine-grained details of implementation: not just who gets hired on a project, for example, but how long their job lasted, what type of labor they performed, and so on. In this way, observing benefits-sharing agreement outcomes is frequently far more complex than simply seeing whether a park was actually built. Frequently, obscured details prove critically important, since they shed light on the extent to which the agreement achieves broader, often complex goals, such as producing career opportunities. Throughout each case, limited transparency prevented stakeholders from understanding the full outcomes produced by these policies.

Whether information is hidden, or conversely, the extent to which community advocates can demand and receive additional vital information, can—and, often, should—critically shape perceptions of the agreement among residents and beyond. Powerholders and agreement administrators should yield to demands for more information wherever possible, to build trust with communities, and to improve information and outcomes. Concessions in transparency can improve public trust and outcomes by enhancing community oversight. This proved true in Los Angeles, where community observations yielded important information on the disparate jobs performed by workers—even though Metro could have still delivered better and more complete information. Agreement participants must understand the history of harm and institutional neglect into which these agreements frequently enter. This perspective can help pro-development interests appreciate that valid transparency demands will likely exceed what they believe is necessary or relevant. Regardless, the history of harmful, and often discriminatory, institutional decisions in disinvested communities makes transparency a vital step toward greater equity in urban development.[5]

To this end, inclusivity and responsiveness are essential ingredients to build trust, to ensure that community priorities are adequately represented and enacted into the agreement and its final outcomes. The nonresponsive community investment that occurred in the Atlanta case illustrates how powerholders during agreement negotiations and implementation—parties with at least some control over decision-making—have a responsibility to promote inclusivity and to respond to community priorities when possible. The moment that representatives in Atlanta bypassed community influence by fast-tracking the benefits plan through the community without its approval represents an extreme case of nonresponsiveness. Such actions can enhance distrust, exacerbate community harm, and minimize community influence over agreements that claim to enhance equity in urban development. However, even less egregious actions, such as avoiding requests for greater transparency or power sharing, or ignoring community preferences, which occurred throughout each case, can similarly undermine the equitable development goals that originally inspired community benefits organizing.

In contrast, the Yesler Terrace agreement illustrates the perils of attempting to represent community interests without significant community inclusion, where exclusion in agreement formulation undermined the agreement results. In Seattle, residents focused their attention on avoiding displacement rather than on capturing the jobs produced by the redevelopment, and therefore never really participated in the agreement. The lack of inclusion and responsiveness to community priorities illustrates how, for agreements to support community development, benefits must reflect and promote community goals. To advance community goals, communities need to drive these agreements in an influential way from the very beginning.

6. Agreements need provisions to protect these policies during leadership, staff, and community transitions.

Individual leadership can greatly shape implementation, by either enhancing or undermining implementation and enforcement capabilities. Leadership, among elected officials but also public managers and community leaders, can ensure that community interests are prioritized and represented throughout implementation. Conversely, when elected officials dominate benefits negotiation and implementation, they can diminish community goals by misrepresenting interests and undermining community power. Indeed, much of the outcomes of these cases—both successes and failures—are directly attributable to leadership decisions—primarily, whether and how local leaders represent and respond to community residents. Agreement successes often resulted from the deliberate efforts of empowered individuals who used their direct control over outcomes or influence over others to advance community interests—sometimes motivated only by a personal commitment to equity and inclusion.

The importance of leadership implies that leadership transitions can threaten implementation of benefits-sharing agreements, by removing key sources of accountability, commitment, and institutional knowledge. This is particularly true for long-term policies including the PERC and the Metro PLA, which require sustained oversight that can effectively endure over time. Benefits-sharing agreements can reduce the impact of leadership transitions by institutionalizing resourced and transparent third-party accountability and oversight within the agreement itself, to protect this role and ensure its persistence over time.

7. While agreement terms necessarily differ based on the local context, communities should consider prioritizing benefits that promote long-term stability, to help residents avoid displacement or other harm.

New development projects enter into larger forces of neighborhood change. These contexts are shaped not just by the development projects that happen locally, to which benefits-sharing agreements may apply, but also by regional and broader dynamics of housing, economic, and job markets, as well as public and private investment. Communities—and even cities and regions—lack full control over these impactful forces. For this reason, large-scale projects often catalyze or amplify broader neighborhood changes that extend far beyond the immediate effects or boundaries of a particular development project.

In this way, benefits-sharing agreements are fundamentally limited by a scale asymmetry. These agreements advance negotiations over inherently local, ad hoc projects, to tackle issues that are influenced by phenomena that range from local to global in scale. A single project—even a multibillion-dollar stadium—cannot distribute sufficient community benefits, even if effectively administered, to offset the displacement and other harms that projects often create or amplify. However, when viewed within broader neighborhood change and investment dynamics, this perspective suggests that some benefits can provide greater stability to existing residents in the face of broader, longer-term displacement pressures.

To accommodate this inherent scale limitation within the agreement, communities should consider pursuing benefits that act as stabilizing forces over the long term (such as affordable housing, community land trusts, job training, and jobs for residents), rather than community benefits that could catalyze gentrification and act as amenities for future, wealthier residents (such as parks and physical design improvements). This is not to say that communities should not pursue benefits like parks, when this is what residents need and want. Whether benefits are appropriate, or the determination of how much is enough to make a project sufficiently equitable, is an inherently context-specific consideration that residents must participate in deciding.[6] However, it is important to recognize that different community benefits offer varying degrees of protection from gentrification and displacement pressures, which these development projects may amplify. To this end, not all community benefits are equal in offering positive change and neutralizing negative project effects. Furthermore, this broader context underscores the essential point that benefits agreements do not buy institutions and pro-growth advocates out of their inherent obligations to work to create systems that advance racial, social, economic, and environmental justice.

8. Planners, public administrators, and other relevant public actors should cultivate and use their expertise to inform and improve, but not dominate, agreement negotiations and implementation.

Earlier research warned that local governments can dominate negotiations and, in the process, reduce community power.[7] Events in Atlanta and Seattle confirm these harmful possibilities, demonstrating the various ways in which the interests of local government bodies and leaders did not necessarily align with community interests. In contrast, evidence from Milwaukee and Los Angeles illustrates the potential for local governments to promote community interests during agreement negotiation and implementation in ways that community advocacy, alone, could not accomplish. Therefore, this research suggests that the public sector can support community benefits organizing, playing an important role by leveraging institutional resources and authority to advance local interests and share power. Throughout, however, local government engagement must supplement inclusive community participation in agreement negotiations and implementation, rather than replace it.

Many of the recommendations specified in this chapter can be more easily achieved with local government resources and expertise, leveraging the inherent longevity and stability of government institutions. Therefore, even for investment led by the private and nonprofit sectors, an important role exists during both agreement formulation and implementation for actors representing the public interest, including planners and public administrators.[8] As the cases in this book demonstrate, how agreement implementation occurs determines whether the benefits that an agreement commits to communities are made real—or, conversely, whether an agreement only delivers false hope and empty promises to communities in exchange for their project support and resources. Planners in community development organizations and public agencies can steward implementation, to ensure that these agreements do more than produce tokenistic deliberations and partial outcomes, but rather offer real opportunities for residents.

Since benefits-sharing agreements have become increasingly common and scaled to govern multiple projects, planners and public actors can use their unique position and expertise to improve policy terms and outcomes. By acting in this way, they can work to carefully structure these policies so that they deliver optimal outcomes for community beneficiaries—operating in an "equity planning" capacity, using their influence and position to advocate for marginalized perspectives.[9] As Marisa Zapata and Lisa Bates (2015) note, "*equity planners are everywhere.* . . . Today's equity planners are not only those working in municipal planning departments, but are found in community-based organizations, labor unions, metropolitan planning organizations (MPOs), and health departments." Benefits-sharing agreement negotiations and implementation can draw on the potential for individuals in these wide-ranging roles to use their positions to promote equity. Their activities cannot be expected to overcome the structural limitations of benefits-sharing agreements, where these policies create fundamentally limited levers of social change. However, these cases illustrate, again and again, how the behavior of individual actors, including local government and agency staff, local leaders, and community organization representatives, can deeply influence policy outcomes. Public actors—acting as equity planners—can support this important work.

9. Communities and local government actors should work together to scale up agreements to broader policies where it is possible to do so without sacrificing community benefits.

As previous research has demonstrated, and events in Milwaukee and Los Angeles confirm, the potential to scale up ad hoc agreements to broader equity-oriented policies can increase the impact of community benefits organizing efforts, avoid additional, resource-intensive negotiations, and make developers more likely to respond to enforcement efforts.[10] Furthermore, the advantage of scale can also make it easier to fund and institutionalize community enforcement efforts, and to create impactful oversight, though these efforts may prove difficult to fund regardless.[11] Because of these advantages and the potential for creating greater impact, cities from Detroit to Portland have attempted to enact broader benefits policies, with some success.

However, many issues arise with the move to scale. Attempts to enact benefits provisions across jurisdictions can further politicize community benefits organizing by opening these activities up to broader public scrutiny, resistance from pro-growth actors, and political processes. With greater politicization, benefits policies such as the City of Seattle priority hire ordinance have faced critique for promising fewer benefits after they emerge through politicized, broader policy deliberations, raising questions about whether these policies will necessarily dedicate the same benefits as ad hoc agreements.[12] Furthermore, when more actors become involved with negotiations, such a move can reduce the relative influence of local communities that use these agreements to increase their leverage and advocate for their needs, specifically. In so doing, broader benefits policies may undermine the very emphasis on spatial, local communities that these agreements were explicitly designed to promote. For this reason, the move toward broader policies, while possibly advantageous, should be undertaken with caution. Scaled policies should not undermine the local benefits distribution processes and goals that agreements were originally intended to achieve.

Why Community Benefits Matter

While it may seem early or even counterintuitive to worry about gentrification in many affected neighborhoods, these projects illustrate that growth interests have already identified the potential profit that exists in the places where projects take place. Even in places where people still grapple with issues created by decades of disinvestment and institutionally sanctioned harm, the local concerns of gentrification and large-scale neighborhood change that frequently exist are both real and valid. Community advocates, local leaders, and institutions must plan in advance of future change to combat its negative effects.

To this end, benefits-sharing agreements offer an important tool to reduce the harmful impacts of new development, protect community residents, and balance community investment and economic growth with community development for existing residents. These policies will not produce the transformational, systemic shifts in power originally envisioned by benefits-sharing agreement innovators, nor will they forestall the neighborhood change pressures that large-scale development can create and intensify. However, carefully crafted, negotiated agreements can realize meaningful change for the intended community beneficiaries and allow a broader set of actors to capture value from local development.[13] To accomplish this, however, all stakeholders must retain accountability, act transparently, and stay motivated to produce community outcomes throughout agreement implementation. When agreements deliver community benefits provisions that meet community goals, these agreements can avoid tokenism and co-optation. Rather, successful agreements can build power sharing with community participants over local outcomes, to improve democracy in the development process.

The Metro PLA in Los Angeles demonstrates how benefits-sharing agreements can generate important opportunities for historically underserved communities and residents to share in the benefits produced by large-scale urban development projects. In many instances, the benefits promised by these agreements may represent the best deal that community activists can secure in many contemporary planning processes, without broader systems change. Under the neoliberal status quo, built on patterns of racial capitalism and accumulation by dispossession, residents face an uphill battle from the start: an urban political context in which community participation is frequently used to create the appearance of democratic decision-making and thus can be co-opted to promote growth.[14]

Throughout, benefits-sharing agreements may promise only incremental changes, but these benefits can prove consequential for underserved residents and communities fighting for institutional support, resources, and investment. Absent broader systems change, low-income residents and communities risk experiencing disproportionate harm from the neighborhood changes associated with adjacent development, without capturing concentrated benefit. From this perspective, benefits-sharing agreements offer an important opportunity for communities to secure access to critical resources, and for their organizing to deliver crucial and impactful wins, however incremental those benefits may ultimately prove.[15]

As a result, the material delivery of community benefits promised by benefits-sharing agreements remains incredibly important. Failed community benefits delivery does not just represent a missed opportunity for community and urban development, or wasted time and resources in negotiations. Rather, the legacy of failed community investment endures in low-income communities and can contribute to persistent marginalization. Development in the Atlanta Westside illustrates the deep impacts of flawed community investment. In Atlanta, the harmful planning process around the Georgia Dome project remained acutely present during the new stadium project development, leaving damaging perceptions about what the community had already received and its capacity to direct future investment. The Atlanta philanthropic community and Atlanta local elected officials cited this history to justify their philanthropic, nonresponsive community investment approach—not concerning just stadium-related benefits, but also future neighborhood investment. In Los Angeles, as well—like many other places—the legacy of harmful development and institutional neglect persists. This ongoing history frequently manifests in community distrust of local institutions that have historically done little to advance their interests. This history shaped the Metro PLA and its implementation—just as it motivated other agreements and shaped events around them, and even inspired community benefits negotiations as a community development strategy.

Therefore, failed community benefits distributions represent more than just another unsuccessful community investment attempt, wasted time, or a missed opportunity. Rather, agreements that do not deliver on their community promises can undermine future community development efforts by contributing to harmful, persistent perceptions about underrepresented communities, while exacerbating ongoing community harm and distrust. As a result, these agreements must do more than offer promises, attempt to create change, or deliver partial results. Benefits-sharing agreements must enact the real opportunities they promise, in an inclusive and transparent manner, to make these development projects worthwhile to the communities that dedicate resources and offer project support. In this way, agreement approval represents only one step toward outcomes delivery and more equitable development. The strategies described in this chapter offer a path forward to realize results.

Beyond dedicating benefits, however, negotiations must allow community residents to call into question whether the development should take place at all—and if so, whether the proposed community benefits sufficiently alter the project's costs and benefits distributions to make the project worth it to communities. In Atlanta, for example, the $15 million designated by the Blank Foundation in this agreement represented less than 1 percent of the final project cost, a small amount for a billionaire and a wealthy franchise that have already substantially profited from the new stadium. While $15 million may be a lot of money, and better than nothing if the project was to proceed regardless, it could not fundamentally shift the aggregate costs and benefits distributions around this impactful project. Instead, the stadium is still a project that, as one resident said, will "enrich those who are already rich"—a statement that captured the sentiment of many.[16] The allocated money, even if it were spent efficiently and impactfully, never involved sufficient funds to protect residents against the project's negative effects—including the gentrification and displacement that many fear that the project has already advanced. Without the possibility for residents to reject or substantially alter the benefits distributions or the project itself, benefits-sharing agreements cannot make substantial progress toward equitable and inclusive urban development.

As community organizations and residents focus attention on strategies to promote equity and inclusion in urban development, scholars need to consider the implications of benefits-sharing agreements as a method to promote this goal. As Laura Wolf-Powers (2010) aptly noted in her highly cited community benefits article, under the community benefits model, the realization of community development outcomes hinges not on need but on opportunity, which depends on real estate demand. The Park East redevelopment project, in particular, demonstrates the risks associated with leaving community development outcomes dependent on a strong real estate market: fluctuations may happen, and benefits may get delayed or never materialize. For communities that work to achieve material community benefits, economic downturns then pose an additional threat beyond the hardship that these cycles already bring. Rather, when community development is tied to economic growth, benefits-sharing agreements cannot move past cyclical investment and disinvestment patterns.

With the COVID-19 epidemic bringing economic instability, a real estate shock, and related potential urban restructuring that threatens to exacerbate existing inequalities, the promise of community benefits that recently existed has suddenly seemed more elusive. And yet, federal and state governments—like so many across the world—dedicated new resources, on a massive scale, toward capital distributions, at least at first. Although the research for this book and its conclusions come from events before the pandemic, the persistent nature of local investment battlegrounds will likely parallel conversations about the struggle to achieve the equity goals underlying benefits-sharing agreements. As a result, the lessons outlined here have never been more relevant.

Throughout, it is important to recognize that benefits-sharing agreements advance a fundamentally ad hoc negotiations model that creates a particular type of community investment. This piecemeal, resource-intensive strategy to promote community development is inherently poorly situated to address the broader housing, employment, and related market forces that operate at a larger scale than the neighborhood level. A well-negotiated and well-implemented benefits-sharing agreement can ensure that a particular development neutralizes at least some of the direct harms it produces and generates additional benefits. However, an individual developer would never—and could never—combat the full effects of the broader neighborhood change, gentrification, and displacement pressures into which a large-scale project frequently enters and amplifies. Therefore, ad hoc benefits-sharing agreements can never be the only tool used to protect communities and promote their interests against these broader, potent forces. Urban development must recognize, and plan in advance of, these broader patterns by advancing institutions and systems that promote social, economic, and racial justice and deploy significant resources accordingly.

For this reason, practitioners and policy makers must continually remember that benefits-sharing agreements should never come at the expense of other forms of community and economic development, which must occur at scale. Rather, benefits-sharing agreements represent only one community development tool, potentially impactful but inherently limited, intended to ensure that wealth-generating development projects share some prosperity with local residents—if they deliver.

APPENDIX 1

Benefits-Sharing Agreements: A New Frontier for Development Conflict

To understand how benefits-sharing agreements have introduced new challenges and opportunities in land development, this appendix clarifies how these agreements relate to and differ from previous forms of land use bargaining. Earlier negotiations between developers and local governments laid the foundation for contractual, negotiated development agreements. However, previous land use bargaining tools involved limited external participation, particularly by affected community residents. In response to this exclusive model, and building off the negotiated land use bargaining tradition, community activists leveraged their influence to win the first benefits-sharing agreements, which involved significant community participation and dedicated local benefits, at least in theory.

This appendix is included to show how benefits-sharing agreements represent a consequential departure in the negotiated land use tradition by involving community representatives as recognized stakeholders and by explicitly promising community benefits. In so doing, this appendix provides a more detailed overview of existing research on both community benefits agreements and project labor agreements.

The community activists who drove the first agreements sought to fundamentally shift the development process from one that favors urban elites and growth interests toward a model that could give communities (more) power to shape development processes and generate local benefits. However, by offering benefits in exchange for project support, benefits-sharing agreements afford developers new opportunities to expedite development by reducing or eliminating community resistance to projects—with no guarantee that community benefits will materialize during implementation, or that the promised benefits equalize community harm. Rather, the core conflicts between elites and local communities over growth frequently remain unresolved.

The Foundation for Benefits-Sharing Agreements

Benefits-sharing agreements emerged out of a long history of negotiated land use decision-making in the United States. Negotiated development is rooted in the tradition of local government exactions: in the late 1800s and early 1900s, local governments began to assess infrastructural and other development-related expenses onto developers as a condition of development to share the cost burden of public improvements. These new development costs, combined with growing local government regulatory influence over the first half of the twentieth century and the need for additional local government revenue, drove developers and local governments to negotiate over specific development terms.[1]

These efforts established the foundation for contractual, negotiated development agreements, first instituted in the 1970s. Development agreements are enforceable negotiated agreements in which local governments and project developers agree to freeze existing land use regulations in exchange for agreed-on concessions by developers, such as infrastructure provisions and fees. Development agreements have become widespread because they effectively benefit both local government (by creating additional revenue and infrastructure and more flexible project terms) and developers (by reducing uncertainty in the development process).[2]

The shift toward bilateral, privately negotiated enforceable contracts altered the land use approval process in important ways, entrenching private processes that lack transparency, include significant discretion, and generally involve minimal participation by third parties—including affected communities. Rather, in private negotiations public interests remain "overlooked" unless they are adequately represented by negotiators or legislators.[3] After private negotiations, participants are "usually heavily invested" in the agreement they created, presented as "done deals" that therefore afford little opportunity for altering the agreement terms in response to public input.[4] This private negotiation-based approach to land development has altered the relationship between local governments and developers away from a hierarchical, adversarial relationship, in which local governments hold significant power and prioritize objectivity and systematic decision-making. Instead, the land development process has moved toward a negotiation format characterized by mutual reliance, necessity, and interest—if not to a particular end, then at least to reaching consensus through "some measure of cooperation."[5]

The shift toward negotiation has benefitted developers in many ways. Simply entering into negotiations implies that local government representatives believe that consensus is possible and indicates "a willingness to compromise" to reach agreement.[6] Well-resourced developers can use negotiations to avoid the local participation mandated in public processes, to gain approval for projects that otherwise would have been rejected or altered, or to secure provisions that benefit their interests.[7] Planners gain more discretion, which can create unequal outcomes, even among similar projects. Even the decision to engage (or not) in negotiations alters outcomes because local governments may treat projects differently, and create varying outcomes, solely on this basis.[8]

Thus, the shift toward negotiated land use decision-making entrenched development processes where decisions largely derive from interactions between developers and local governments. Affected communities may have little input, transparency, or accountability—even though the decisions reached during negotiation constrain a municipality's future abilities to address resident needs and changing conditions, potentially reproducing existing inequalities. Community engagement may become "little more than a pro forma exercise" such as involvement at a public meeting, after agreement specifics have been decided, and with little influence over the outcome.[9] Development negotiations can generate mistrust and suspicion among residents, as the developer and the local government are motivated to avoid public "scrutiny" and to enact the agreement delineated during negotiations.[10] This situation illustrates the "asymmetrical access to planning decisions" experienced by "financially powerful interests in municipal decisionmaking" as compared to community interests.[11] These deficits generated calls for more inclusion and democratic participation in development agreements and the development process.[12]

The Emergence of Benefits-Sharing Agreements

In the late 1990s and early 2000s, community activists started to fight for new agreements to govern land development, responding to a land use approval process that frequently excluded affected residents, and which often produced outcomes that exacerbated urban inequality. These activists created a category of agreements that I call *benefits-sharing agreements*, defined as negotiated agreements with project owners or developers that leverage large-scale, adjacent urban development projects to benefit local community residents. Two specific, but related, types have emerged: community benefits agreements (CBAs) and project labor agreements (PLAs). CBAs exist between developers and communities, and sometimes involve participation by local governments; communities exchange their project support for dedicated local benefits. PLAs are labor contracts between developers or project owners and labor unions, which govern labor terms for a project or set of projects. PLAs often include local workforce development provisions for communities such as training and targeted hire and involve community advocacy to shape the agreement terms. The next section describes CBAs and PLAs in greater depth, to show how these agreements operate in theory and in practice.

CBAs

CBAs refer to legally binding contracts where developers dedicate community benefits and frequently involve significant community participation. Community representatives exchange project support for dedicated local benefits, though agreements take different forms. Private CBAs exist between a developer and community groups, and both can enforce the agreement terms. Local governments may participate, but not as an agreement signatory. Public CBAs occur within the land use approval process, through development agreements, and lack community enforceability. Public agencies sign on to the agreements and retain enforcement capabilities. Both parties can change the agreement later *without* community input.[13] Across agreements, benefits have ranged widely, including affordable housing, workforce development provisions such as targeted jobs and training programs, housing loans, and community services such as childcare, youth centers, health clinics, parks, and neighborhood improvement funds.[14]

In theory, CBAs enable communities to influence the development process through inclusive deliberations where developers are held accountable to the commitments they make in negotiations.[15] CBAs that meet this standard can enhance democratic participation in the development process, include residents and groups that would otherwise not participate, and improve public outcomes by taking a broader range of interests into consideration.[16]

Through dedicated benefits, CBAs create "value capture" opportunities, whereby communities can directly acquire some of the value created by new development projects and mitigate some of the negative project effects.[17]

COMMUNITY AND LOCAL GOVERNMENT PARTICIPATION IN CBAs

CBAs alter traditional forms of community and local government participation in the development process. CBAs are intended to involve influential community participation, often achieved through community coalitions, to increase community pressure during negotiations.[18] However, coalitions are vulnerable to fragmentation from conflicting interests. Developers may exploit this weakness, particularly since residents frequently lack adequate representation and experience in formal negotiations.[19] Without a unified coalition, developers or elected officials may be able to pick the groups with which they want to negotiate. For example, community stakeholders claim that this occurred in multiple New York City agreements.[20]

CBAs shift the local government role, as well, in varying ways. Local governments may not even participate in developing some CBAs, potentially creating a "parallel process" to the public approval process.[21] Local governments retain a vested interest in benefits negotiations, since government agencies and officials can directly benefit from CBAs that produce consensus, expedite development, and improve community outcomes. When they participate, local governments can enhance CBA negotiations and implementation by assembling and mediating between groups, sharing development expertise, and promoting enforcement.[22]

However, local government participation can also harm community interests: participation by government officials or public agencies gives CBAs the perception that they are institutionally sanctioned. Moreover, CBAs with significant leadership from elected officials tend to tackle fewer issues, lack substantial monitoring and enforcement, and involve less transparent and open processes. Politicians may take positions that conflict with community interests and may sway the final agreement in their direction.[23] For this reason, some scholars are careful to specify a more circumspect role for elected officials, to oversee negotiations but not direct decision-making. Furthermore, some argue that, with significant participation by local governments, CBAs simply replicate the land use approval process and redistribute exactions without the institutional checks of public processes.[24]

Altogether, CBAs foster new policy formulation means, with a vague and context-driven role for local government, and frequently through opaque processes. With sufficient public support, negotiated CBAs may encourage local governments to approve projects that would otherwise have been rejected or altered, even though agreement deliberations lack the public protections embedded in the public approval process. Therefore, CBAs risk creating harm if residents lack the expertise and information to adequately weigh the agreement and the project's benefits and costs.[25]

CBAS: CHALLENGES AND FAILURES

CBAs face many criticisms, including disagreement about whether they create benefits beyond those that communities would secure within the land use approval process. In contrast, some argue that developers have conceded more benefits to communities in CBAs than the land use approval process would otherwise generate, that CBAs incorporate broader interests, and that these agreements can produce more efficient outcomes.[26] However, in the first comprehensive account of CBA outcomes, Marantz (2015) finds that the exemplar Los Angeles Live agreement produced roughly the same outcomes as the public land use approval process, raising doubts about the added value that CBAs offer.

Furthermore, scholars dispute the participatory benefits and achievements of CBAs, questioning whether agreements produce influential community participation and authentic and adequate representation. Many express concern with the extent to which negotiating stakeholders espouse, act in accordance with, or are recognized to advance the interests of those individuals or groups they claim to represent. Rather, developers can co-opt what is intended to be a community-driven process by minimizing or avoiding inclusive, representative, and influential participation.[27] In one example, with the Atlantic Yards project in New York, some community organizations were formed just to negotiate for a CBA, and others were "hand-picked" by the developer to represent the community in negotiations. Critics contend that most groups actually opposed the project, which included eminent domain, and that the process lacked transparency.[28]

Without a legislative check on process, CBAs can provide an additional venue for developers to exert power. Developers retain disproportionate influence during deliberations, including whether and how to engage in CBA negotiations, and over the agreement terms. Further, communities need significant resources and expertise to negotiate adequate agreements and to monitor and enforce agreements. If undertaken, community-based monitoring generally occurs informally, which burdens underresourced communities and may prevent sustained monitoring over time.[29]

Altogether, therefore, CBAs emerged as a means to leverage urban development projects for community development through transformative processes and outcomes. Evidence indicates, however, that these ad hoc agreements vary widely in terms of their formulation and implementation processes and outcomes. Many agreements have failed to meet the standards espoused, in terms of participation, oversight, and outcomes.[30]

When outcomes lag, agreements have offered varying opportunities for recourse. Some agreements have not allowed communities or local governments to fine the developer for failing to achieve certain goals.[31] Others have prevented penalties above a certain dollar amount, such as the Bronx Terminal Market CBA, in which developer penalties could not surpass $600,000.[32] Only parties to the contract can legally enforce it—and only if the agreement is binding. This context limits potential enforcement, since signatories are often fragmented and shifting coalitions of community groups, comprising nonprofit organizations with limited funds to launch expensive monitoring and enforcement efforts. For this reason, ensuring funding for monitoring and enforcement efforts, as well as creating institutional memory in the face of personnel turnover, remains critically important but inherently difficult to achieve.[33]

The next section reviews the research to date on PLAs. While far less research exists on PLAs, this work similarly suggests that community stakeholders have minimal control over community benefits delivery.

PLAs

PLAs are construction agreements between contractors or owners and unions that govern labor terms including hiring policies, labor conditions, and dispute resolution. PLAs arose in the early 1900s to ensure that projects do not experience labor delays from worker and union disputes, nonstreamlined work between trades, and inadequate supplies of skilled labor. PLAs exist on both private and public projects.[34]

Under PLAs, unions give up their right to strike, with provisions for avoiding disputes and timely resolution, under threat of large penalties. In exchange for this additional certainty and efficiency, project owners and/or contractors commit to hiring a minimum percentage of union workers on the project. Further, all contractors on the project must follow the collective bargaining agreement, including nonunion contractors, which ensures higher wages and representation for all workers in the union grievance process. These terms improve job quality and make union contractors more competitive in the bidding process. For this reason, PLAs are controversial and have become highly politicized.[35]

PLA supporters argue that these agreements provide developers with access to skilled workers, streamline work sites with many rules and firms working simultaneously, and minimize work stoppage. In contrast, PLA opponents claim that agreements favor union bidders, discourage competition, and increase project costs through higher wages.[36] However, efficiency assertions remain difficult to test because of the methodological challenge of directly comparing across highly varied construction projects. Nevertheless, some research has found that PLAs do not reduce the number of project bidders, nor do they contribute to higher bids.[37]

Regardless of the cumulative impacts of PLAs, construction unions and their members clearly benefit from these agreements, particularly in an era of declining unionization. In construction, unionization rates fell from approximately 50 percent union density in the 1950s to its current levels, where roughly 13 percent of private-sector construction workers are union members or are represented by unions.[38] Lower unionization rates have reduced the supply of skilled workers in construction, since unions have historically provided the industry's workforce development through apprenticeships and training. Adequate skill development takes many years, particularly for certain trades, often lagging construction booms.[39]

With billions of dollars in contracts at stake, creating intense competition between union and nonunion contractors, PLAs have become highly politicized.[40] Presidents George H. W. Bush and George W. Bush both signed executive orders to essentially prevent PLAs on public projects, while Presidents Clinton and Obama signed executive orders overturning the bans. President Obama specifically advocated for PLAs through Executive Order 13502 (2009), arguing that PLAs improve construction efficiency and timeliness.[41] After facing sustained pressure from construction lobbying groups, President Trump issued Executive Order 13495 on October 21, 2019, to revoke President Obama's Executive Order 13502 enabling PLAs on federal projects.[42] President Biden issued his own executive order in February 2022 to promote the use of PLAs on federal projects with construction contracts worth $35 million or more.[43]

PLAS AND COMMUNITY DEVELOPMENT

Since the Port of Oakland PLA in the early 2000s, PLAs have often been used to deliberately foster community development by leveraging large projects and, frequently, public contracts for community workforce provisions such as targeted hire. Since then, PLAs with community workforce provisions have become standard practice, with the vast majority including at least one community workforce provision, and almost half including between four and nine such provisions.[44] Community workforce provisions have involved stipulations to direct jobs distributions to underrepresented workers, provide job training, and target resources to local disadvantaged business enterprises and minority and women-owned business enterprises,[45] which tend to employ underrepresented workers at higher rates and involve opportunities for wealth creation and local economic spillovers. However, these businesses may prove more difficult to use since they often require additional business support.[46] Many PLAs also include provisions for health and safety on project sites, since construction work is extremely dangerous and has among the highest fatality rates of any industry sector.[47]

PLAs with community workforce provisions aim to foster community development through quality job creation and spatially targeted hiring to local residents who would otherwise lack the skills or opportunity to access these jobs, as well as through workforce development provisions and local economic spillovers. While construction jobs are often viewed as temporary, construction unions offer a pipeline of training and work that generates high-paying careers with benefits and retirement opportunities. Apprenticeship requirements are the central mechanism to improve access, by mandating that contractors hire workers often without construction work experience, who must complete on-the-job training hours to advance within the industry. Eligible community residents can enter the industry and progress through these preapprenticeship and apprenticeship programs, which direct motivated residents into construction unions and help workers gain the workforce and technical skills required in construction.[48]

Despite important opportunities offered by construction work, many issues can undermine community benefits delivery as PLAs get implemented. Targeted hire hinges on effective coordination among the various contractors and unions across trades that are needed at different project stages, to ensure that sufficiently trained workers are available as need arises. Unemployment and temporary employment are serious concerns, since real estate and related construction demand reflect larger economic conditions.[49] Graduates of job training programs must withstand periodic lulls and booms in regional construction, as well as a competitive and expansive construction labor market.[50]

Furthermore, targeted hire is difficult to achieve, requiring sufficient pools of skilled local workers at precise times in the construction process. In response to critiques of skills gaps—where local workers are perceived to lack the skills to perform the necessary work—community groups and other entities sometimes create preapprenticeship or boot camp programs. Such programs screen residents and teach participants the workforce and technical skills necessary to succeed in apprenticeship programs, from interview, safety, and math skills to basic fitness. Preapprenticeship programs "identify and funnel workers" into the construction trades; in general, the trades are more willing to take on candidates who have completed a preapprenticeship program, as they are perceived to be more reliable, more dedicated, and more likely to pursue a long-term construction career.[51] Once enrolled in an apprenticeship program, most trades require a basic training that lasts a few weeks. Afterward, workers are placed on the out-of-work list from which unions refer workers onto jobsites. Throughout, timing is crucial to ensure that a sufficiently qualified ironworker apprentice who meets the disadvantaged worker classification, for example, is on the out-of-work list and ready to work at the exact moment that a contractor seeks an ironworker apprentice. This process is extremely difficult, complicated by many nuanced, overlapping factors. Successful targeted hire requires coordination among preapprenticeship programs, unions, contractors, and the project owner.[52]

PLA NEGOTIATION, IMPLEMENTATION, AND (HIGHLY VARIED) OUTCOMES

The existence and terms of PLAs vary widely. PLAs are more common on large-scale projects with an organized community, and in places with a history of previous PLAs, existing training programs, in regions with insufficient labor supplies, and in places where these policies have backing from elected officials. PLAs are less likely in areas without community-labor coalitions, which are a primary force behind PLA advocacy.[53] While many unions and local negotiators have developed expertise and standardized terms, ad hoc agreement negotiations still produce significant local variation, sometimes necessarily, to tailor PLAs to local conditions. Participants expend considerable resources on negotiation. Local engagement and relationships are essential for effective negotiation and implementation.[54]

Minimal research has examined PLA implementation, including whether and how agreements produce stated community goals. Some research has focused on identifying characteristics that enhance implementation, including "clear policy language" and other factors such as specified, measurable goals, consequences for noncompliance, flexible outcomes measurement that accounts for variation between subcontractors, partnerships, and political support for enforcement.[55] Preapprenticeship programs have come to play an important role in providing eligible workers with necessary skills and directing them into construction careers. Flexibility and coordination among unions, contractors, and workers is essential, to enable actors to adapt to unexpected barriers.[56] Local characteristics can also improve outcomes, where local actors have a commitment to PLA objectives, existing relationships that support coordination, and connections to training programs and support services.[57]

Monitoring and enforcement vary between projects, agreements, and locations. Monitoring can occur by the staff of the project owner or by external groups. These efforts can include the community in a formalized capacity such as by designating on-site representatives (such as with the Sound Transit PLA in Seattle) or through inclusion on a committee to oversee and influence implementation (such as with the Port of Oakland PLA). Key considerations include the reporting structure, access to data, including on-site observations, and the extent to which a PLA includes the ability to sanction noncompliance.[58]

Therefore, PLAs frequently need, but often do not include, outside compliance mechanisms, to enable third parties to observe implementation and determine whether outcomes materialize. Some research suggests that incentives or penalties to promote compliance are the most important factor to determine whether outcomes are produced. Without mechanisms for ensuring compliance to clearly delineated outcomes, including wide participation and dedicated resources for proactive oversight and compliance targeted hire goals may not be met.[59]

As they are not a signatory party, community groups often can only enforce agreements informally as third parties, without institutional resources or support. While little research has examined community participation in PLAs, evidence indicates that community organizations have participated in implementation through monitoring and enforcement, including labor-community coalitions.[60] Community participation in enforcement often requires enterprising community-based organizations to act as implementation watchdogs. Thus, community-based organizations "have stepped in to fill the vacuum created by the withdrawal of the federal government from affirmative action in construction," though community-driven efforts tend to prioritize geographically targeted hire rather than racially targeted hire to underrepresented groups, with important implications for benefits distributions.[61]

Therefore, PLAs now largely include community benefits provisions, including stipulations for targeted workforce development and local economic spillovers. Research on the community outcomes produced by these agreements is extremely limited, but it indicates that similar to CBAs, PLA outcomes vary widely between agreements. Some agreements fulfill their stated goal of delivering community benefits, while others produce only partial outcomes. While community groups are not agreement signatories, they sometimes monitor and enforce agreements out of concern that their desired outcomes will not materialize otherwise. Pressure from community actors appears to contribute to better results, which underscores the varying outcomes produced by these agreements and their broader contexts.[62]

APPENDIX 2

Methods

Case Selection

Table 4 reviews the relevant variations and controls between the Park East Redevelopment Compact (PERC) and the Atlanta Falcons Community Benefits Plan to demonstrate that these cases are reasonably comparable. At the time of data collection, these cases were similarly in the implementation stage, which allowed me to trace implementation as it unfolded. Further, both agreements involved agreement administration by public agencies and, included the local government as a signatory party with some discretion during implementation, with oversight from a local government legislative body. Both agreements also included some direct community oversight of agreement processes through an established committee. These cases also vary in important ways, including that the Milwaukee agreement was approved far before the Atlanta agreement, and the latter also involves agreement administration by a private entity (the Blank Foundation). Further, the PERC is a county resolution broader than only one development project and has included penalties for noncompliance. Finally, the Atlanta project does not specify precise benefits but rather a monetary investment, leaving further discretion to the administering parties.

Table 4. Community Benefits Agreement Case Study Characteristics

	Park East Redevelopment Compact	*Atlanta Falcons Community Benefits Plan*
Time Line	Agreement approved in 2004	Plan approved in 2013
Project Stage (at Time of Data Collection)	Implementation	Implementation
Project	Land sale and redevelopment of the Park East Redevelopment Corridor: sixteen acres of county-owned land near downtown Milwaukee	New $1.6 billion stadium project for the Atlanta Falcons NFL team
Public Agency	County of Milwaukee, which sells land, divided into parcels, for private development	City of Atlanta, which had development approval over the project and public financing
Private Interest	Project developer, which differs across parcels and projects	Atlanta Falcons and owner Arthur M. Blank
Public Investment in Project	Sixteen acres of county land, able to be sold at far below market price, within a tax incremental district established by the City of Milwaukee	$200 million from the City of Atlanta's hotel-motel tax
Agreement Scope	County resolution that specifies benefits (prevailing wage, affordable housing by the county, local hire, disadvantaged business utilization, green design, and a community fund) that were to be written into development contracts	Designates $15 million investment each from Invest Atlanta and the Arthur M. Blank Foundation. The benefits plan made recommendations about projects and identified desired benefits, but did not identify specific projects or parties to receive funding
Signatory Parties	County of Milwaukee passed the PERC; developers have signed onto benefits when written into development agreements	Invest Atlanta enacted a resolution and the Arthur M. Blank Foundation board committed to funds allocation. The benefits plan was approved by the Atlanta City Council after deliberation occurred under the Community Benefits Plan Committee, which included community representatives

	Park East Redevelopment Compact	*Atlanta Falcons Community Benefits Plan*
Agreement Administrator(s)	County of Milwaukee economic development division	Invest Atlanta and the Arthur M. Blank Foundation have directly administered their different investments, with some coordination
Oversight	Reporting to the County of Milwaukee Board of Supervisors; the PERC establishes a community advisory committee to review development proposals	Plan specifies that Invest Atlanta or its designee monitor and report to the City of Atlanta Community Development/Human Resources Committee, meet with the Community Benefit Plan Committee quarterly, and regularly update website with all project activities
Stakeholder Discretion in Implementation?	Yes, as county employees responsible for administration negotiate agreement terms into development agreements	Yes, as Invest Atlanta and the Arthur M. Blank Foundation retain discretion over which projects get funded
Penalties for Noncompliance?	Yes, when written into development agreements	No
Ad Hoc Agreement, or Part of a Broader Community Benefits Strategy?	Part of a broader strategy: county resolution that governs many different developments within the Park East Redevelopment Corridor; in 2015, the PERC terms were extended to all county land through a separate county ordinance	Ad hoc policy
Was Agreement Formulation Community Led (at Least in Part)?	Yes	Yes

Table 5 shows the various characteristics of the project labor agreement case studies. Los Angeles and Seattle were selected because they share important characteristics that would likely influence PLA and CWA implementation. In particular, both regions already had a history of formulating, approving, and implementing innovative, large-scale, and nationally prominent PLAs.

Among these, Los Angeles has important PLAs around the Port of Los Angeles and the Los Angeles Unified School District. Seattle has an agreement around Sound Transit, the regional transportation provider.[1] These existing policies suggested some local expertise in project labor agreement negotiation and administration. Seattle and Los Angeles stakeholders were similarly constrained by state laws banning public institutions from engaging in affirmative action, including preference based on race, ethnicity, and gender.[2] Both Seattle and Los Angeles have strong real estate markets, with many large-scale projects recently built, planned, or under construction. Therefore, the regions have active construction industries. Each case covers a public agreement, with a public agency serving as the project owner and master developer. The public agency was also tasked with internally administering the agreement (that is, the agency would be directly responsible for implementation and did not outsource this responsibility to a third party). Further, these cases were both in the implementation stage at the time of data collection, with construction ongoing. Therefore, I could observe implementation as it unfolded. Both agreements have governed high-profile and controversial projects, involving dynamics that contributed to agreement formulation.[3]

Table 5. Project Labor Agreement Case Study Characteristics

	Metro PLA	*Yesler Terrace CWA*
State Context	California: affirmative action prohibited by Proposition 209 (1996)	Washington: affirmative action prohibited by Initiative 200 (1998)
Regional Context	Strong unions; regional history of large-scale, innovative PLAs; strong real estate market	Strong unions; regional history of large-scale, innovative PLAs; strong real estate market
Project Controversy?	Yes	Yes
High-Profile Project?	Yes	Yes
Project Type	Transportation	Residential
Project Owner	Regional public agency: Los Angeles County Metropolitan Transportation Authority	Public agency: Seattle Housing Authority

	Metro PLA	*Yesler Terrace CWA*
Project Cost	Entire PLA covers projects funded by a $40 billion sales tax measure; the case focuses on the Crenshaw/LAX Transit Corridor Project, which costs roughly $2.1 billion	CWA covers the $300 million public housing construction, funded by the Seattle Housing Authority (including land sale) and a HUD choice neighborhoods grant
Project Stage (at Time of Data Collection)	Implementation	Implementation
Agreement Goals	Target work to "disadvantaged workers" and apprentices	Target work to Yesler Terrace residents, public housing residents, and Section 3 workers and businesses (economically eligible for public housing)
Implementation Structure	Internal with third-party administrative support (the jobs coordinator)	Internal; first CWA within the agency
Oversight	Metro board of supervisors (comprising public officials)	Section 3 Advisory Committee (includes community stakeholders and union members)
Penalties for Noncompliance?	Yes, and Metro has previously assessed penalties	Not for the community benefits provisions
Ad Hoc Agreement, or Part of a Broader Strategy?	Yes, PLA covers Measure R projects	No, CWA concerns only Yesler Terrace
Was Agreement Formulation Community Led (at Least in Part)?	Yes	Not to a significant extent

Source: California Voter Foundation, 1996; Herrera et al., 2014; Interview with Respondents 3, 12, 14, and 27; League of Women Voters, 1998; Los Angeles Metropolitan Transportation Authority, 2012c; Seattle Housing Authority, 2013a.

However, these agreements also differ along many characteristics, including the project scale, the construction type, and the constraints attached to the various funding sources. The Los Angeles case addresses a roughly $2.1 billion transportation project, including federal and state money. The Seattle agreement covered a $300 million public housing redevelopment project, funded by a federal grant and money from the Seattle Housing Authority. Further, implementation was structured slightly differently; implementation for both projects involved formal oversight bodies, though these groups differed in influence, including their ability to assess penalties for noncompliance regarding the community benefits provisions. While the Yesler Terrace CWA was ad hoc, the Metro PLA governs multiple projects across the agency, advancing a broader strategy. Finally, community involvement has differed across the projects, including whether the community drove agreement formulation.

Methods

To construct these case studies, I conducted semistructured interviews that generally lasted between sixty and ninety minutes with forty-eight individuals (see Table 6) representing community advocates, local government, and private interests and, for the project labor agreements specifically, project owners, administrators, building trades representatives and construction companies. Table 6 provides information about the interview subjects. Interviews followed a semistructured format. If given permission to record, interviews were transcribed and coded using a grounded coding approach and ATLAS.ti qualitative coding software.

I triangulated these data with available archival data from in-person library visits and online sources. For the Atlanta case, this included minutes from the Community Benefits Plan Committee, relevant local government plans, newsletters, press releases, and grant reporting from the Blank Foundation, and some radio and television transcripts. For the Milwaukee case, archival research involved minutes from the Milwaukee County Board of Supervisors, as well as relevant plans and proposals related to the Park East area and the development projects. For both cases, I conducted content analyses of media mentions related to the agreements, which produced important news articles, blog posts, and website mentions. I used the search

Table 6. Interviews

	Milwaukee	Atlanta	Seattle	Los Angeles	Total
Local Government/ Public Agency Representative	3	3	5	5	16
Third-Party Administrator	N/A	N/A	1	1	2
Community Representatives	2	6	3	4	15
Developers/Contractors/ Private Interests	2	0	2	2	6
Building Trades/ Unions			5	1	6
Other[4]			3		3
Total	7	9	19	13	48

terms "Atlanta Falcons" and "community benefits plan" plus "Atlanta Falcons" and "Mercedes-Benz Stadium" for the Atlanta case and two searches for the Milwaukee case: Milwaukee and "Park East Redevelopment Compact" plus Milwaukee and "Park East Redevelopment." After my initial search, I set Google alerts to inform me of new articles that emerged after this effort.

Further, the Milwaukee case offered a significant body of existing research from which to draw. As the first successful attempt to create a community benefits ordinance, which uniquely codified community benefits into legislation that covered more a single development project, the PERC has received significant attention in the community benefits agreement literature.[5] However, since implementation of the PERC was delayed by the economic recession and other factors, these studies occurred almost exclusively before implementation fully proceeded, such that none examine the long-term processes and outcomes produced by this innovative and important agreement. As a result, to construct this case study, I relied on an existing body of research to provide background context.

Table 7. Archival Documents for Community Benefits Agreement Cases

Atlanta Falcons Community Benefits Plan	Park East Redevelopment Compact
Minutes and agendas from City Council and Community Benefits Plan Committee Meetings (when available)	Minutes and agendas from Milwaukee County Board of Supervisors
Media reporting	Media reporting
Systematic online searches, including project and construction firm websites	Systematic online searches, including project and construction firm websites
Newsletters, press releases, and annual reports from the Arthur Blank Foundation	Existing literature
Relevant city plans	Relevant city and county plans
Reports from Invest Atlanta	

Table 8. Archival Documents for Project Labor Agreement Cases

Metro PLA Documents	Yesler Terrace CWA Documents
Minutes and agendas from Metro board meetings (when available)	Minutes and agendas from citizen review committee (when available)
Media reporting	Media reporting
Systematic online and library searches, including project and firm websites	Systematic online searches, including project and firm websites
PLA symposium video	Environmental impact reporting
Metro Source blog	Seattle Housing Authority blog
Hiring reports (available online)	Hiring reports (requested from Seattle Housing Authority)
Reports produced by community stakeholders (available online)	

I triangulated data from interviews with available archival data from in-person library visits and online sources, documents provided by stakeholders, and media reporting. For the Los Angeles case, I searched for all documents related to the PLA formulation and implementation process. For the Seattle case, I visited the Seattle Public Library and Seattle Municipal Archives and searched for relevant documents related to the Yesler Terrace redevelopment project and the community workforce agreement (CWA). These documents included environmental impact reports with extensive public comments. Also included are any available meeting agendas and minutes, including from the Yesler Terrace Citizen Review Committee.

I conducted web searches on both the Google and Bing search engines. For the Los Angeles case, I conducted two searches, using two terms: "Los Angeles" and Metro and "project labor agreement" plus "project labor agreement" and Crenshaw. For the Yesler Terrace case, I also conducted two searches each: "Yesler Terrace" and "community workforce agreement" plus "Yesler Terrace redevelopment." I examined each web hit and downloaded and identified relevant documents and news articles. I then coded these documents and articles using a grounded coding approach and the ATLAS.ti coding software. I also set up a Google alert for each search term, so that I was aware of new articles that met the search terms after the web searches that I performed. This enabled me to remain up to date on articles.

I also extensively searched organization websites, including the administering agency, developers, and community organizations. This endeavor yielded important public documents such as press releases, meeting minutes, guiding plans, agreement reporting, agency blog posts, and construction updates (see Table 8). In contrast to the Metro agreement, Yesler Terrace agreement outcomes were not publicly reported. I requested and received reporting documents, to analyze construction hiring outcomes.

For the Los Angeles case, I also drew data from over three years of action research with a Los Angeles–based community organization involved in this PLA, such that observing their work enabled me to examine events around this policy. This effort included participation in organizational meetings, activities, events, and public meeting attendance.

APPENDIX 3

Westside Neighborhood Prosperity Fund Grants Funded by the Arthur M. Blank Foundation

Grantee	Year	Grant Amount
Inclusiv dba National Federation of CDCUs	2019	$583,500
Historic Westside Gardens ATL, Inc.	2019	$45,000
Quest Community Development Organization	2019	$350,000
Atlanta Volunteer Lawyers Foundation, Inc.	2019	$100,000
Westside Future Fund	2019	$300,000
First Step Staffing	2019	$130,000
Westside Future Fund	2018	$250,000
National Federation of Community Development Credit Unions	2018	$75,000
Historic Westside Gardens ATL, Inc.	2018	$45,000
Good Samaritan Health Center, Inc.	2018	$100,000
YMCA of Metro Atlanta	2018	$2,000,000
Urban Land Institute	2018	$50,000
Urban Land Institute	2018	$75,000
Enterprise Community Partners	2018	$150,000
Community Foundation of Greater Atlanta	2018	$116,000

Grantee	Year	Grant Amount
Big Brothers Big Sisters of Metro Atlanta	2018	$125,000
Center for Civic Innovation	2018	$125,000
United Way of Greater Atlanta	2018	$25,000
Access to Capital for Entrepreneurs	2018	$135,000
CHRIS 180	2018	$320,350
Salvation Army Boys and Girls Clubs of Greater Atlanta—Bellwood Unit	2018	$125,000
The Center for Working Families	2018	$270,000
Per Scholas	2018	$230,000
Literacy Action	2018	$150,000
Integrity Transformations Community Development Corporation, Inc.	2018	$1,665,000
Construction Education Foundation of Georgia (CEFGA)	2018	$340,000
Urban League of Greater Atlanta	2018	$48,000
Quest Community Development Organization	2018	$350,000
Curry Davis Consulting Group, LLC	2018	$50,000
The Mosaic Group	2018	$155,000
Quest Community Development Organization, Inc.	2017	$2,000,000
EcoDistricts	2017	$4,520
Street Smart Youth Project, Inc.	2017	$50,000
CommunityBuild Ventures	2017	$20,000
Atlanta Volunteer Lawyers Foundation, Inc.	2017	$200,000
Park Pride, Inc.	2017	$50,000
Integrity Transformations Community Development Corporation, Inc.	2017	$622,260
Atlanta Police Foundation	2017	$1,000,000

Grantee	Year	Grant Amount
Construction Education Foundation of Georgia (CEFGA)	2017	$140,000
Per Scholas	2017	$90,000
Westside Future Fund, Inc.	2017	$70,000
Salvation Army Boys and Girls Clubs of Greater Atlanta – Bellwood Unit	2017	$30,000
Center for Civic Innovation	2017	$125,000
The Mosaic Group	2017	$155,000
1Q	2017	$20,000
The Mission Continues	2017	$75,000
The Center for Working Families	2017	$135,000
Curry Davis Consulting Group, LLC	2017	$52,000
Atlanta Public Schools c/o Atlanta Partners for Education	2017	$193,440
CommunityBuild Ventures	2017	$94,000
Georgia Center for Nonprofits	2017	$51,000
Families First	2016	$95,000
Juma Ventures	2016	$50,000
Castleberry Hill Neighborhood Association	2016	$68,675
Street Smart Youth Project, Inc.	2016	$50,000
Health Education Assessment and Leadership, Inc.	2016	$206,000
Center for Land Reform, Inc.	2016	$18,000
WonderRoot, Inc.	2016	$80,750
Literacy Action	2016	$66,729
Integrity Transformations Community Development Corporation, Inc.	2016	$210,000
Community Foundation for Greater Atlanta	Westside Roots Fund	2016	$390,155

Grantee	Year	Grant Amount
Atlanta Habitat for Humanity	2016	$30,000
Trust for Public Land	2016	$700,000
Regionerate, LLC	2016	$90,000
The Mosaic Group	2016	$142,500
HOME Training Institute	2016	$75,000
Bellwether Education Partners, Inc.	2016	$125,000
Project for Public Spaces, Inc.	2016	$63,100
New Hope Enterprises	2016	$75,000
Atlanta Police Foundation	2016	$737,567
Quest Community Development Organization, Inc.	2015	$1,250,000
The Conservation Fund	2015	$50,000
Vine City Civic Association	2015	$75,000
Georgia Appleseed	2015	$140,000
21st Century Science Technology Engineering and Math Foundation	2015	$15,558.85
Phoenix Boys Association, Inc.	2015	$75,000
West Atlanta Watershed Alliance	2015	$150,000
People Partnering for Progress	2015	$25,000
Fulton County Sheriff Reserve	2014	$25,000
KIPP Metro Atlanta Collaborative	2014	$225,000
City of Refuge	2014	$115,000
		$19,079,104.85

Source: Blank Foundation reporting: The Arthur M. Blank Foundation, n.d.a.

NOTES

Introduction

1. Following Canon (2014), I use the term "developers" to refer to "the diversity of individuals and entities, and combinations of those individuals and entities that enter into development agreements with local governments. Developers may be individual property owners, financers, or developers under contract with property owners, partnerships of property owners and financers, or holding companies that include combinations of these different parties" (p. 782).
2. For a more detailed review of existing literature on CBAs and PLAs, including how these agreements differ from previous forms of land use bargaining, please see Appendix 1.
3. Wolf-Powers, 2010, p. 141.
4. Marantz, 2015; Saito and Truong, 2015; Wolf-Powers, 2010.
5. Rau, 2019; Garrison, 2018; Saito and Truong, 2015; Belko, 2014; Wolf-Powers, 2010.
6. City of Detroit, 2020; Rihl, 2018.
7. U.S. General Accounting Office, 1998, p. 1.
8. Given the range of issues that PLAs now address, the terminology concerning PLAs can be somewhat unclear. PLAs that specifically seek to promote community development through community workforce provisions are sometimes called community workforce agreements but elsewhere are called project labor agreements. I use the term project labor agreement, but specifically address agreements with community workforce provisions, which have become the dominant agreement type (Herrera et al., 2014; Figueroa, Grabelsky, and Lamare, 2011; Belman and Bodah, 2010).
9. Parkin, 2004; Johnston-Dodds, 2001.
10. Figueroa, Grabelsky, and Lamere, 2011.
11. Herrera et al., 2014; Figueroa, Grabelsky, and Lamere, 2011. "'Targeted hire' is a policy initiative aimed at increasing employment opportunities for disadvantaged workers, who often experience difficulty accessing the construction workforce pipeline. The value of targeted hire is that it creates institutional mechanisms to increase the availability and accessibility of opportunities for these workers" (Herrera et al., 2014, p. 12).
12. Herrera et al., 2014; Figueroa, Grabelsky, and Lamere, 2011.
13. City of Seattle Purchasing and Contracting, 2015.
14. Johnston-Dodds, 2001; Los Angeles Unified School District, 1999.
15. Belongie and Silverman, 2018.
16. Including work such as Belongie and Silverman, 2018; Doussard, 2015; Saito and Truong, 2015; Wolf-Powers, 2010; Swanstrom and Banks, 2009; Baxamusa, 2008.

17. Rosen and Schweitzer, 2018; Purcell, 2009. Following Purcell (2009), neoliberalism refers to the political economic shift toward economic liberalization policies associated with laissez-faire economics.

18. Saito and Truong, 2015; Haas, 2012; Saito, 2012; Wolf-Powers, 2010; Baxamusa, 2008. Similar to Liegeois and Carson (2003), here *leverage* refers to the use of influence, opportunities, and/or resources to achieve, or attempt to achieve, a desired outcome.

19. Haas, 2012, p. 273, emphasis mine.

20. Marantz, 2015; Haas, 2012; Wolf-Powers, 2010.

21. Saito and Truong, 2015; Haas, 2012; Wolf-Powers, 2010.

22. Partnership for Working Families, 2007; Interview with Respondent [not specified to maintain confidentiality].

23. Allison, Cline, and Reese, 2018; Parkin, 2004; Johnston-Dodds, 2001; Interview with Respondent [not specified to maintain confidentiality]. The Partnership for Working Families is a nationwide umbrella advocacy coalition whose member community organizations frequently employ community benefits strategies. These include organizations in Atlanta (Georgia STAND-UP), Milwaukee (Citizen Action of Wisconsin Education Fund, which merged with the Good Jobs and Livable Neighborhoods Coalition), Seattle (Puget Sound Sage), and Los Angeles (Los Angeles Alliance for a New Economy, or LAANE) (Partnership for Working Families, 2007; Partnership for Working Families, n.d.), among many others.

24. Interview with Respondent [not specified to maintain confidentiality].

25. Logan and Molotch, 1987.

26. Doussard and Fulton, 2020; Lesniewski and Doussard, 2017; Doussard and Lesniewski, 2017; Doussard, 2015; Swanstrom and Banks, 2009.

27. Lucas-Darby, 2012; Saito, 2012; Figueroa, Grabelsky, and Lamare, 2011; Wolf-Powers, 2010.

28. Figueroa, Grabelsky, and Lamare, 2011; Chimienti, 2010, Wolf-Powers, 2010. For more information on these agreements and their relationship to land use bargaining, see Appendix 1.

29. Saito and Truong, 2015; Canon, 2014; Wolf-Powers, 2010; Baxamusa, 2008; Liegeois and Carson, 2003.

30. Saito and Truong, 2015; Baxamusa, 2008; Liegeois and Carson, 2003. Some research has viewed PLAs and CBAs similarly, though this perspective is not widespread. This work acknowledges important similarities between these agreements, and sometimes other policies, which leverage public contracts and/or subsidies for local benefits. Liegeois and Carson (2003) classify development agreements, PLAs, and CBAs together as policies that similarly aim to ensure that communities benefit from projects that include public contracts and/or subsidies. They also include neutrality agreements, in which employers remain neutral to organizing activities, and different types of legislation, including living wages. Cummings (2009) also positions CBAs and PLAs within a broader strategy aimed at enacting local protections for low-wage workers, which have largely emerged in response to insufficient protections in federal legislation. These local protections have taken many forms, including efforts to influence local contracting and land use regulation. Cummings views CBAs and PLAs as land use tactics that advance this broader goal. To this end, benefits-sharing agreements frequently leverage local government authority over land development to enact protections for low-wage workers.

31. Saito and Truong, 2015; Canon, 2014; Wolf-Powers, 2012.

32. Rosen and Schweitzer, 2018.

33. Implementation scholars have viewed policy making as occurring in multiple stages, including policy formulation, implementation, and reformulation (Mazmanian and Sabatier, 1989; Pressman and Wildavsky, 1984).

34. Margerum (2011) defines deliberative processes as "allowing everyone to fully explore and debate the issues" (p. 7).

35. Saito and Truong, 2015; Been, 2010; Erie, Kogan, and MacKenzie, 2010; Wolf-Powers, 2010. Consensus refers to "a process of seeking unanimous agreement. It involves a good-faith effort to meet the interests of all stakeholders. Consensus has been reached when everyone agrees they can live with whatever is proposed after every effort has been made to meet the interests of all stakeholding parties" (Susskind, McKearnan, and Thomas-Larmer, 1999, p. 6).

36. Nugent, 2017; Saito and Truong, 2015; Been, 2010; Erie, Kogan, and MacKenzie, 2010; Wolf-Powers, 2010; Baxamusa, 2008.

37. Nugent, 2017; Marantz, 2015; Saito and Truong, 2015; Lucas-Darby, 2012; Wolf-Powers, 2010; Salkin and Lavine, 2008; Gross, 2007.

38. Rosen and Schweitzer, 2018; Janssen-Jansen and van der Veen, 2017; Marantz, 2015; Saito and Truong, 2015; Hutson, 2015; Saito, 2012; Chimienti, 2010; Nadler, 2011; Baxamusa, 2008; Salkin and Lavine, 2008; Gross, 2007; Parkin, 2004.

39. Fox-Rogers and Murphy, 2015; Schrock, 2014; Lester and Reckhow, 2013; Wolf-Powers, 2012.

Chapter 1

1. deMause, 2017; 11Alive Staff, 2013; Tierney, 2012; City of Atlanta, n.d.a.; Invest Atlanta, n.d.c.; Interview with Respondents 30, 31, 34, and 41.

2. Blau, 2013b; Leslie, 2013a; Leslie, 2013b; Pendered, 2013a; Pendered, 2013b; Shapiro, 2013b; Shapiro, 2013c; Interview with Respondents 31, 32, and 35.

3. Blau, 2013b; Leslie, 2013a; Leslie, 2013b; Pendered, 2013a; Pendered, 2013b; Shapiro, 2013c; Interview with Respondents 31, 32, and 35.

4. Leslie, 2013a; Pendered, 2013a; Shapiro, 2013c; Interview with Respondents 31, 32, and 34. See Shapiro (2013c) for audio recordings of the meeting.

5. Rodriguez, 2021; Keating, 2001; Interview with Respondents 30, 31, 32, and 34.

6. See also Rodriguez, 2021; Wheatley, 2012a; Keating, 2001; Rutheiser, 1996.

7. Rodriguez, 2021; Albright, 2017; Wheatley, 2012a; Keating, 2001.

8. National Parks Service, n.d.; Rodriguez, 2021; Carnes, 2019; Saporta, 2014b; Burns, 2013; Gibson and Jung, 2005; Keating, 2001.

9. City of Atlanta, n.d.b.

10. Rodriguez, 2021; Shelton and Poorthuis, 2019; Isaf, 2015; City of Atlanta, n.d.b.; Interview with Respondent 34.

11. Burns, 2013; Keating, 2001.

12. Burns, 2013.

13. Green, 2019; Mariano, 2015a; Burns, 2013; Georgia STAND-UP, 2013; 11Alive Staff, 2013; Keating, 2001; Kunerth, 1991; Invest Atlanta, n.d.a.; Interview with Respondents 30, 31, 33, and 41.

14. Invest Atlanta, n.d.a.

15. Green, 2019; Mariano, 2015a; Burns, 2013; Georgia STAND-UP, 2013; 11Alive Staff, 2013; Keating, 2001; Kunerth, 1991; Interview with Respondents 30, 31, 33, and 41.

16. Invest Atlanta, n.d.a.; Green, 2019; Mariano, 2015a; 11Alive Staff, 2013; Interview with Respondents 31, 33, and 34.
17. Interview with Respondents 31, 33, and 34; Mariano, 2015b.
18. Invest Atlanta, n.d.a.; Green, 2019; Mariano, 2015a; 11Alive Staff, 2013; Interview with Respondents 31, 33, and 34.
19. Keating, 2001; Kunerth, 1991.
20. Rodriguez, 2021; Lohr, 2011; Keating, 2001; Newman, 1999. See Rodriguez (2021) and Keating (2001) for additional analysis on the political conflicts surrounding the Atlanta Olympics and the event's impacts.
21. WSB Web Staff, 2013.
22. Mariano, 2015a; 11Alive Staff, 2013; Wheatley, 2012a; Interview with Respondents 31, 33, and 34.
23. Dolan, Wang, and Peterson-Withorn, 2020; City of Atlanta, 2013; Pendered, 2013a; Shapiro, 2013a; Tierney, 2012; City of Atlanta, n.d.a.; Interview with Respondents 30 and 33.
24. City of Atlanta, n.d.
25. Atlanta United, 2017; Belson, 2017; Fennessy, 2017; Kahn, 2017; Bluestein, 2013; Partnership for Working Families, 2013; Leslie, 2013b; Tucker, 2013a; City of Atlanta, n.d. As Tucker (2013a) clarifies, "How much public money eventually goes into the stadium depends on how much revenue Atlanta hotel rooms generate through 2050. That's because 39.3 percent of the city's 7 cents-per-dollar hotel-motel tax is committed by law to the stadium—the same percentage that has gone into the Georgia Dome for the past 21 years. The tax money would be used first to make the annual principal and interest payments on the bonds that would fund $200 million of the construction cost. And whatever is left after that—potentially hundreds of millions of dollars over 30 years, according to some projections—would go to offset the Falcons' expenses of operating and maintaining the stadium. In another use of public money, the GWCCA is responsible for acquiring the land on which the stadium would be built."
26. Belson, 2017; Fennessy, 2017; Mariano, 2015a; Burns, 2013; Keating, 2001; Rutheiser, 1996.
27. Holmes and Berube, 2016; Immergluck, 2016; Bertrand, 2015; The Annie E. Casey Foundation, 2015; Burns, 2014; Burns, 2013; Severson, 2013; Wheatley, 2012a; Wheatley, 2012b.
28. Interview with Respondent [not specified to maintain confidentiality].
29. American Community Survey, 2010–2014 (5-Year Estimates); Interview with Respondents 32 and 34.
30. Immergluck, 2016.
31. Household income refers to 2014 inflation adjusted dollars.
32. Mariano, 2014.
33. Leslie, 2016; Mariano, 2016; Mariano, 2014.
34. Leslie, 2016; Mariano, 2016; Lee, 2015; Diamant, 2014; Mariano, 2014; Invest Atlanta, 2013a; Interview with Respondent [not specified to maintain confidentiality].
35. Tierney, 2014; Green, 2013; Saporta, 2013a; Severson, 2013; Tucker, 2013a.
36. Georgia World Congress Center Authority, n.d.; Green, 2013; Saporta, 2013a; Saporta and Wenk, 2013; Severson, 2013; Tucker, 2013b; Tucker, 2013c; Tucker, 2013d.
37. Interview with Respondents [not specified to maintain confidentiality].
38. Interview with Respondents [not specified to maintain confidentiality].
39. Wheatley, 2012a.
40. Burns, 2013.

41. Burns, 2013; Leslie, 2013a; Leslie, 2013b; Interview with Respondents 30, 31, 33, and 34.

42. City of Atlanta Resolution 13-R-3783, adopted December 2, 2013; Partnership for Working Families, 2013; Leslie, 2013b; Interview with Respondents 31, 33, and 34.

43. City of Atlanta Resolution 13-R-3783, adopted December 2, 2013; Leslie, 2013a; Partnership for Working Families, 2013; Pendered, 2013a; Pendered, 2013b; City of Atlanta, 2013; Interview with Respondents 30 and 34.

44. Archbold, 2014; City of Atlanta, 2013; Invest Atlanta, 2013a; Leslie, 2013a; Pendered, 2013a; Pendered, 2013b; Shapiro, 2013b; Interview with Respondents [not specified to maintain confidentiality]. As Archbold (2014) explains, Invest Atlanta aims "to strengthen Atlanta's economy and global competitiveness in order to create increased opportunity and prosperity for the people of Atlanta. Chaired by [then] Mayor Reed and governed by a nine-member board of directors, Invest Atlanta's programs and initiatives focus on developing and fostering public/private partnerships to create jobs, grow the economy, revitalize neighborhoods, attract investment, spur innovation, and encourage entrepreneurship. To achieve these goals, Invest Atlanta leverages the benefits of bond financing, revolving loan funds, housing financing, tax increment financing (TIF), and tax credits."

45. Archbold, 2014; City of Atlanta, 2013; Invest Atlanta, 2013b; Invest Atlanta, 2013c; Leslie, 2013a; Pendered, 2013a; Pendered, 2013b; Shapiro, 2013b; Wheatley, 2012b; Interview with Respondents [not specified to maintain confidentiality].

46. Blau, 2013a; Shapiro, 2013b; Interview with Respondents 30, 31, and 33. The plan committee meetings were open to the public, with public agendas, but there are no public minutes available for most meetings. However, some transcripts and audio recordings of particularly contentious moments are available online (Blau, 2013a; Shapiro, 2013c).

47. Leslie and Tucker, 2014; Blau, 2013a; Leslie, 2013a; Leslie, 2013b; Pendered, 2013a; Pendered, 2013b; Shapiro, 2013b; Interview with Respondents 30, 31, and 34.

48. Interview with Respondent [not specified to maintain confidentiality].

49. Interview with Respondent [not specified to maintain confidentiality].

50. Blau, 2013b; Pendered, 2013a; Pendered, 2013b; Shapiro, 2013a; Shapiro, 2013b; Shapiro, 2013d; Shapiro, 2013e; Interview with Respondents [not specified to maintain confidentiality].

51. Interview with Respondent [not specified to maintain confidentiality].

52. Blau, 2013a; Blau, 2013b; Shapiro, 2013b; Shapiro, 2013d; Shapiro, 2013e.

53. Blau, 2013b; Pendered, 2013a; Pendered, 2013b; Shapiro, 2013b; Shapiro, 2013c.

54. Leslie, 2013a; Leslie, 2013b; Pendered, 2013a; Pendered, 2013b; Shapiro, 2013b; Shapiro, 2013c; Shapiro, 2013d; Interview with Respondents [not specified to maintain confidentiality].

55. Leslie, 2013a; Pendered, 2013a.

56. Shapiro, 2013d; Shapiro, 2013f.

57. Leslie, 2013a; Pendered, 2013a; Shapiro, 2013c; Interview with Respondents [not specified to maintain confidentiality].

58. Rabouin, 2013; Shapiro, 2013e.

59. Pendered, 2014; Blau, 2013b; Interview with Respondent 41.

60. Belson, 2017; Wickert, 2016; Shapiro, 2013d; Interview with Respondents [not specified to maintain confidentiality].

61. Interview with Respondent [not specified to maintain confidentiality].

62. Blau, 2013b; Shapiro, 2013d; Shapiro, 2013f; Interview with Respondents [not specified to maintain confidentiality].

63. Belson, 2017; Kahn, 2015a; Mariano, 2015a; 11Alive Staff, 2013; Interview with Respondents 30, 31, 33, and 34.
64. Green, 2019; Abdulahi, 2017; Immergluck, 2016; Respondents [not specified to maintain confidentiality].
65. Blau, 2013b; Leslie, 2013b; Interview with Respondent [not specified to maintain confidentiality].
66. Chick-fil-A Peach Bowl, 2020; Trubey and Leslie, 2016.
67. Belson, 2017; Trubey and Leslie, 2016; Leslie, 2013a; Leslie, 2013b; Pendered, 2013a; Interview with Respondents 30 and 34.
68. Interview with Respondents 30, 31, 33, and 41.
69. City of Atlanta, Georgia, Mayor's Office of Communication, 2014.
70. Kahn, 2015b.
71. City of Atlanta, Georgia, Mayor's Office of Communication, 2015.
72. Green, 2019; Belson, 2017; Trubey & Leslie, 2016; Leslie, 2013a; Leslie, 2013b; Pendered, 2013a; Interview with Respondents 30 and 34.
73. Green, 2019; Belson, 2017; Trubey and Leslie, 2016; Leslie, 2013a; Leslie, 2013b; Pendered, 2013a; Interview with Respondents 30 and 34.
74. Georgia World Congress Center Authority, n.d.; Mercedes-Benz Stadium, n.d.b.; Green, 2016; Invest Atlanta, 2013a.
75. Green, 2016.
76. deMause, 2017; Caldwell, 2016; Leslie, 2013b.
77. City of Atlanta, n.d.a.
78. Kahn, 2017; Trubey, 2017; Tucker, 2013a; Tucker, 2013c; Interview with Respondent 30.
79. Chambers, 2019; deMause, 2017; Tucker, 2013a.
80. Invest Atlanta, 2013a.
81. Invest Atlanta, 2013a, p. 1.
82. Invest Atlanta, 2013a, p. 8.
83. Invest Atlanta, 2013a.
84. According to the plan, regarding the Blank Foundation's funding, "These charitable contributions will be made solely at the discretion of the trustees of The Arthur M. Blank Family Foundation and will be guided by the Community Benefits Plan Framework approved by the City of Atlanta Council" (Invest Atlanta, 2013a, p. 2). The language surrounding Invest Atlanta's activities is less explicit: "A $15 million fund to be provided by Invest Atlanta in capital projects of varying sizes that remove blighted conditions, expand redevelopment efforts, leverage other public and private funding sources and result in job creation and quality of life enhancement for residents of Vine City, English Avenue and Castleberry Hill" (Invest Atlanta, 2013a, p. 2).
85. According to the Westside TAD neighborhoods strategic implementation plan, "These goals will be accomplished by: Identifying specific recommendations for connections to downtown and surrounding areas; Improving and increasing walkability within the project area; Addressing watershed management issues while maximizing park and greenspace opportunities; Reducing crime within the project area; Improving the quality and mix of housing stock; Identifying three to five key short term development opportunities as priority projects; Integrating job creation opportunities into redevelopment scenarios; Promoting public/private partnership opportunities among developers and interest groups; [and] Identifying opportunities for development of a resource center in a central location that could provide access to the human services needed by residents" (Invest Atlanta, 2013c, p. 6).

86. Invest Atlanta, 2013c; Saporta, 2013b; Shapiro, 2013b.

87. Invest Atlanta, n.d.b.; Archbold, 2014; Invest Atlanta, 2014a; Invest Atlanta, 2014b; Invest Atlanta, 2013c. The Westside Neighborhood Strategic Implementation Plan decision-making matrix evaluates projects based on the following criteria: "Housing conditions (large rehab potential and demolition potential); Property ownership (site control); Vacant land; Adequate zoning and approvals of other entitlements; High number of foreclosures; Proximity to existing homeowners; Condition of existing infrastructure; Proximity to transit (within ¼ mile); Access to food (within ¼ mile); Access to open space (within ¼ mile); Proximity to funded projects (or recently completed projects); Proximity to services (health, police, retail) (within ¼ mile); Proximity to education (within ¼ mile); On or close to major thoroughfares; Feasible market conditions; Direct economic impact; Job creation (construction and permanent); Encourages new development; Encourages innovation and growth service; Indirect economic impact; Encourages public and private partnerships; Utilizes transit network improvements; Attracts private investment; "But for" public/private leverage (Feasibility); [and] Sustainability efforts (water management, urban gardening, parks and open space)" (Invest Atlanta, 2013c, p. 66).

88. Invest Atlanta, 2021a; Green, 2014; Interview with Respondent [not specified to maintain confidentiality].

89. Invest Atlanta, n.d.b.; Interview with Respondent [not specified to maintain confidentiality].

90. Invest Atlanta, 2016c; Green, 2014; Interview with Respondent [not specified to maintain confidentiality].

91. Invest Atlanta, n.d.b.; Invest Atlanta, 2017; Invest Atlanta, 2016a; Reddy 2016; Invest Atlanta, 2013c; Interview with Respondents 30, 31, and 34.

92. Invest Atlanta, 2016a; Invest Atlanta, 2013a; Reddy, 2016; Interview with Respondents 30, 31, and 34.

93. Arthur M. Blank Foundation, n.d.a.; Invest Atlanta, 2017; Invest Atlanta, 2016b; Invest Atlanta, 2016c; Interview with Respondents [not specified to maintain confidentiality].

94. Invest Atlanta, 2017; Invest Atlanta, 2016.

95. Kahn, 2015c.

96. Kahn, 2015c; Saporta, 2014a.

97. Invest Atlanta, 2017; Invest Atlanta, 2016b; Mariano, 2015b.

98. Invest Atlanta, 2018a; Invest Atlanta, 2018b; Invest Atlanta, 2013a.

99. Invest Atlanta, 2021b; Invest Atlanta, 2020a; Invest Atlanta, 2020b.

100. Interview with Respondents [not specified to maintain confidentiality].

101. Interview with Respondent [not specified to maintain confidentiality].

102. Saporta, 2014b; Wheatley, 2012b.

103. Saporta, 2014b; Wheatley, 2012b; Interview with Respondents 32 and 34. According to the Blank Foundation, grants would emphasize "Helping community members receive the training and opportunities they need to secure stable, good-paying jobs or start small businesses; Creating a safer environment that will lead to lower crime and a greater sense of community; Increasing and improving the educational opportunities available to kids in these neighborhoods; Providing safe, quality, affordable housing for long-time residents who need assistance; Improving the ability of local residents to live healthier lives in healthier environments; and [m]ore broadly, connecting neighborhood residents to the socio-economic opportunities they need to succeed" (Saporta, 2014b).

104. Arthur M. Blank Foundation, n.d.a.; Atlanta Police Foundation, n.d.; Invest Atlanta, 2013a; Interview with Respondent [not specified to maintain confidentiality].
105. Saporta, 2014b.
106. Saporta, 2015; Georgia Center for Nonprofits, n.d.a.
107. Georgia Center for Nonprofits, n.d.a.; Georgia Center for Nonprofits, n.d.b. Georgia Center for Nonprofits, 2015.
108. Georgia Center for Nonprofits, n.d.a.; Georgia Center for Nonprofits, n.d.b.; Georgia Center for Nonprofits, 2015; Interview with Respondent 32.
109. Interview with Respondents 31, 32, and 34.
110. Interview with Respondents 31, 32, and 34.
111. Interview with Respondent [not specified to maintain confidentiality].
112. Rodriguez, 2021; Keating, 2001; Interview with Respondents 30, 31, 32, and 34.
113. Interview with Respondent [not specified to maintain confidentiality].
114. Mercedes-Benz Stadium, n.d.a.; Trubey and Leslie, 2016.
115. Interview with Respondent [not specified to maintain confidentiality].
116. Mariano, 2015b; Shapiro, 2013b; Shapiro, 2013g; Interview with Respondents 30, 31, and 33.
117. Mariano, 2015b; Interview with Respondents 30, 31, and 33.
118. Interview with Respondent [not specified to maintain confidentiality].
119. Interview with Respondent 30, 31, and 34.
120. Mariano, 2015b; Interview with Respondents 33 and 34.
121. Mariano, 2015a; Mariano, 2015b; Interview with Respondents 32 and 34.
122. Mariano, 2015b.
123. Interview with Respondents 31, 33, and 34.
124. Interview with Respondents 31, 33, 34, and 35.
125. Interview with Respondents 31, 33, 34, and 35.
126. Interview with Respondent [not specified to maintain confidentiality].
127. Interview with Respondent [not specified to maintain confidentiality].
128. Interview with Respondents 31, 33, 34, and 35.
129. Mariano, 2015a; 11Alive Staff, 2013; Wheatley, 2012b; Interview with Respondents 30, 31, 33, 34, 35, and 41.
130. Mariano, 2015b; Interview with Respondents 30, 31, 33, 34, and 35.
131. Interview with Respondents 31, 32, 34, and 35.
132. Mercedes-Benz Stadium, n.d.a.

Chapter 2

1. Eskenazi, 2002; Seattle Housing Authority, 2002; Harris v. United States Department of Housing and Urban Development, CA No. 1481C 2002.
2. Fox, 2011; Seattle Housing Authority, 2007b; Fox, 2006; National Housing Law Project, 2003.
3. Fox, 2006; Eskenazi, 2002; Seattle Housing Authority, 2002; Harris v. United States Department of Housing and Urban Development, CA No. 1481C 2002.
4. Seattle Housing Authority, 2007b; National Housing Law Project, 2003; Seattle Housing Authority, 2002; Harris v. United States Department of Housing and Urban Development, CA No. 1481C 2002; Interview with Respondents 12, 13, and 15.
5. Fox and O'Donnell, 2007; Seattle Housing Authority, 2007b; National Housing Law Project, 2003; Seattle Housing Authority, 2002.

Notes to Pages 55–64

6. Interview with Respondent 13; U.S. Department of Housing and Urban Development, 2015; U.S. Department of Housing and Urban Development, 2013; Seattle Housing Authority, 2012c.

7. Beekman, 2016b; Seattle Housing Authority, 2015; Curbed Staff, 2014; Seattle University, 2013; Seattle Housing Authority, 2008.

8. Seattle Housing Authority, 2008.

9. Black, 2013a; Seattle Housing Authority, 2008.

10. Seattle Housing Authority, 2008.

11. Seattle Housing Authority, 2015; Seattle Housing Authority, 2008.

12. Young, 2011; Interview with Respondents 12 and 13.

13. Dierwechter, 2017; Seattle Housing Authority, 2015; Caldbick, 2014; Curbed Staff, 2014; Seattle University, 2014; Young, 2011; Seattle Housing Authority, 2008; Interview with Respondents 12, 13, 14, and 15.

14. Albertson et al., 2020; Pulkkinen, 2019; Stubbs, 2018; Vulcan Real Estate, 2018; Stiles, 2017; Stiles and Parkhurst, 2016; Stiles, 2015; Seattle Housing Authority, 2014; Wang, 2013; Young, 2011; Interview with Respondents 12 and 13.

15. Seattle Housing Authority, 2013a; Interview with Respondents 13 and 14.

16. Seattle Housing Authority, 2013a, p. 8; Seattle Housing Authority, 2011a.

17. Keeley, 2016; Curbed Staff, 2014; Seattle Housing Authority, 2013a; Interview with Respondent 13.

18. Pulkkinen, 2019; Keeley, 2016; Stiles, 2016; Curbed Staff, 2014; Mudede, 2013; Seattle Housing Authority, 2013a; Interview with Respondents 12 and 13.

19. Pulkkinen, 2019; Stiles, 2017; Stiles, 2016; Stiles, 2015; Curbed Staff, 2014; SCIDpda, 2014; Mudede, 2013; Interview with Respondents 12, 13 and 14.

20. Stiles, 2017; Stiles, 2016; Stiles, 2015; Interview with Respondents 12, 13, and 14.

21. Vulcan Real Estate, n.d.; Stiles, 2017; Whitely, 2017; Stiles, 2016; Stiles, 2015.

22. Stiles, 2015.

23. Edwards, 2019; Pulkkinen, 2019; Stubbs, 2018; Stiles, 2017; Daily Journal of Commerce Staff, 2016; Stiles, 2016; Seattle Housing Authority, 2011a.

24. Upstream Artist Coalition for Equitable Development, n.d.; Sears, 2017.

25. Pulkkinen, 2019; Oluo, 2015; Curbed Staff, 2014; Mudede, 2013.

26. Mudede, 2013.

27. Stiles, 2015; Mudede, 2013. Yesler Terrace crime statistics support the contention that before redevelopment, Yesler Terrace and its surrounding area did not experience significantly more crime than the rest of Seattle (Seattle Police Department, 2014; Seattle University, n.d.).

28. Pulkkinen, 2019; Oluo, 2015; Young, 2015; Curbed Staff, 2014; Mudede, 2013.

29. Black, 2013b; Young, 2011.

30. These include *Even the Walls* and *Hagereseb* (Oluo, 2015).

31. Pulkkinen, 2019; Graves, 2016a; Black, 2013b.

32. Pulkkinen, 2019; Seattle Housing Authority, 2007b, p. 9, bold formatting removed; Seattle Housing Authority, 2011b; Interview with Respondents 12 and 14.

33. Pulkkinen, 2019; Interview with Respondent [not specified to maintain confidentiality].

34. Interview with Respondent 47.

35. Interview with Respondent 48.

36. Pulkkinen, 2019.

37. Seattle City Council, 2012; Seattle Housing Authority, 2012b; Seattle Housing Authority, 2012c; Interview with Respondents 12, 14, 20, and 24.

38. Logan and Molotch, 1987.
39. Interview with Respondents [not specified to maintain confidentiality].
40. Many other CWAs exist in the region, including large-scale agreements around Sound Transit projects, the Port of Seattle, and the Elliot Bay Seawall project, which is the largest public works project in the history of the city of Seattle (Kinney, 2016; Interview with Respondents 24, 26, and 29).
41. Interview with Respondents 12, 16, 18, and 24.
42. Interview with Respondents 12, 18, and 21.
43. Interview with Respondents 12, 20, and 23.
44. Interview with Respondents 12, 20, 23, 24, 47, and 49.
45. Seattle Housing Authority, 2013a.
46. Seattle Housing Authority 2013a, p. 7. According to the U.S. Department of Housing and Urban Development (n.d.), "The Section 3 program requires that recipients of certain HUD financial assistance, to the greatest extent possible, provide training, employment, contracting and other economic opportunities to low- and very low-income persons, especially recipients of government assistance for housing, and to businesses that provide economic opportunities to low- and very low-income persons."
47. Seattle Housing Authority, 2013a, p. 7.
48. Seattle Housing Authority, 2013a, p. 7.
49. Seattle Housing Authority, 2013a. Specifically, the CWA establishes that signatories to the agreement "agree that: 1) Section 3-eligible persons seeking pre-apprenticeship training will be given preference for entry into these programs. 2) Qualified Section 3-eligible persons who successfully complete approved pre-apprenticeship programs, mutually agreed upon by SHA and the Unions, will be given preference for entry into the Union-sponsored apprenticeship programs. 3) Qualified Section 3-eligible persons enrolled in Union-sponsored apprenticeship programs will be given preference in dispatch to Contractors working on the Project. 4) Section 3-eligible persons who qualify and possess the requisite skills as a journeyman as evaluated by the Local Unions will be given preference in employment by Contractors working on the Project. These evaluations by the Unions will be offered frequently and in close proximity to the Project. Any person denied journeyman status by any of the Local Unions may appeal this decision to the Administrator. The Administrator has sole discretion to accept or deny the decision of the Local Union" (Seattle Housing Authority 2013a, p. 9).
50. Seattle Housing Authority, 2013a; League of Women Voters, 1998; Interview with Respondents 12 and 14.
51. As the CWA clarifies, "The Seattle Housing Authority intends to use the term 'Yesler Terrace Redevelopment Project' ... to refer collectively to a number of individual projects ... that they will build, or fund. These projects are an integral and important part of the overall Yesler Terrace Master Planned Community, but distinctly separate from other Master Plan projects that will be built by non-profits, or market-rate developers, as the work on the Project will be covered by the Yesler Terrace Redevelopment Project Community Workforce Agreement.... Although this program is quite comprehensive, the intention of this CWA is that only the work bid out and awarded by the Seattle Housing Authority, or work funded by the Seattle Housing Authority and contracted to another government entity, on or before December 31, 2017, will be considered Covered Work. However, it is also the intention of the Parties to offer the CWA to contractors working on projects for non-profits or market-rate developers within the Master Plan on a voluntary basis" (Seattle Housing Authority 2013a, p. 8).

52. Pulkkinen, 2019; Turnbull, 2017; Stiles, 2016; Interview with Respondents 12, 14, 16, 18, and 24.
53. Interview with Respondents 12, 14, 16, 18, 24, 50, and 51; Stiles, 2016.
54. Based on summary data for community participation reports; Interview with Respondents 12, 14, and 19.
55. Interview with Respondents 12, 13, 14, 17, 18, 21, and 24.
56. Interview with Respondents 13, 15, 17, and 18.
57. Interview with Respondent 49.
58. Interview with Respondents 16, 17, and 18.
59. As with other PLAs, targeted worker hiring depends on a functional pipeline to funnel potential workers through training and onto jobsites. This process requires commitment and good communication between the project owner, contractors, and unions, to predict upcoming worker needs and quickly dispatch targeted workers. It is difficult to ensure that a pool of eligible workers exists in advance of contractor needs. Many unions are reluctant to enroll workers before jobs exist, since these workers would have to wait, potentially for a long time, on the out-of-work list. Without sufficient work, such as during recessions when construction slows, many workers are forced leave construction work altogether if they cannot wait for a job opening to arise. Further, various trades have different commitments to inclusion of historically marginalized workers, such that some unions are more willing to confront the challenges that arise with community inclusion. Throughout, coordination and communication are critical; as one respondent stated, "When there's breakdown either way [in communication], the whole thing falls apart" (Interview with Respondents 1, 12, 14, 16, 18, and 21).
60. U.S. Department of Housing and Urban Development, n.d.; Interview with Respondents 12, 14, 17, and 21. Although the Section 3 requirement exists regardless of the CWA, SHA staff noted that the CWA systematized the process of hiring Section 3 workers and "takes it a step farther" through additional compliance. Union stakeholders expressed that they felt like they had an unfair burden placed on them, since normally the Section 3 requirement did not receive so much attention from the agency, but it was scrutinized on this union agreement (Interview with Respondents 12, 14, and 24).
61. Interview with Respondents 12, 14, 17, 18, and 24.
62. Interview with Respondents 12, 16, 18, and 24.
63. Interview with Respondents 12, 14, 16, and 24.
64. Interview with Respondents 12, 16, 18, 21, 24, and 29.
65. This presentation occurred at a January 2013 meeting. Section 3 construction job opportunities were also discussed in a March 2012 meeting, before the community workforce agreement was approved. Seattle Housing Authority, n.d.; Seattle Housing Authority, 2013b; Seattle Housing Authority, 2012a; Seattle Housing Authority, 2007a; Interview with Respondents 13, 14, and 22.
66. Interview with Respondents 12, 13, 14, 22, and 49.
67. Specifically, the CWA states that the Section 3 Advisory Committee "will serve these purposes:

1) Monitor contractors' compliance efforts with the social equity requirements and goals for all Covered Work on the Yesler Terrace Project.
2) Advise SHA and its contractors on how best to meet those goals as appropriate as well as address areas of deficiency and corrective measures.

3) By its representative composition, the Committee will help interested community members understand the requirements and goals, and SHA's and the Parties' commitment to them.
4) Through the Committee's involvement, increase the community's confidence in the effort being made and make success more likely" (Seattle Housing Authority 2013a, p. 16).

68. Interview with Respondents 12, 14, 17, and 22.
69. Interview with Respondents 12, 13, 14, 15, 17, and 22.
70. Interview with Respondents 12, 14, 15, 17, 22, and 24.
71. Daily Journal of Commerce Staff, 2017.
72. Interview with Respondents 14, 15, 17, and 24.
73. Kinney, 2016; Interview with Respondents 12, 14, 16, 23, and 24.
74. Pulkkinen, 2019; Turnbull, 2017; Interview with Respondent 49.
75. Albertson et al., 2020; Farquhar et al., 2018.
76. Fowler, 2020; Pulkkinen, 2019; Beekman, 2016a; Mudede, 2013; Gillis, 2009; Interview with Respondents 13, 14, and 49.
77. Fowler, 2020; KIRO 7 News Staff, 2020.
78. Madrid, 2012.
79. Lloyd, 2018.
80. Pulkkinen, 2019.
81. Graves, 2016b.

Chapter 3

1. City of Milwaukee Department of City Development, n.d.; Congress for the New Urbanism, n.d.; Wisconsin Highways, 2016; Larsen, 2009.
2. Preservation Institute, n.d.; Wisconsin Highways, 2016; Snyder, 2016. For a more thorough review of the Park East freeway project, please see Snyder (2016).
3. Wolf-Powers, 2010, p. 151; Snyder, 2016.
4. Rose & Mohl, 2012, p. 109; Snyder, 2016; Wolf-Powers, 2012.
5. Wolf-Powers, 2012, p. 224; City of Milwaukee Department of City Development, n.d.; Preservation Institute, n.d.; Wisconsin Highways, 2016; Redevelopment Authority of the City of Milwaukee, 2004.
6. Wisconsin Highways, 2016; Rose and Mohl, 2012; Chiuchiarelli, 2011; Wolf-Powers, 2010; Henry, 2009; Larsen, 2009; Napolitan, 2007; Preservation Institute, 2007; Redevelopment Authority of the City of Milwaukee, 2004; Interview with Respondent 36.
7. Wolf-Powers, 2010; Henry, 2009; Parker, 2005; City of Milwaukee Department of City Development, n.d.
8. City of Milwaukee Department of City Development, n.d.; Preservation Institute, n.d.; Henry, 2009; Parker, 2005, p. 1; Redevelopment Authority of the City of Milwaukee, 2004.
9. Wolf-Powers, 2010; Larsen, 2009; Partnership for Working Families, 2007.
10. Redevelopment Authority of the City of Milwaukee, 2004.
11. Wolf-Powers, 2010; Larsen, 2009; Partnership for Working Families, 2007; Parker, 2005.
12. This body is equivalent to a city council (City of Milwaukee, n.d.).
13. McKean, 2015; Wolf-Powers, 2010; Larsen, 2009; Partnership for Working Families, 2007; Parker, 2005.

14. McKean, 2015; Wolf-Powers, 2010; Larsen, 2009; Partnership for Working Families, 2007; Parker, 2005; Interview with Respondents 37 and 38.

15. Ryan, 2015b; Larsen, 2009; Parker, 2005; Millard, 2003; Interview with Respondents 37 and 38.

16. Larsen, 2009; Parker, 2005. Larsen (2009) details this process and the different competing explanations given for the policy's failure before the Common Council.

17. McKean, 2015; Larsen, 2009; Ho, 2007; Parker, 2005; Interview with Respondents 37 and 38.

18. Parker, 2005; Ryan, 2005; Ryan, 2004; Interview with Respondents 37 and 38.

19. File no. 04-492 (Park East Milwaukee, 2004).

20. Interview with Respondents 36 and 37; Wolf-Powers, 2010; Larsen, 2009; Parker, 2005; Park East Milwaukee, 2004.

21. Ryan, 2004.

22. Interview with Respondents 36, 37, 38, and 39.

23. McKean, 2015; Wolf-Powers, 2010; Partnership for Working Families, 2007; Parker, 2005.

24. This research includes McKean (2015); Rosado (2014); Severin (2013); Wolf-Powers (2012); Larsen (2009); Pastor, Benner, and Matsuoka (2009); De Sousa (2008); Gross (2007); McGahey and Vey (2008); Salkin and Lavine (2008); and Sheikh (2008).

25. County of Milwaukee, 2004.

26. Wolf-Powers, 2010; Larsen, 2009; Parker, 2005; County of Milwaukee, 2004; Interview with Respondents 36, 37, 38, and 39.

27. County of Milwaukee, 2004, p. 2.

28. McKean, 2015; Larsen, 2009; Parker, 2005; County of Milwaukee, 2004; Interview with Respondents [not specified to maintain confidentiality].

29. Smith and Davey, 2018; Umhoefer, 2016; Wolf-Powers, 2010; Rosen, 2009; Ryan, 2005; Interview with Respondents 37, 38, and 39.

30. County of Milwaukee, 2004.

31. Interview with Respondents 36 and 39.

32. County of Milwaukee, 2004.

33. Park East Milwaukee, 2004, p. 1. The PERC specifies "some possible uses of the CED Fund: Minority Business Working Capital; Small & Minority Business Contract Financing; Housing Development; Neighborhood Business Development; Economic Development; Environmental Mitigation/Brownfields" (County of Milwaukee, 2004, p. 2).

34. Interview with Respondent [not specified to maintain confidentiality].

35. Wolf-Powers, 2010; Larsen, 2009; Parker, 2005. Interview with Respondent [not specified to maintain confidentiality].

36. Wolf-Powers, 2010; Larsen, 2009; Rosen, 2009; Ryan, 2005. Interview with Respondents 37, 38, and 39.

37. Wolf-Powers, 2010, p. 224; Wolf-Powers, 2012; Interview with Respondents 36 and 37.

38. Wolf-Powers, 2012; Interview with Respondents 36, 37, and 39.

39. Wolf-Powers, 2010; Larsen, 2009; Interview with Respondent 36, 38, 39, and 40.

40. Wolf-Powers, 2010; Larsen, 2009; Holloway, 2005; County of Milwaukee, 2004; Interview with Respondents 36 and 38.

41. Daykin, 2014; Daykin, 2013; Wolf-Powers, 2010; Daykin, 2009; Larsen, 2009.

42. Wolf-Powers, 2010; Daykin, 2009.

43. Weiland, 2018; City of Milwaukee, 2014; Daykin, 2012a; Daykin, 2012b.

44. Daykin, 2013; Daykin, 2012a; Ryan, 2012a; Daykin, 2009; Interview with Respondents [not specified to maintain confidentiality].

45. Jannene, 2014; Daykin, 2013; Daykin, 2012a; Ryan, 2012a; Daykin, 2009; Interview with Respondents [not specified to maintain confidentiality].

46. Interview with Respondents [not specified to maintain confidentiality].

47. See also McKean (2015); Larsen (2009).

48. Park East Milwaukee, n.d.; Daykin, 2015; Daykin, 2013; Ryan, 2012b; Interview with Respondents [not specified to maintain confidentiality].

49. Park East Milwaukee, n.d.; Daykin, 2015; Daykin, 2013; Ryan, 2012b; Interview with Respondents [not specified to maintain confidentiality].

50. Jannene, 2014; Daykin, 2012a; Interview with Respondents 36 and 37.

51. Milwaukee County File No. 15-288; Daykin, 2015; McKean, 2015; Jannene, 2014; Interview with Respondents [not specified to maintain confidentiality].

52. Interview with Respondents [not specified to maintain confidentiality].

53. Ryan, 2015b; Larsen, 2009; Parker, 2005; Millard, 2003; Interview with Respondents 36, 39, and 42.

54. Jannene, 2014; Daykin, 2013.

55. Jannene, 2014.

56. Daykin, 2013.

57. Murphy, 2021; Murphy, 2019; Daykin, 2015; Jannene, 2014; Daykin, 2013; Interview with Respondents 36 and 37.

58. Zillgitt, 2018; Marklein, 2017; Ryan, 2016b; Murphy, 2015; Powell, 2015.

59. Bayatpour, 2015; Daykin, 2015; Ryan, 2015b.

60. Zillgitt, 2018; Weis, 2017; Marklein, 2017; Schneider, 2017; Daykin, 2015; Kirchen, 2015. According to Kirchen (2015), these sources include "state income tax, a ticket surcharge at the new arena, $4 million annually in Milwaukee County funding, $47 million from the city of Milwaukee and $203 million-plus in new bonding from the Wisconsin Center District."

61. Marklein, 2017; Schneider, 2017; CBS58 Staff, 2015; Ryan, 2015b; Kirchen, 2015.

62. Powell, 2015; Ryan, 2015b; Interview with Respondents [not specified to maintain confidentiality]. The estimated cost of the project has risen since this interview.

63. Murphy, 2019; Jannene, 2017; Marklein, 2017; Kirchen, 2016; Kirchen, 2015; Bauer, 2015; Powell, 2015.

64. Powell, 2015.

65. Jannene, 2019; Schneider, 2017; Daykin, 2015; Interview with Respondent [not specified to maintain confidentiality].

66. Schneider, 2017; Reid, 2015; Interview with Respondents [not specified to maintain confidentiality]; Daykin, 2013.

67. Wolf-Powers, 2010; Interview with Respondents [not specified to maintain confidentiality].

68. Jannene, 2019; Fiserv, 2018; Jannene, 2018; Weiland, 2018; Schneider, 2017; Kirchen, 2016; Ryan, 2016a; Ryan, 2016b; Kirchen, 2015; Daykin, 2012b.

69. Daykin, 2019; Weiland, 2018; Daykin, 2018.

70. Wolf-Powers, 2010; Larsen, 2009; Parker, 2005; Interview with Respondents [not specified to maintain confidentiality].

71. Interview with Respondents [not specified to maintain confidentiality].

72. Interview with Respondents [not specified to maintain confidentiality].

73. Interview with Respondents [not specified to maintain confidentiality].
74. Jannene, 2018; Kirchen, 2018; Weis, 2017; Daykin, 2016; Jannene, 2015.
75. Gores, 2018; Jannene, 2018; Thompson, 2018; Gores, 2017.
76. Murphy, 2021; Badenhausen, 2019; Murphy, 2019; Zillgitt, 2018.
77. Interview with Respondents [not specified to maintain confidentiality].
78. Interview with Respondents [not specified to maintain confidentiality].
79. Interview with Respondents 36, 37, and 38.
80. In one example, administrators switched to tracking workers by hours performed, rather than total number of workers hired, to avoid incentivizing contractors to hire targeted workers for only short periods to inflate numbers (Interview with Respondents [not specified to maintain confidentiality]).
81. Interview with Respondents [not specified to maintain confidentiality].
82. Interview with Respondents [not specified to maintain confidentiality].
83. Interview with Respondents [not specified to maintain confidentiality].
84. Interview with Respondents [not specified to maintain confidentiality]. See Rosen and Schweitzer (2018) for a discussion about the challenges of competing narratives in urban development and community benefits delivery. This discussion covers the often asymmetric access to influential media reporting, where development interests have access to more powerful media outlets. This context creates the potential for rhetorical trickery, where proponents claim to produce outcomes that do not necessarily occur.
85. Interview with Respondents 36, 38, and 39.
86. Interview with Respondents 36, 38, and 39.
87. Interview with Respondents [not specified to maintain confidentiality].
88. Delong, 2015; Interview with Respondents [not specified to maintain confidentiality].
89. Interview with Respondents 36, 38, and 39.
90. Inflation-adjusted total income; Vasquez, 2020; Chowdhury, 2017; Keith, 2017; Interview with Respondents [not specified to maintain confidentiality].
91. Wisconsin Legislative Council, 2013; Schultze, 2013; Schultze and Stein, 2013; Interview with Respondents [not specified to maintain confidentiality].
92. Smith and Davey, 2018.
93. Small, 2016; Act 55, Section 1907M.59.17 (Wisconsin State Legislature, 2015); Interview with Respondents [not specified to maintain confidentiality].
94. Ryan, 2015a; Milwaukee County Ordinance 15-13, File No. 15-352; Supervisor John Weishan, 2015; Interview with Respondents [not specified to maintain confidentiality].
95. Ryan, 2015a; Milwaukee County Ordinance 15-13, File No. 15-352; Supervisor John Weishan, 2015; Interview with Respondents [not specified to maintain confidentiality].
96. Interview with Respondents [not specified to maintain confidentiality].

Chapter 4

1. Los Angeles County Metropolitan Transportation Authority, 2012b; Los Angeles County Metropolitan Transportation Authority, n.d.d.
2. Sides, 2013; Bakewell, 2012; Interview with Respondents 3 and 4.
3. Los Angeles County Metropolitan Transportation Authority, 2012b.
4. U.S. Bureau of Labor Statistics, 2013b; Bakewell, 2012; Griffin, 2012; Los Angeles County Metropolitan Transportation Authority, 2012c.
5. Interview with Respondents 3, 4, and 10.

6. Newton, 2016; Soja, 2010; Griffin, 2012.

7. Newton, 2016; Bakewell, 2012; Griffin, 2012; Author field notes, 2012; Newton, 2011; Soja, 2010. Soja (2010) documents the fractured relationship between Metro and low-income residents, which culminated in the 1996 court case *Labor/Community Strategy Center et al. v. Los Angeles Metropolitan Transit Authority*.

8. Chiland, 2020; Newton, 2016; Kudler, 2013; Miller, 2013; Newton, 2011.

9. Kudler, 2013; Miller, 2013; Bakewell, 2012; Stoltze, 2011.

10. Fleischer, 2021; Bermudez, 2016; Newton, 2016; Newton, 2011.

11. County of Los Angeles Supervisor Mark Ridley-Thomas, n.d.b.; County of Los Angeles Supervisor Mark Ridley-Thomas, 2020; Streeter, 2013; Soja, 2010; Interview with Respondents 7 and 8.

12. County of Los Angeles Supervisor Mark Ridley-Thomas, 2020; Interview with Respondent [not specified to maintain confidentiality].

13. Interview with Respondent [not specified to maintain confidentiality].

14. Streeter, 2013; Soja, 2010; Interview with Respondents 2, 7, and 8.

15. County of Los Angeles Supervisor Mark Ridley-Thomas, 2020; Author field notes, 2014; Streeter, 2013; Griffin, 2012; Interview with Respondent [not specified to maintain confidentiality].

16. Kofman and Cuevas, n.d.; Los Angeles Alliance for a New Economy, n.d.; Los Angeles Black Worker Center, n.d.b.; County of Los Angeles Supervisor Mark Ridley-Thomas, 2020; Interview with Respondents 2, 7, 8, and 44.

17. Interview with Respondents 4, 7, 8, and 44.

18. Bakewell, 2012; Griffin, 2012; Interview with Respondents 4, 7, 8, and 44.

19. Los Angeles Black Worker Center, n.d.a.; Los Angeles Black Worker Center, n.d.b.; Fine, 2018; Fine, 2015; UCLA Labor Center, 2014; Kofman, 2013; Interview with Respondents 1, 2, 4, 8, and 44.

20. See Appendix; Interview with Respondents 1, 4, 8, and 9.

21. Los Angeles County Metropolitan Transportation Authority, n.d.e.; Interview with Respondents 2 and 44.

22. Kofman, 2013; Bakewell, 2012; Griffin, 2012; Interview with Respondents 1, 2, 3, 4, 8, and 44.

23. Los Angeles County Metropolitan Transportation Authority, n.d.e.; Ubaldo, 2014; Griffin, 2012; Weikel, 2012.

24. Foxx, 2015; Nelson, 2014; Bakewell, 2012; Griffin, 2012; Weikel, 2012.

25. Bakewell, 2012; Griffin, 2012; Interview with Respondents 1, 2, 4, and 10.

26. Los Angeles County Metropolitan Transportation Authority, n.d.e.

27. Foxx, 2015; Sulaiman, 2013; Interview with Respondents [not specified to maintain confidentiality]. In March 2015, U.S. Secretary of Transportation Anthony Foxx developed a one-year pilot program to enable local hire on federal projects, as a means to test potential changes to federal limitations on local hire. Foxx used the Metro PLA to argue for the policy change (Foxx, 2015). Metro amended the PLA to enable a local hire pilot, to run during the larger FTA pilot project, from February to September 2015 (Los Angeles County Metropolitan Transportation Authority, 2015b; Vock, 2015). The U.S. Department of Transportation ended the local pilot hire program in 2017 and reinstituted it in 2021 (U.S. Department of Transportation, 2021; Los Angeles County Metropolitan Transportation Authority, n.d.e.; Los Angeles County Metropolitan Transportation Authority, 2017).

28. Los Angeles County Metropolitan Transportation Authority, n.d.e.; Interview with Respondents 2, 8, and 44.

29. California Legislative Analyst's Office, 1996; Los Angeles County Metropolitan Transportation Authority, 2012c; Interview with Respondents 1, 2, and 44. The term "disadvantaged worker" concerns "an individual who, prior to commencing work on the project, resides in an Economically Disadvantaged Area or Extremely Economically Disadvantaged Area as defined in 1.9 and 1.10 below, and faces at least two of the following barriers to employment: (1) being homeless; (2) being a custodial single parent; (3) receiving public assistance; (4) lacking a GED or high school diploma; (5) having a criminal record or other involvement with the criminal justice system (as more specifically described in Section 3.8 of the Construction Careers Policy); (6) suffering from chronic unemployment (as more specifically described in Section 3.28 of the Construction Careers Policy); (7) emancipated from the foster care system; (8) being a veteran of the Iraq/Afghanistan war; or (9) being an apprentice with less than 15% of the apprenticeship hours required to graduate to journey level in a program" (Los Angeles County Metropolitan Transportation Authority, 2012c, p. 3). "Local targeted worker" is defined as a "Local Resident, Community Area Resident or a Disadvantaged Worker whose primary place of residence is within Los Angeles County" (Los Angeles County Metropolitan Transportation Authority, 2012c, p. 4). "Community area resident" refers to "a Local Resident whose primary place of residence is within an Economically Disadvantaged Area or an Extremely Economically Disadvantaged Area and is within a 5-mile radius of the covered project in question" (Los Angeles County Metropolitan Transportation Authority, 2012c, p. 2).

30. Interview with Respondents 1, 2, 7, and 44.

31. Griffin, 2012; Los Angeles County Metropolitan Transportation Authority, 2012a; Los Angeles County Metropolitan Transportation Authority, 2012c; Weikel, 2012; Interview with Respondents 1, 2, 3, 4, 7, 8, 44, and 46. Targeted hire is "a policy initiative aimed at increasing employment opportunities for disadvantaged workers, who often experience difficulty accessing the construction pipeline.... Targeted hire refers to hiring requirements for target groups, such as minorities, women, or low-income workers. In other words, local hire is tied solely to a specific geographic region, while targeted hire is broader, encompassing different segments of the population across geographic regions" (Herrera et al., 2014, pp. 12–13).

32. Los Angeles County Metropolitan Transportation Authority, 2012c, p. 14; Interview with Respondents 2, 4, and 7.

33. Los Angeles County Metropolitan Transportation Authority, 2012c, p. 14.

34. Los Angeles County Metropolitan Transportation Authority, 2012c. "Apprentice" concerns "those apprentices registered and participating in Joint Labor/Management Apprenticeship Programs approved by the State of California, Department of Industrial Relations, Division of Apprenticeship Standards ("DAS"), or in the case of Projects with federal funding, approved by the US Department of Labor ("DOL") and DAS" (Los Angeles County Metropolitan Transportation Authority, 2012c, p. 2).

35. Herrera et al., 2014; Los Angeles County Metropolitan Transportation Authority, 2012c; Interview with Respondents 1, 8, and 9.

36. Miller, 2013; Los Angeles County Metropolitan Transportation Authority, 2012a; Interview with Respondents 1, 8, and 9.

37. Herrera et al., 2014; Kofman, 2013; Philips, 2010.

38. Boarnet and Crane, 1998; Interview with Respondents 2, 3, and 7.

39. Bloomekatz, 2012; League of Women Voters of California, 2012; Interview with Respondents 2, 3, and 7.

40. Rudick, 2015; Interview with Respondents 2 and 3.

41. Los Angeles County Metropolitan Transportation Authority, 2016b; Interview with Respondents 2, 3, and 7.

42. Weikel, 2012.

43. Nelson, 2014; Miller, 2013; Streeter, 2013; Griffin, 2012; Weikel, 2012.

44. Foxx, 2015; Ubaldo, 2014.

45. FTA policy effectively prohibited local hire on projects using federal funding by preventing "certain contracting provisions that do not directly relate to the bidder's performance of work in a competent and responsible manner," which encompassed local and geographically targeted hire. The pilot, enacted on March 6, 2015, which some partially attributed to the Metro PLA's success with local hire, suspended the prohibition on local hire for one year. The initial pilot was extended for one year, and then an additional five years, though the Trump Administration later rescinded this policy (Federal Register, 2021; Federal Register, 2017a; Federal Register, 2017b; Foxx, 2015; Ebeling, 2014; Interview with Respondents 1, 2, and 44).

46. Rosen and Schweitzer, 2018.

47. Linton, 2022; Chiland, 2020; Nelson, 2020; Chiland, 2018; Los Angeles County Metropolitan Transportation Authority, n.d.f.; Los Angeles County Metropolitan Transportation Authority, 2019; Nelson, 2014.

48. Chiland, 2020; Los Angeles County Metropolitan Transportation Authority, n.d.a.; Los Angeles County Metropolitan Transportation Authority, n.d.b.; Los Angeles County Metropolitan Transportation Authority, n.d.f.; Los Angeles County Metropolitan Transportation Authority, 2019.

49. Flores, 2019; Muhammad, 2018.

50. American Community Survey, 2008-2012, 5-Year Estimates. Census tracts 2340, 2342, 2343, 2345.01, 2345.02, 2346, 2347, 2348, 2349.01, 2349.02, 2352.01, 2352.02; ACS 2008–2012 (5-Year Estimates) roughly correspond with the Crenshaw area.

51. American Community Survey, 2008-2012, 5-Year Estimates.

52. Kudler, 2013.

53. Jennings, 2014; Kudler, 2013.

54. Jennings, 2014; Los Angeles County Metropolitan Transportation Authority, 2014c; Los Angeles County Metropolitan Transportation Authority, n.d.g.

55. Los Angeles County Metropolitan Transportation Authority, n.d.c.; Los Angeles County Metropolitan Transportation Authority, n.d.g.; Jennings, 2014.

56. Rosen et al., 2020; Flores, 2019; Jennings, 2019; Miller, 2017; McGahan, 2017.

57. Redfin, 2021a; Redfin, 2021b.

58. Hymon, 2014; Sulaiman, 2013; Interview with Respondents 3 and 7.

59. Interview with Respondents 2, 3, 4, 7, and 8.

60. Hymon, 2014; Los Angeles County Metropolitan Transportation Authority, 2014a; Sulaiman, 2013; Los Angeles County Metropolitan Transportation Authority, 2012c; Interview with Respondents 3 and 24.

61. Hymon, 2014; Sulaiman, 2013; Interview with Respondents 2, 3, 4, 7, 8, and 24.

62. Interview with Respondents 1, 2, 3, 4, and 8.

63. Interview with Respondents 1, 2, 3, 4, 8, 44, and 45.

64. Interview with Respondents [not specified to maintain confidentiality].

65. Los Angeles Black Worker Center, n.d.b.; Los Angeles Black Worker Center, n.d.d.; Fine, 2018; Fine, 2015; Newman, 2014; Kofman, 2013; Interview with Respondents 2, 4, 8, and 46; Author field notes, 2015.

66. Los Angeles Black Worker Center, n.d.b.; Los Angeles Black Worker Center, n.d.d.; Fine, 2018; Race Forward, 2016; Newman, 2014; Kofman, 2013; UCLA Labor Center, 2012; Interview with Respondents 1, 2, 4, and 5; Author field notes, 2015.

67. Fine, 2018; Kofman, 2013; Interview with Respondents [not specified to maintain confidentiality]; Author field notes, 2015.

68. Fine, 2018; Fine, 2015; Kofman, 2013; Interview with Respondents 1, 2, 4, 6, 7, and 8.

69. Los Angeles County Metropolitan Transportation Authority, 2021.

70. Los Angeles County Metropolitan Transportation Authority, 2021; Los Angeles County Metropolitan Transportation Authority, 2016a; Author field notes, 2015; Los Angeles County Metropolitan Transportation Authority, 2015c; Los Angeles County Metropolitan Transportation Authority, 2014b.

71. In the 2018 and 2021 reports, the "Other" and "Not Specified" categories are merged.

72. Los Angeles County Metropolitan Transportation Authority, 2021; Los Angeles County Metropolitan Transportation Authority, 2017; Fine, 2018; Fine, 2015; Los Angeles County Metropolitan Transportation Authority, 2015c; Interview with Respondents 3, 4, and 8.

73. Fine, 2015; Interview with Respondents 1, 2, 10, 11, and 44.

74. Metro aggregated hiring data by total work hours rather than by individual worker in order to standardize across the different lengths of worker employment. Either reporting by total work hours or by individual worker can obscure important details related to hiring outcomes (Fine, 2018; Rosen and Schweitzer, 2018; Fine, 2015; Hymon, 2014; Los Angeles County Metropolitan Transportation Authority, 2014a; Interview with Respondents 1, 2, 3, 4, 7, and 8).

75. Fine, 2018; U.S. Bureau of Labor Statistics, 2014; U.S. Bureau of Labor Statistics, 2013b; Interview with Respondents 1, 2, 3, 4, 7, and 8.

76. Interview with Respondents 1, 2, 3, 4, 7, and 8.

77. Los Angeles County Metropolitan Transportation Authority, 2021; Fine, 2018; Los Angeles County Metropolitan Transportation Authority, 2016a; Fine, 2015; Los Angeles County Metropolitan Transportation Authority, 2015c; Interview with Respondents 1 and 4.

78. Fine, 2018; Fine, 2015; Kofman, 2013; Interview with Respondents 1, 2, 4, 7, 8, and 44.

79. Fine, 2018; Fine, 2015; Sklar, 2015; Newman, 2014; Interview with Respondents 1, 2, 4, 7, 8, and 10; Author field, notes, 2014.

80. Foxx, 2015; Kirkham, 2015; Ubaldo, 2014; Interview with Respondents 1, 2, 4, and 8; Author field notes, 2014.

81. Fine, 2018; Rosen and Schweitzer, 2018; Fine, 2015; Kofman, 2013; Interview with Respondents 1, 2, 3, 4, 7, 8, and 10; Author field notes, 2015; Author field notes, 2014.

82. Interview with Respondent [not specified to maintain confidentiality]; Author field notes, 2015.

83. Interview with Respondent [not specified to maintain confidentiality].

84. Fine, 2018; Los Angeles Black Worker Center, 2016; Fine, 2015; Los Angeles Black Worker Center, 2015; Los Angeles Black Worker Center, 2014; Kofman, 2013; Author field notes, 2014; Los Angeles Black Worker Center, n.d.c.

85. Kofman and Cuevas, n.d.; Fine, 2018; Fine, 2015; Kofman, 2013; Interview with Respondents 1, 3, 4, 10, and 11.

86. Fine, 2018; Fine, 2015; Kofman, 2013; Interview with Respondent [not specified to maintain confidentiality].
87. Fine, 2018; Fine, 2015; Kofman, 2013; Los Angeles Black Worker Center, n.d.b.; Los Angeles Black Worker Center, n.d.c.; Interview with Respondents 1, 2, 3, and 4; Author field notes, 2015.
88. Los Angeles County Metropolitan Transportation Authority, 2012c; Interview with Respondents 1, 2, 6, 7, and 10.
89. Fine, 2018; Fine, 2015; Kofman, 2013; Los Angeles County Metropolitan Transportation Authority, 2012a; Los Angeles County Metropolitan Transportation Authority, 2012c; Interview with Respondents, 1, 2, 4, 7, and 10.
90. Fine, 2018; Fine, 2015; Sklar, 2015; Newman, 2014; Kofman, 2013; Kudler, 2013.
91. Fine, 2018; Fine, 2015; Kofman, 2013; Interview with Respondents 1, 2, 3, 4, 5, 7, 8, and 44.
92. Miller, 2013; Sulaiman, 2013; Interview with Respondents 1, 3, 7, and 8.
93. Interview with Respondent [not specified to maintain confidentiality].
94. Herrera et al., 2014; Interview with Respondents 2, 3, 4, 8, and 9.
95. Kofman and Cuevas, n.d.; Los Angeles Black Worker Center, n.d.b.; Freeman and Richards, 2020; Sentinel News Service, 2018; Fine, 2018; Los Angeles Black Worker Center, 2016; Ubaldo, 2016; Fine, 2015; Los Angeles Black Worker Center, 2015; Los Angeles Black Worker Center, 2014; Kofman, 2013; UCLA Labor Center, 2012; Interview with Respondents 4, 6, 8, and 10.
96. Fine, 2018; Fine, 2015; Kofman, 2013; Interview with Respondents [not specified to maintain confidentiality].
97. Los Angeles Alliance for a New Economy, n.d.; Interview with Respondents 2, 7, 10, and 46.
98. Interview with Respondents 1, 6, 9, 10, and 11.
99. Fine, 2018; Fine, 2015; Kofman, 2013; Interview with Respondents 1, 3, and 10. The Women Build Metro LA (WBMLA) initiative set an agency goal of 6.9 percent female worker hiring. As of 2017, 3.4 percent of workers on Metro projects were women, which was above the national average of 3 percent. The 6.9 percent goal was consistent with Executive Order 11246, which concerned equal opportunity in employment (Los Angeles County Metropolitan Transportation Authority, 2017).
100. Los Angeles County Supervisor Mark Ridley-Thomas, 2020.
101. Interview with Respondents 1, 2, and 6.

Chapter 5

1. Rosen and Schweitzer, 2018; Purcell, 2009; Surborg, VanWynsberghe, and Wyly 2008; Stone, 1993; Logan and Molotch, 1987.
2. Doussard and Fulton, 2020; Lesniewski and Doussard, 2017; Doussard and Lesniewski, 2017; Doussard, 2015; Swanstrom and Banks, 2009.
3. Doussard and Fulton 2020; Doussard, 2015; Saito and Truong, 2015; Bornstein, 2010; Swanstrom and Banks, 2009.
4. According to Fisher and Ury (1991), "[n]egotiation is a process of communicating back and forth for the purpose of reaching a joint decision" (p. 32).
5. Collaboration is "an approach to solving complex problems in which a diverse group of autonomous stakeholders deliberates to build consensus and develop networks for translating consensus into results" (Margerum, 2011, p. 6).

6. Margerum, 2011; Susskind, McKearnan, and Thomas-Larmer, 1999. Margerum (2011) explains consensus as "in most cases it means an agreement that everyone can live with" (p. 7).
7. Innes and Booher, 2010.
8. Innes and Booher, 2010; Wolf-Powers, 2010.
9. See Fung (2020) for a discussion of the four levels of power. He defines policy power as "the general laws and policies (from government and other organizations) that make it more or less difficult for individuals to advance their interests" (p. 132). Structural power refers to "rules of engagement—the parameters and terrain—that govern contests between groups and organizations that advocate for individuals at the first level and seek to shape the covering laws and policies constituting the second level of power" (p. 132). This is contrasted with everyday power, where individuals can resist "challenges to their interests" (p. 132).
10. Margerum (2011) defines deliberative processes as "allowing everyone to fully explore and debate the issues" (p. 7).
11. For example, Innes and Booher, 2010; Fatima, Woolridge, and Jennings, 2004; Susskind, McKearnan, and Thomas-Larmer, 1999; Mnookin and Susskind, 1999; Faratin, Sierra, and Jennings, 1997; Carnevale and Pruitt, 1992; Sebenius, 1992; Fisher and Ury, 1991. The term "mutually beneficial outcomes" refers to what Forester (1989) calls "both-gain" or ideally "win-win" results (p. 100). In both scenarios, all parties experience some benefit from collaboration that exceeds participation costs.
12. Innes and Booher, 2010.
13. Rosen and Alvarez León, 2022; Fischel, 2005; Logan and Molotch, 1987.
14. Saito and Truong, 2015; Surborg, VanWynsberghe, and Wyly, 2008; Stone, 1993; Logan and Molotch, 1987.
15. Urbinati, 2010; Selmi, 2010; Purcell, 2009; Sager, 2005.
16. Urbinati, 2010; Brand and Gaffikin, 2007; Fung, 2006; Bengs, 2005a; Bengs, 2005b.
17. Bond, 2011; Purcell, 2009; Brand and Gaffikin, 2007; Sager, 2005; Abram, 2000.
18. Urbinati, 2010, p. 74; Purcell, 2009.
19. Doussard, 2015; Swanstrom and Banks, 2009.
20. Purcell, 2009; Sager, 2009; Brand and Gaffikin, 2007.
21. Purcell, 2009, p. 153.
22. Purcell, 2009; Brand and Gaffikin, 2007; Bengs, 2005a; Bengs, 2005b.
23. Rosen and Schweitzer, 2018.
24. Mazmanian and Sabatier, 1989, p. 20.
25. Matland, 1995; Mazmanian and Sabatier, 1989; Stoker, 1989; Pressman and Wildavsky, 1984; Hjern, 1982; Lipsky, 1980.
26. Lowe and Morton, 2008.
27. Fine, 2014; Luce, 2012; Fine and Gordon, 2010; Luce, 2005; O'Rourke, 2002.
28. Fine, 2014; Luce, 2012; Fine and Gordon, 2010; Luce, 2005; O'Rourke, 2002.
29. Doussard, 2015; Swanstrom and Banks, 2009.
30. Been, 2010; Wolf-Powers, 2010; Parks and Warren, 2009; Salkin and Lavine, 2008; Gross, 2007.

Chapter 6

1. Interview with Respondents 1, 14, 18, and 21. While the costs obviously vary between agreements and settings, many individuals maintained that third-party administrators can operate at a higher efficiency sufficient to equalize their additional cost.

2. Interview with Respondents 8, 16, 20, 21, and 24; personal communication, 2015.

3. See Fine, 2014; Fine and Gordon, 2010; Luce, 2012, 2005; and O'Rourke, 2002. Co-enforcement research and the accountability recommendations described in this chapter have important parallels to the influential work of Elinor Ostrom in *Governing the Commons* (1990), albeit in substantively different contexts.

4. Chen et al., 2012.

5. Rosen and Schweitzer, 2018.

6. Rosen and Schweitzer, 2018.

7. Been, 2010; Wolf-Powers, 2010; Parks and Warren, 2009; Salkin and Lavine, 2008; Gross, 2007.

8. Rosen, O'Neill, and Hutson, 2018.

9. See Zapata and Bates, 2015; Krumholz, 2011.

10. Doussard and Fulton, 2020; Lesniewski and Doussard, 2017; Doussard and Lesniewski, 2017; Doussard, 2015; Swanstrom and Banks, 2009.

11. Belongie and Silverman, 2018.

12. Interview with Respondents 16, 18, and 24.

13. Wolf-Powers, 2012.

14. Rosen and Schweitzer, 2018; Pulido, 2017; Purcell, 2009.

15. Rosen and Schweitzer, 2018.

16. Interview with Respondents 31, 34, and 41.

Appendix 1

1. Rosenberg, 2006; Ryan, 2002; Cullingworth, 1993; Been, 1991; Marsh, 1989; Holliman, 1981.

2. Canon, 2014; Callies, Curtin, and Tappendorf, 2003; Cowart, 1989; Marsh, 1989; Holliman, 1981.

3. Selmi, 2010; Cowart, 1989, p. 35.

4. Cowart, 1989, p. 35.

5. Callies, Curtin, and Tappendorf, 2003, 3; Selmi, 2010; Funk, 1997.

6. Selmi, 2010, p. 614; Canon, 2014; Camacho, 2005.

7. Selmi, 2010; Camacho, 2005; Cowart, 1989; Porter, 1989.

8. Selmi, 2010; Ryan, 2002.

9. Camacho, 2005, p. 44; Canon, 2014; Selmi, 2010; Larsen, 2002.

10. Canon, 2014, p. 809; Camacho, 2005.

11. Camacho, 2005, p. 43.

12. Canon, 2014; Selmi, 2010; Larsen, 2002.

13. Camacho, 2013; Wolf-Powers, 2010; Gross, 2007.

14. Saito and Truong, 2015; Camacho, 2013; Wolf-Powers, 2010; Salkin and Lavine, 2008; Gross, 2007; Salkin and Lavine, 2007.

15. Lucas-Darby, 2012; Saito, 2012; Baxamusa, 2008; Gross, 2007. Gross (2007) defines inclusiveness as occurring when "the CBA negotiation process provides a mechanism to ensure that a broad range of community concerns are heard and addressed prior to project approval" (p. 37). Accountability "means that promises made by redevelopment agency staff, public officials, and developers regarding community benefits should be treated seriously, made legally binding, and enforced against the party that committed to them" (pp. 38–39).

16. Camacho, 2013; Saito, 2012; Parks and Warren, 2009; Baxamusa, 2008; Lowe and Morton, 2008.

17. Wolf-Powers, 2012.
18. Saito and Truong, 2015; Parks and Warren, 2009; Gross, 2007.
19. Saito and Truong, 2015; Wolf-Powers, 2010; Salkin and Lavine, 2008.
20. Saito and Truong, 2015; Wolf-Powers, 2010; Gross, 2007.
21. Baxamusa, 2008, p. 266; Been, 2010.
22. Been, 2010; Wolf-Powers, 2010; Gross, 2007; Salkin and Lavine, 2007.
23. Been, 2010; Wolf-Powers, 2010; Parks and Warren, 2009; Gross, 2007.
24. Been, 2010; Wolf-Powers, 2010; Salkin and Lavine, 2008; Gross, 2007.
25. Saito and Truong, 2015; Camacho, 2013; Been, 2010; Wolf-Powers, 2010.
26. Saito and Truong, 2015; Seigel, 2014; Been, 2010; Baxamusa, 2008.
27. Lucas-Darby, 2012; Wolf-Powers, 2010; Salkin and Lavine, 2008; Salkin and Lavine, 2007; Gross, 2007.
28. Wolf-Powers, 2010, p. 155; Saito, 2012; Been, 2010; Salkin and Lavine, 2008; Salkin and Lavine, 2007.
29. Rosen and Schweitzer, 2018; Herrera et al., 2014; Lucas-Darby, 2012; Saito, 2012; Wolf-Powers, 2010; Salkin and Lavine, 2008; Gross, 2007.
30. Saito and Truong, 2015; Wolf-Powers, 2010; Baxamusa, 2008; Salkin and Lavine, 2008.
31. Marantz, 2015; Saito, 2012; Gross, 2007.
32. Salkin and Lavine, 2007.
33. Rosen and Schweitzer, 2018; Salkin and Lavine, 2008.
34. Belman and Bodah, 2010; Johnston-Dodds, 2001; Siegel, 2001.
35. Belman and Bodah, 2010; Johnston-Dodds, 2001; Siegel, 2001; Langworthy, 1995.
36. Nonunion firms rely on lower wages and benefits to maintain a competitive advantage over union firms. Rather, the union model emphasizes workforce training through apprenticeships. Therefore, PLAs require nonunion contractors to significantly alter their normal business practices, including paying higher wages and providing benefits, requirements that necessitate higher worker productivity (Brubeck, 2019; The Truth About PLAs, 2015; Belman and Bodah, 2010; Northrup and Alario, 1998; Langworthy, 1995; U.S. General Accounting Office, 1998).
37. Philips and Waitzman, 2020; Johnston-Dodds, 2001; U.S. General Accounting Office, 1998.
38. U.S. Bureau of Labor Statistics, 2019; Kosla, 2014.
39. Herrera et al., 2014; Belman and Bodah, 2010; Johnston-Dodds, 2001; Northrup and Alario, 1998.
40. PLAs have been contested and consistently upheld in the courts, including at the U.S. Supreme Court in the Boston Harbor case (507 U.S. 218 1993). While somewhat disputed, the prevailing legal interpretation maintains that the Boston Harbor ruling upholds PLAs as legal (Johnston-Dodds, 2001; Langworthy, 1995).
41. Kussy and Cooke, 2010; Mayer, 2010; Northrup and Alario, 1998; Langworthy, 1995.
42. Brubeck, 2019; The White House, 2019; Brubeck, 2018.
43. The White House, 2022.
44. In a content analysis of 185 PLAs over 15 years, Figueroa, Grabelsky, and Lamare (2011) found that only 3 percent of PLAs had no community workforce provisions, and almost half had between four and nine provisions. All of the most recent PLAs included at least one community workforce provision.
45. PLAs can effectively target work because they create a legal means to alter normal union dispatching procedures. In contrast to the traditional hiring process, in which unions refer workers sequentially according to an out-of-work list, PLAs enable preferential hiring of targeted

individuals such that unions do not have to dispatch in sequential order. The dispatch process is the way in which individual trade unions refer workers onto jobsites and varies across trades. In general, it is structured to promote predictable and fair hiring for members. Union members cannot take a job on a union site without being dispatched by the union hall to which they belong. When an eligible union member is out of work, because a job has ended or because the worker was terminated or finished apprenticeship training, the worker is placed at the bottom of the out-of-work list. Workers advance up the dispatch list when the preceding individuals are hired, so a slow construction market creates little movement up the list. Construction contractors contact the union hall when they need a worker, and the union hall is required to send the worker at the top of the dispatch list. Once the worker's employment with that contractor ends, the worker returns to the union hall and is placed at the bottom of the out-of-work list. Some unions make exceptions for brief hires. PLAs are unique and effective at targeting jobs because these agreements allow unions to leverage their pool of workers while prioritizing hiring based on socioeconomic or geographic characteristics, a practice that is otherwise not permitted. Under a PLA that targets work to local residents, for example, a union dispatcher sends the local worker that is highest on the dispatch list, even if they are not at the top of the list overall. The rationale for unions is that under PLAs, more union workers get hired overall, which benefits all workers on the list (Herrera et al., 2014; Figueroa, Grabelsky, and Lamare, 2011; Belman and Bodah, 2010; Garland and Suafai, 2002).

46. Rosen and Schweitzer, 2018; Herrera et al., 2014.
47. U.S. Bureau of Labor Statistics, 2013a; Belman and Bodah, 2010.
48. Herrera et al., 2014; Figueroa, Grabelsky, and Lamare, 2011; Philips, 2010.
49. Herrera et al., 2014; Belman and Bodah, 2010; Kotler, 2009.
50. Giuliano, Blanco, and Bahl, 2013; Belman and Bodah, 2010.
51. Herrera et al., 2014; Interview with Respondents 1, 2, 3, 12, and 24. Preapprenticeship programs have become increasingly necessary for unions because many high schools and community colleges cut technical classes. These classes taught students basic construction skills and enabled them to learn about different construction careers. Without these programs, many potential candidates know little about construction work or even which trade they want to pursue. This inexperience increases the risk that unions will expend resources on candidates who may not finish apprenticeship programs.
52. Herrera et al., 2014; Interview with Respondents 1, 2, 3, 12, and 24.
53. Herrera et al., 2014; Chimienti, 2010; Garland and Suafai, 2002.
54. Rosen and Schweitzer, 2018; Herrera et al., 2014; Belman and Bodah, 2010.
55. Herrera et al. 2014, p. 70; Chimenti, 2010; Belman and Bodah, 2010; Philips, 2010.
56. Herrera et al., 2014; Figueroa, Grabelsky, and Lamare, 2011; Belman and Bodah, 2010.
57. Herrera et al., 2014; Belman and Bodah, 2010; Philips, 2010; Garland and Suafai, 2002.
58. Herrera et al., 2014; Garland and Suafai, 2002.
59. Herrera et al., 2014; Chimienti, 2010; Garland and Suafai, 2002.
60. Herrera et al., 2014; Garland and Suafai, 2002.
61. Swanstrom and Banks, 2009, p. 364; Rosen and Schweitzer, 2018.
62. Rosen and Schweitzer, 2018; Herrera et al., 2014.

Appendix 2

1. Herrera et al., 2014; Los Angeles Unified School District, 1999; Sound Transit, 1999.
2. In 1996, California voters enacted this policy through Proposition 209, a constitutional amendment (California Legislative Analyst's Office, 1996). In 1998, Washington voters approved

this law through Initiative 200, which also prohibits preference based on national origin (League of Women Voters, 1998).

3. Interview with Respondents 1, 4, 12, and 14.

4. This includes individuals engaged in agreement negotiation and administration of other agreements in the region who had important information about the Yesler Terrace Agreement and/or the regional context.

5. Other work that discusses the PERC includes McKean, 2015; Severin, 2013; Wolf-Powers, 2012; Larsen, 2009; Pastor, Benner, and Matsuoka, 2009; De Sousa, 2008; Gross, 2007; McGahey and Vey, 2008; Salkin and Lavine, 2008; and Sheikh, 2008.

REFERENCES

11Alive Staff. (2013, September 25). *No more broken promises for new Falcons stadium neighbors?* WXIA Atlanta. http://www.11alive.com/story/money/economy/2014/03/06/1948638/.

Abdulahi, N. (2017, November 10). *"Housing is just getting so unaffordable": Westside residents fear gentrification*. 11Alive. https://www.11alive.com/article/news/local/west-side/housing-is-just-getting-so-unaffordable-westside-residents-fear-gentrification/85-490889926.

Abram, S. A. (2000). Planning the public: Some comments on empirical problems for planning theory. *Journal of Planning Education and Research*, 19(4), 351–357. DOI: 10.1177/0739456X0001900404.

Albertson, E. M., Chen, R., Matheson, A., Ursua, M. G., Fliss, M. D., and Farquhar, S. (2020). Effect of public housing redevelopment on reported and perceived crime in a Seattle neighborhood. *Crime Prevention and Community Safety*, 22, 381–398.

Albright, C. (2017, November 10). Gentrification is sweeping through America: Here are the people fighting back. *Guardian*. https://www.theguardian.com/us-news/2017/nov/10/atlanta-super-gentrification-eminent-domain.

Allison, J., Cline, N., and Reese, E. (2018). *The need for a better deal for workers and residents in Inland Southern California: A case study of QVC Inc.'s 2015 operating covenant agreement with Ontario, California*. UCLA Institute for Research on Labor and Employment. https://irle.ucla.edu/wp-content/uploads/2018/02/IRLE-Research-and-Policy-Brief-40_-Final-PDF.pdf.

Annie E. Casey Foundation. (2015, June 24). *Changing the odds: The race for results in Atlanta.* https://www.aecf.org/resources/changing-the-odds.

Archbold, H. (2014, January 15). *Next steps: Transforming Atlanta's Westside neighborhoods.* Patch. http://patch.com/georgia/cascade/next-steps-transforming-atlantas-westside-neighborhoods.

Arthur M. Blank Foundation. (n.d.a.). *Grants*. https://blankfoundation.org/grants-page/.

Atlanta Police Foundation. (n.d.). *Atlanta Police Foundation*. https://atlantapolicefoundation.org.

Atlanta United. (2017, September 21). *Behind the stripes, Arthur Blank*. https://www.atlutd.com/post/2017/09/21/behind-stripes-arthur-blank.

Badenhausen, K. (2019, February 6). NBA team values 2019: Knicks on top at $4 billion. *Forbes*. https://www.forbes.com/sites/kurtbadenhausen/2019/02/06/nba-team-values-2019-knicks-on-top-at-4-billion/#5896ddc4e667.

Bakewell, D. J. (2012, July 12). Will Black political leaders deliver on the Crenshaw Line? *Los Angeles Sentinel*. Accessed via Proquest.

Bauer, S. (2015, June 4). *Half of $500M Bucks arena financing to come from taxpayers*. ESPN. https://www.espn.com/nba/story/_/id/13012213/taxpayers-pay-half-500-million-cost-new-milwaukee-bucks-arena.

Baxamusa, M. H. (2008). Empowering communities through deliberation: The model of community benefits agreements. *Journal of Planning Education and Research, 27*(3), 261–276. DOI: 10.1177/0739456X07308448.

Bayatpour, A. J. (2015, September 24). *Land sold to Bucks for $1 for arena project; but first, it must be prepared for construction.* Fox 6 News. http://fox6now.com/2015/09/24/land-in -park-east-corridor-sold-to-bucks-for-1-for-arena-project-but-first-it-must-be-prepared -for-construction/.

Beekman, D. (2016a, July 11). Yesler Terrace transition: Many families leave area. *Seattle Times.* http://www.seattletimes.com/seattle-news/politics/yesler-terrace-transition-many-families -leave-area/.

Beekman, D. (2016b, December 6). City wants help naming new park in Yesler Terrace. *Seattle Times.* http://www.seattletimes.com/seattle-news/politics/city-wants-help-naming-new -park-in-yesler-terrace/.

Been, V. (1991). "Exit" as a constraint on land use exactions: Rethinking the unconstitutional conditions doctrine. *Columbia Law Review, 91*(3), 473–545. DOI: 10.2307/1122797.

Been, V. (2010). Community benefits agreements: A new local government tool or another variation on the exactions theme? *University of Chicago Law Review, 77*(1), 5–35. https://www .jstor.org/stable/40663024.

Belko, M. (2014, July 14). Recession leaves taxpayers paying much more of Consol Energy Center debt. *Pittsburgh Post-Gazette.* https://www.post-gazette.com/business/2014/07 /15/Taxpayers-paying-more-of-costs-for-Consol-Energy-Center-than-expected/stories /201407150069.

Belman, D., and Bodah, M. M. (2010). *Building better: A look at best practices for the design of project labor agreements* (No. 274; EPI Briefing Paper). Economic Policy Institute. https:// files.epi.org/page/-/pdf/BP274.pdf.

Belongie, N., and Silverman, R. M. (2018). Model CBAs and community benefits ordinances as tools for negotiating equitable development: Three critical cases. *Journal of Community Practice, 26*(3), 308–327. DOI: 10.1080/10705422.2018.1476427.

Belson, K. (2017, January 12). Building a stadium, rebuilding a neighborhood. *New York Times.* https://www.nytimes.com/2017/01/12/sports/football/atlanta-falcons-stadium-arthur -blank-neighborhood.html?_r=0.

Bengs, C. (2005a). Planning theory for the naive? *European Journal of Spatial Development,* 1–12.

Bengs, C. (2005b). Time for a critique of planning theory. *European Journal of Spatial Development, 3*, 1–3.

Bermudez, E. (2016, November 5). Why these Southeast L.A. cities are banding together to fight Measure M, the transportation tax. *Los Angeles Times.* http://www.latimes.com/local /california/la-me-ln-measure-m-southeast-20161101-story.html.

Bertrand, A. (2015, March 20). *Atlanta is the most unequal city in America — here's why.* Business Insider. http://www.businessinsider.com/atlanta-is-the-most-unequal-city-in-america --heres-why-2015-3.

Black, D. (2013a, January 13). *From Profanity Hill to Yesler Terrace.* KUOW. http://kuow.org/post /profanity-hill-yesler-terrace.

Black, D. (2013b, March 25). *After 40 years, one resident looks to the future.* KUOW. http://kuow .org/post/after-40-years-yesler-terrace-one-resident-looks-future.

Blau, M. (2013a, August 26). *Reed, English Avenue pastor spar over community benefits package for neighborhoods near new Falcons stadium.* Creative Loafing Atlanta. http://clatl

.com/freshloaf/archives/2013/08/26/reed-english-avenue-pastor-spar-over-community-benefits-package-for-neighborhoods-near-the-new-falcons-stadium.

Blau, M. (2013b, December 3). *Council OKs community benefits plan for Falcons stadium neighborhoods*. Creative Loafing Atlanta. http://clatl.com/freshloaf/archives/2013/12/03/council-oks-community-benefits-plan-for-falcons-stadium-neighborhoods.

Bloomekatz, A. (2012, November 7). This just in. *Los Angeles Times*. http://latimesblogs.latimes.com/lanow/2012/11/measure-j-la-county-transit-tax-extension-fails.html.

Bluestein, G. (2013, January 12). Falcons stadium will be a hard sell, legislators say. *Atlanta Journal-Constitution*. https://www.ajc.com/news/falcons-stadium-will-hard-sell-legislators-say/YIcfGcIHY4dcirz9DCSTiI/.

Boarnet, M., and Crane, R. (1998). Public financing and transit-oriented planning: New evidence from Southern California. *Journal of Planning Education and Research*, 17(3), 206–219. DOI: 10.1177/0739456X9801700302.

Bond, S. (2011). Negotiating a "democratic ethos": Moving beyond the agonistic-communicative divide. *Planning Theory*, 10(2), 161–186. DOI: 10.1177/1473095210383081.

Bornstein, L. (2010). Mega-projects, city-building and community benefits. *City, Culture and Society*, 1(4), 199–206. DOI: 10.1016/j.ccs.2011.01.006.

Brand, R., and Gaffikin, F. (2007). Collaborative planning in an uncollaborative world. *Planning Theory*, 6(3), 282–313. DOI: 10.1177/1473095207082036.

Brubeck, B. (2018, July 24). *House lawmakers ask President Trump to eliminate Obama policy promoting project labor agreements*. The Truth About PLAs. https://thetruthaboutplas.com/2018/07/24/u-s-house-lawmakers-ask-president-trump-to-eliminate-obama-policy-promoting-project-labor-agreements/.

Brubeck, B. (2019, June 24). *Trump can still score an infrastructure win*. The Hill. https://thehill.com/blogs/congress-blog/labor/449955-trump-can-still-score-an-infrastructure-win.

Burns, R. (2013, March 13). It's going to take more than $45 million* to help Vine City. *Atlanta Magazine*. http://www.atlantamagazine.com/civilrights/its-going-to-take-more-than-45-million-to-help-vine-city/.

Burns, R. (2014, March 17). Atlanta's food deserts leave its poorest citizens stranded and struggling. *Guardian*. https://www.theguardian.com/cities/2014/mar/17/atlanta-food-deserts-stranded-struggling-survive.

Caldbick, J. (2014, March 27). *Seattle Housing Authority—Part 2*. History Link. https://www.historylink.org/File/10761.

Caldwell, C. (2016, June 17). Officials: Mercedes-Benz Stadium cost rises to $1.6 billion. *Atlanta Business Chronicle*. https://www.bizjournals.com/atlanta/morning_call/2016/06/officials-mercedes-benz-stadium-cost-rises-to-1-6.html.

California Legislative Analyst's Office. (1996). *Proposition 209*. https://lao.ca.gov/ballot/1996/prop209_11_1996.html.

Callies, D. L., Curtin, D. J., and Tappendorf, J. A. (2003). *Bargaining for development: A handbook on development agreements, annexation agreements, land development conditions, vested rights, and the provision of public facilities*. Environmental Law Institute.

Camacho, A. E. (2005). Mustering the missing voices: A collaborative model for fostering equality, community involvement and adaptive planning in land use decisions. *Stanford Environmental Law Journal*, 24(1), 3–70.

Camacho, A. E. (2013). Community benefit agreements: A symptom, not the antidote, of bilateral land use regulation. *Brooklyn Law Review*, 78(2), 355–383.

Canon, R. G. (2014). Participatory democracy and the entrepreneurial government: Addressing process efficiencies in the creation of land use development agreements. *Chicago-Kent Law Review, 89*(2), 781–821.

Carnes, J. (2019, February 18). *Why is Atlanta considered the mecca of the Civil Rights Movement?* 11 Alive News. https://www.11alive.com/article/news/why-is-atlanta-considered-the-mecca-of-the-civil-rights-movement/85-6d59b82b-d340-4664-9ff6-2c632aeb70a3.

Carnevale, P. J., and Pruitt, D. G. (1992). Negotiation and mediation. *Annual Review of Psychology, 43*(1), 531–582. DOI: 10.1146/annurev.ps.43.020192.002531.

CBS58 Staff. (2015). *Milwaukee County agrees to sell Park East plots for $1 to Bucks.* CBS58. https://www.cbs58.com/news/milwaukee-county-agrees-to-sell-park-east-plots-for-1-to-bucks.

Chambers, D. (2019, January 31). The billionaire's stadium next door. *New York Times*. https://www.nytimes.com/2019/01/31/sports/english-avenue-atlanta-mercedes-benz-stadium.html.

Chen, N. T. N., Dong, F., Ball-Rokeach, S. J., Parks, M., and Huang, J. (2012). Building a new media platform for local storytelling and civic engagement in ethnically diverse neighborhoods. *New Media and Society, 14*(6), 931–950. https://doi.org/10.1177/1461444811435640.

Chick-fil-A Peach Bowl. (2020, December 30). *Peach Bowl renews sponsorship with Chick-fil-A.* https://chick-fil-apeachbowl.com/news/2020/12/30/general-peach-bowl-renews-sponsorship-with-chick-fil-a.aspx.

Chiland, E. (2018, November 16). *Metro's Crenshaw/LAX Line opening delayed to 2020.* Curbed Los Angeles. https://la.curbed.com/2018/11/16/18097780/metro-crenshaw-lax-line-opening-date-2020-delay.

Chiland, E. (2020, April 13). *A guide to the Crenshaw Line—opening in 2021.* Curbed Los Angeles. https://la.curbed.com/2019/12/4/20992333/crenshaw-lax-line-opening-map-stops.

Chimienti, E. A. (2010). *Breaking down barriers, building up communities: Implementing project labor agreements with targeted hiring goals.* Master's thesis, Massachusetts Institute of Technology. https://dspace.mit.edu/bitstream/handle/1721.1/59718/669026787-MIT.pdf?sequence=2.

Chiuchiarelli, K. (2011, March 1). Past and future of Park East development. *Marquette Wire.* http://marquettewire.org/3785513/tribune/tribune-featured/development-kw1-rp2-dac3/.

Chowdhury, A. (2017, June 6). Repeal of prevailing wage would hurt Wisconsin economy. *Milwaukee Journal Sentinel.* https://www.jsonline.com/story/opinion/contributors/2017/06/06/chowdhury-repeal-prevailing-wage-would-hurt-wisconsin-economy/373668001/.

City of Atlanta. (n.d.a). *A new stadium: An economic driver.* http://www.atlantaga.gov/modules/showdocument.aspx?documentid=6824.

City of Atlanta. (n.d.b.). Neighborhood planning unit (NPU). https://www.atlantaga.gov/government/departments/city-planning/office-of-zoning-development/neighborhood-planning-unit-npu.

City of Atlanta. (2013). *Resolution 13-R-3783.* http://atlantacityga.iqm2.com/Citizens/Detail_LegiFile.aspx?MeetingID=1237andID=3346.

City of Atlanta, Georgia, Mayor's Office of Communication. (2014, December 19). *Mayor Kasim Reed and Atlanta Committee for Progress announce board of Westside Future Fund* [Press release]. https://www.atlantaga.gov/Home/Components/News/News/3208/.

City of Atlanta, Georgia, Mayor's Office of Communication. (2015, September 28). *City of Atlanta wins $30 million HUD Choice Neighborhood Grant* [Press release]. https://www.atlantaga.gov/Home/Components/News/News/3897/.

City of Detroit. (2020). *Community benefits ordinance.* https://detroitmi.gov/departments/planning-and-development-department/design-and-development-innovation/community-benefits-ordinance.

City of Milwaukee. (n.d.). *Common Council.* http://city.milwaukee.gov/CommonCouncil#.VpXfGzbEiQc.

City of Milwaukee. (2014, March 7). *Downtown proposed, under construction and completed public and private projects.* http://city.milwaukee.gov/ImageLibrary/Groups/cityDCD/DownTownMilwaukee/Development/pdfs/3.7.14Projects.pdf.

City of Milwaukee Department of City Development. (n.d.). *Park East freeway—history and removal.* https://city.milwaukee.gov/DCD/Projects/ParkEastredevelopment/Park-East-History.

City of Seattle Purchasing and Contracting. (2015). *Community workforce agreement.* http://www.seattle.gov/Documents/Departments/FAS/PurchasingAndContracting/Labor/Seattle_CWA_final.pdf.

Congress for the New Urbanism. (n.d.). *Park East Freeway.* https://www.cnu.org/what-we-do/build-great-places/park-east-freeway.

County of Los Angeles Supervisor Mark Ridley-Thomas. (n.d.a.). *Hon. Mark Ridley-Thomas.* https://ridley-thomas.lacounty.gov/index.php/supervisors-biography/.

County of Los Angeles Supervisor Mark Ridley-Thomas. (n.d.b.). *Second Supervisorial District.* http://ridley-thomas.lacounty.gov/index.php/2nd-supervisorial-district/.

County of Los Angeles Supervisor Mark Ridley-Thomas. (2020). *The Legacy of Mark Ridley-Thomas, Second District Supervisor 2008–2020.* https://ridley-thomas.lacounty.gov.

County of Milwaukee. (2004). *Park East Redevelopment Compact.* http://county.milwaukee.gov/ImageLibrary/Groups/cntySupervisors/dimitrijevic/PERC.PDF.

Cowart, R. (1989). Experience, motivations and issues. In D. R. Porter and L. L. Marsh (Eds.), *Development agreements: Practice, policy and prospects* (pp. 9–39). Washington, DC: Urban Land Institute.

Cullingworth, J. (1993). *The political culture of planning.* New York: Routledge.

Cummings, S. L., and Boutcher, S. A. (2009). Mobilizing local government law for low-wage workers. *University of Chicago Legal Forum, 1,* 187–246.

Curbed Staff. (2014, July 7). *A fresh look at Yesler Terrace's redevelopment.* Curbed Seattle. http://seattle.curbed.com/archives/2014/07/an-indepth-look-at-yesler-terraces-redevelopment.php.

Daily Journal of Commerce Staff. (2016, February 2). SHA opens 83 more apartments and a hillclimb at Yesler Terrace. *Daily Journal of Commerce Staff.* http://www.djc.com/news/re/12085909.html.

Daily Journal of Commerce Staff. (2017, September 21). SHA receives national honor. *Daily Journal of Commerce.* http://www.djc.com/news/re/12104389.html?cgi=yes.

Daykin, T. (2009, January 13). Park East project dropped. *Milwaukee Journal Sentinel.* http://www.jsonline.com/business/37502349.html.

Daykin, T. (2012a, February 18). Building on loss of Kohl's for Park East. *Milwaukee Journal Sentinel.* http://archive.jsonline.com/business/building-on-loss-of-kohls-for-park-east-1v47lkv-139564308.html.

Daykin, T. (2012b, September 20). Cleanup loan for Park East apartment project approved. *Milwaukee Journal Sentinel.* http://www.jsonline.com/business/cleanup-loan-for-park-east-apartment-project-approved-hj6ufr6-170562906.html.

Daykin, T. (2013, May 18). Park East development kicks into high gear with a new marketing campaign. *Milwaukee Journal Sentinel.* http://www.jsonline.com/business/park-east-development-kicks-into-high-gear-with-a-new-marketing-campaign-709v4j3-208008131.html.

Daykin, T. (2014, October 4). But Marcus still hopes to make cinema happen. *Milwaukee Journal Sentinel.* http://www.jsonline.com/business/successful-movie-theater-plan-eludes-downtown-milwaukee-b99362293z1-278124101.html.

Daykin, T. (2015, June 3). Bucks development plan would tie up Park East parcels for 9 years. *Milwaukee Journal Sentinel.* http://www.jsonline.com/blogs/business/305932371.html.

Daykin, T. (2016, February 18). City, Bucks to team up on arena workforce training fund. *Milwaukee Journal Sentinel.* https://www.jsonline.com/story/money/blogs/land-and-space/2016/02/18/city-bucks-to-team-up-on-arena-workforce-training-fund/84835448/.

Daykin, T. (2018, December 3). Downtown Milwaukee's Avenir apartments, early Park East strip project, sold to Seattle-area group. *Milwaukee Journal Sentinel.* https://www.jsonline.com/story/money/real-estate/commercial/2018/12/03/downtown-milwaukees-avenir-apartments-sold-seattle-area-group/2162053002/.

Daykin, T. (2019, April 23). Milwaukee County puts downtown Park East site on sale block after mixed-use development plan falls through. *Milwaukee Journal Sentinel.* https://www.jsonline.com/story/money/real-estate/commercial/2019/04/23/milwaukee-county-puts-downtown-park-east-project-site-sale-block/3547868002/.

deMause, N. (2017, September 29). Why are Georgia taxpayers paying $700 million for a new NFL stadium? *Guardian.* https://www.theguardian.com/sport/2017/sep/29/why-are-georgia-taxpayers-paying-700m-for-a-new-nfl-stadium.

De Sousa, C. A. (2008). *Brownfields redevelopment and the quest for sustainability.* Oxford: Elsevier.

Delong, K. (2015, December 30). *Milwaukee County officials plan to sell last full block of Park East land to Wangard Partners Inc.* Fox 6 News. http://fox6now.com/2015/12/30/milwaukee-county-officials-plan-to-sell-last-full-block-of-park-east-land-to-wangard-partners-inc/.

Diamant, A. (2014, February 26). Atlanta's top code violation offender has "master plan." WSBTV Atlanta. https://www.wsbtv.com/news/local/man-buying-vine-city-properties-hold-several-viola/138213906/.

Dierwechter, Y. (2017). *Urban sustainability through smart growth: intercurrence, planning, and geographies of regional development across greater Seattle.* New York: Springer.

Dolan, K. A., Wang, J., and Peterson-Withorn, C.(2020). World's billionaires list. #432 Arthur Blank. *Forbes.* https://www.forbes.com/profile/arthur-blank/#3bcea9f5749c.

Doussard, M. (2015). Equity planning outside city hall: Rescaling advocacy to confront the sources of urban problems. *Journal of Planning Education and Research, 35*(3), 296–306. DOI: 10.1177/0739456X15580021.

Doussard, M., and Fulton, B. R. (2020). Organizing together: Benefits and drawbacks of community-labor coalitions for community organizations. *Social Service Review, 94*(1), 36–74.

Doussard, M., and Lesniewski, J. (2017). Fortune favors the organized: How Chicago activists won equity goals under austerity. *Journal of Urban Affairs, 39*(5), 618–634. DOI: 10.1080/07352166.2016.1262684.

Ebeling, M. (2014, January 27). *Protecting federal taxpayer interest; training a local workforce—L.A. Crenshaw Line.* State Smart Transportation Initiative. https://www.ssti.us/2014

/01/protecting-federal-taxpayer-interest-training-a-local-workforce-l-a-crenshaw-light-rail-line/.
Edwards, I. (2019, April 18). SCIDpda leads Yesler Terrace redevelopment with new affordable housing project for 2021. *International Examiner*. https://iexaminer.org/scidpda-leads-yesler-terrace-redevelopment-with-new-affordable-housing-project-for-2021/.
Erie, S. P., Kogan, V., and MacKenzie, S. A. (2010). Redevelopment, San Diego style: The limits of public-private partnerships. *Urban Affairs Review*, 45(5), 644–678. DOI: 10.1177/1078087409359760.
Eskenazi, S. (2002, December 25). Rainier Vista lawsuit settled; demolition can begin. *Seattle Times*. http://community.seattletimes.nwsource.com/archive/?date=20021225andslug=vista25m.
Faratin, P., Sierra, C., and Jennings, N. R. (1997). Negotiation decision functions for autonomous agents. *Robotics and Autonomous Systems*, 24(3), 159–182.
Farquhar, S. A., Chen, R., Matheson, A., Forsyth, J., and Ursua, M. (2019). Seattle's Yesler Terrace redevelopment: Assessing the impact of multisector strategies on redevelopment plans and community health. *Housing Policy Debate*, 29(3), 489–500. DOI: 10.1080/10511482.2018.1490795.
Fatima, S. S., Woolridge, M., and Jennings, N. R. (2004). An agenda-based framework for multi-issue negotiation. *Artificial Intelligence*, 154, 1–45. DOI: 10.1016/S0004-3702(03)00115-2.
Federal Register. (2017a, January 18). Contracting initiative. https://www.federalregister.gov/documents/2017/01/18/2017-00984/contracting-initiative.
Federal Register. (2017b, October 6). Geographic-based hiring preferences in administering federal awards. https://www.federalregister.gov/documents/2017/10/06/2017-21574/geographic-based-hiring-preferences-in-administering-federal-awards.
Federal Register. (2021, October 6). Geographic-based hiring preferences in administering federal awards. https://www.federalregister.gov/documents/2017/10/06/2017-21574/geographic-based-hiring-preferences-in-administering-federal-awards.
Fennessy, S. (2017, August 15). American cathedral: The story behind Mercedes-Benz stadium. *Atlanta Magazine*. https://www.atlantamagazine.com/great-reads/american-cathedral-mercedes-benz-stadium/.
Figueroa, M., Grabelsky, J., and Lamare, R. (2011). *Community workforce provisions in project labor agreements: A tool for building middle-class careers*. Ithaca, NY: Cornell University, ILR School.
Fine, J. (2014). Strengthening labor standards compliance through co-production of enforcement. *New Labor Forum*, 1–7. DOI: 10.1177/1095796014527260.
Fine, J. (2015). *Co-production: Bringing together the unique capabilities of government and society for strong labor standards enforcement*. Labor Innovations for the 21st Century (LIFT) Fund. https://theliftfund.org/wp-content/uploads/2022/05/LIFTReportCoproductionOct_ExecSumm-rf_4.pdf.
Fine, J. (2018). New approaches to enforcing labor standards: How co-enforcement partnerships between government and civil society are showing the way forwards. *University of Chicago Legal Forum*, 2017(7), 143–176.
Fine, J., and Gordon, J. (2010). Strengthening labor standards enforcement through partnerships with workers' organizations. *Politics and Society*, 38(4), 552–585. DOI: 10.1177/0032329210381240.
Fischel, W. A. (2005). *The homevoter hypothesis: How home values influence local government taxation, school finance, and land-use policies*. Cambridge, MA: Harvard University Press.

Fiserv. (2018, July 26). *Fiserv Forum is the new home of the Milwaukee Bucks*. https://newsroom.fiserv.com/news-releases/news-release-details/fiserv-forum-new-home-milwaukee-bucks.

Fisher, R., Ury, W. L., and Patton, W. (1991). *Getting to yes* (2nd ed.). New York: Houghton Mifflin.

Fleischer, M. (2021, April 1). Opinion: L.A. wants to bulldoze Latino neighborhoods to expand a freeway. Biden shouldn't help. *Los Angeles Times*. https://www.latimes.com/opinion/story/2021-04-01/opinion-l-a-wants-to-bulldoze-latino-neighborhoods-to-expand-a-freeway-biden-shouldnt-help.

Flores, J. (2019, September 30). "'We are at war': Crenshaw residents organizing to fight development. *Curbed Los Angeles*. https://la.curbed.com/2019/9/30/20885553/gentrification-south-la-crenshaw-subway-coalition.

Forester, J. (1989). *Planning in the face of power*. Berkeley: University of California Press.

Fowler, L. (2020, July 30). *Black pastors and activists want Central District land as reparations*. Crosscut. https://crosscut.com/equity/2020/07/black-pastors-and-activists-want-central-district-land-reparations.

Fox, J. V. (2006, November 23). Public Housing [Letter to the editor]. *Seattle PI*. https://www.seattlepi.com/news/article/Letters-to-the-Editor-1220625.php.

Fox, J. V., and O'Donnell, K. (2007, May 17). *Copy of the language contained in the Rainier Vista legal agreement outlining the role of the Yesler Terrace CRC and its responsibilities and my comments in that regard*. Seattle Displacement Coalition. http://www.zipcon.net/~jvf4119/Yesler%20Minority%20Report.htm.

Fox, J. (2011, March 16). Yesler Terrace and SHA are on the wrong track. *International Examiner*. http://www.iexaminer.org/2011/03/yesler-terrace-sha-wrong-track/.

Fox-Rogers, L., and Murphy, E. (2015). From brown envelopes to community benefits: The co-option of planning gain agreements under deepening neoliberalism. *Geoforum, 67*, 41–50.

Foxx, A. (2015, March 3). *Local hiring just makes sense*. U.S. Department of Transportation Fastlane. https://www.dot.gov/fastlane/local-hiring-just-makes-sense.

Freeman, K., and Richards, D. (2020). *Environmental career worker training program celebrates 25 years*. Environmental Factor: National Institute of Environmental Health Sciences. https://factor.niehs.nih.gov/2020/8/feature/3-feature-worker-training/index.htm.

Fung, A. (2006). Varieties of participation in complex governance. *Public Administration Review, 66*, 66–75.

Fung, A. (2020). Four levels of power: A conception to enable liberation. *Journal of Political Philosophy, 28*(2), 131–157.

Funk, W. (1996). Bargaining toward the new millennium: Regulatory negotiation and the subversion of the public interest. *Duke Law Journal, 46*, 1351–1388.

Garland, L., and Suafai, S. (2002). *Getting to the table: A project labor agreement primer*. National Economic Development and Law Center.

Garrison, J. (2018, August 27). Nashville MLS ownership reaches terms on community benefits agreement for stadium project. *Tennessean*. https://www.tennessean.com/story/news/2018/08/27/nashville-soccer-stadium-mls-fairgrounds/1115093002/.

Georgia Center for Nonprofits. (n.d.a.). *Momentum: Westside*. https://www.gcn.org/WestsideMomentum.

Georgia Center for Nonprofits. (n.d.b.). *Momentum: Westside cohort*. https://www.gcn.org/WestsideMomentum/Cohort.

Georgia Center for Nonprofits. (2015, January 8). *Westside Neighborhood Prosperity Fund accepting applications for capacity building grants through February 13, 2015*. http://www.gcn.org/Westside-Neighborhood-Prosperity-Fund-Accepting-Applications-for-Capacity-Building-Grants-Through.

Georgia World Congress Center Authority. (n.d.). *Mercedes-Benz Stadium*. https://www.gwcca.org/mercedes-benz-stadium.

Gibson, C., and Jung, K. (2005). *Historical census statistics on population totals by race, 1790 to 1990, and by Hispanic origin, 1970 to 1990, for large cities and other urban places in the United States*. Population Division, US Census Bureau.

Gillis, C. (2009, March 12). With funds dry, Rainier Vista changes plans. Real Change News. https://www.realchangenews.org/news/2009/03/12/funds-dry-rainier-vista-changes-plans.

Giuliano, G., Blanco, H., and Bahl, D. (2013). *Promoting employment in transit construction projects by members of minority and low-income communities*. Los Angeles: University of Southern California.

Gores, P. (2017, August 3). Wisconsin would offer Fiserv $12.5 million incentive to stay in state. *Milwaukee Journal Sentinel*. https://www.jsonline.com/story/money/2017/08/03/wisconsin-would-offer-fiserv-12-5-million-incentive-stay-state/537616001/.

Gores, P. (2018, July 26). Bucks arena naming deal will "elevate" Fiserv's brand, CEO says. *Milwaukee Journal Sentinel*. https://www.jsonline.com/story/news/2018/07/26/fiserv-inc-brookfield-based-financial-technology-firm-has-agreement-new-milwaukee-bucks/843373002/.

Graves, J. (2016a, November 30). Seattle artists race to document cultures gentrification is erasing. The Stranger. https://www.thestranger.com/slog/2016/12/02/24709926/the-buildings-the-high-rise-are-not-for-us-inside-the-yesler-terrace-community-meeting.

Graves, J. (2016b, December 2). "The buildings, the high-rise, are not for us.": Inside the Yesler Terrace community meeting. The Stranger. https://www.thestranger.com/film/2016/12/02/24709926/the-buildings-the-high-rise-are-not-for-us-inside-the-yesler-terrace-community-meeting.

Green, J. (2013, May 14). *Falcons stadium dilemma: Tale of two old churches*. Curbed Atlanta. https://atlanta.curbed.com/2013/5/14/10243934/falcons-stadium-dilemma-tale-of-two-old-churches.

Green, J. (2014, June 13). *On downtown fringe, $15M offered for strong developments*. Curbed Atlanta. http://atlanta.curbed.com/archives/2014/06/13/on-downtown-fringe-15m-offered-for-strong-developments.php.

Green, J. (2016, January 5). *Atlanta Falcons stadium touted as absolute game-changer*. Curbed Atlanta. http://atlanta.curbed.com/archives/2016/01/05/atlanta-falcons-stadium-game-changer.php.

Green, J. (2019, January 31). *Five years after Mercedes-Benz Stadium broke ground, is Atlanta's Westside revival working?* Curbed Atlanta. https://atlanta.curbed.com/atlanta-photo-essays/2019/1/31/18201601/super-bowl-liii-atlanta-gentrification-poverty-blank.

Griffin, C. E. (2012, February 2). Disadvantaged workers win in new MTA agreement. *Our Weekly*. http://ourweekly.com/news/2012/feb/01/disadvantaged-workers-win-in-new-mta-agreement/.

Gross, J. (2007). Community benefits agreements: Definitions, values and legal enforceability. *Journal of Affordable Housing and Community Development Law, 17*(1/2), 35–58.

Haas, G. 2012. Community benefits, negotiations, and (in)justice. In D. S. Sloane (Ed.), *Planning Los Angeles* (pp. 272–278). Chicago: American Planning Association.

Henry, K. T. (2009). *Deconstructing elevated expressways: An evaluation of the proposal to remove the Interstate 10 Claiborne Avenue Expressway in New Orleans, Louisiana*. Paper 1016. University of New Orleans Theses and Dissertations.

Herrera, L. E., Waheed, S., Koonse, T., and Ovando-Lacroux, C. (2014). *Exploring targeted hire: An assessment of best practices in the construction industry*. UCLA Labor Center. http://ccaucla-laborcenter.electricembers.net/wp-content/uploads/downloads/2014/04/Exploring-Targeted-Hire.pdf.

Hjern, B. (1982). Implementation research: The link gone missing. *Journal of Public Policy*, 2(3), 301–308.

Ho, W. (2007). Community benefits agreements: An evolution in public benefits negotiation processes. *Journal of Affordable Housing and Community Development Law*, 17(1/2), 7–34.

Holliman, W. G. (1981). Development agreements and vested rights in California. *Urban Lawyer*, 44–64.

Holloway, L. (2005). *Milwaukee County Board Chairman Lee Holloway announces the Park East Redevelopment Compact's (PERC) Community Advisory Committee's first organizational meeting*. County Board of Supervisors Lee Holloway. http://www.wispolitics.com/1006/Holloway_announces_Park_East_Community_Advisory_Committee_Organizational_Meeting.pdf.

Holmes, N., and Berube, A. (2016, January 14). *City and metropolitan inequality on the rise, driven by declining incomes*. Brookings Institution. https://www.brookings.edu/research/city-and-metropolitan-inequality-on-the-rise-driven-by-declining-incomes/.

Hutson, M. A. (2015). *Deepening their roots: The urban struggle for economic, environmental and social justice*. New York: Routledge.

Hymon, S. (2014, January 21). And so it begins: Ground is broken for 8.5-Mile Crenshaw-LAX Line. *The Source*. http://thesource.metro.net/2014/01/21/and-so-it-begins-ground-is-broken-for-8-5-mile-crenshawlax-line/.

Immergluck, D. (2016). *Affordability first: Concerns about preserving housing options for existing and new residents on Atlanta's Westside*. WCA Online Library. http://wcadatadashboard.iac.gatech.edu/library/items/show/189.

Innes, J. E., and Booher, D. E. (2010). *Planning with complexity: An introduction to collaborative rationality for public policy*. New York: Routledge.

Invest Atlanta. (n.d.a). *Developer Funding Incentives*. https://www.investatlanta.com/assets/invest_atlanta_developer_incentives_brochure_2017_qN5EWnl.pdf.

Invest Atlanta. (n.d.b). *Westside TAD Community Improvement Fund (round I) fact sheet*. http://www.boarddocs.com/ga/investatlanta/Board.nsf/files/9QNNE371C47A/$file/CIF%20Fact%20Sheet_20141106.pdf.

Invest Atlanta. (2013a). *Community Benefits Plan*. http://investatlanta.com/wp-content/uploads/Community-Benefits-Plan.pdf.

Invest Atlanta. (2013b, August 21). *Community Benefits Plan Committee meeting*. https://www.investatlanta.com/assets/cbp-meeting-presentation---august-21-2013_38X9BMP.pdf.

Invest Atlanta. (2013c, September 10). *Westside TAD Neighborhoods Strategic Implementation Plan*. http://westsidetad.com/appendices/Westside%20TAD%20Final%20Report%20091013%20(1).pdf.

Invest Atlanta. (2014a, January 13). *Invest Atlanta announces application process for Westside Tax Allocation District community improvement fund*. https://www.investatlanta.com/about

-us/news-press/invest-atlanta-announces-application-process-for-westside-tax-allocation-district-community-improvement-fund.

Invest Atlanta. (2014b, February 27). *Community Benefits Plan Committee meeting.* http://www.investatlanta.com/wp-content/uploads/CBP-Minutes-022714.pdf.

Invest Atlanta. (2016a, November 17). *New home for Westside Works opens in Vine City.* https://www.investatlanta.com/impact-insights/new-home-for-westside-works-opens-in-vine-city.

Invest Atlanta. (2016b, November 17). *New opportunities for stronger communities in Westside Atlanta.* https://www.investatlanta.com/assets/westside_neighborhood_development_booklet_OPqp4ro.pdf.

Invest Atlanta. (2016c). *Westside TAD program guidelines.* https://www.investatlanta.com/assets/westside-tad-program-guidelines-final-1_BxkgEMO.pdf.

Invest Atlanta. (2017). *Invest Atlanta Westside Projects Update.* https://www.investatlanta.com/assets/cbp_committee_meeting_final_presentation_jan_2017_qN9LjDo.pdf.

Invest Atlanta. (2018a, May 17). *Hagar CTM set to transform vacant Westside properties into affordable housing.* https://www.investatlanta.com/impact-insights/hagar-ctm-set-to-transform-vacant-westside-properties-into-affordable-housing.

Invest Atlanta. (2018b, May 18). *Board approves $2.4 million for Westside TAD resident retention effort.* https://www.investatlanta.com/impact-insights/board-approves-24-million-for-westside-tad-resident-retention-effort.

Invest Atlanta. (2020a, January 23). *TAD funds allocated to help provide school-adjacent affordable rental housing in English Ave.* https://www.investatlanta.com/impact-insights/tad-funds-allocated-to-help-provide-school-adjacent-affordable-rental-housing-in-english-ave.

Invest Atlanta. (2020b, February 26). *TAD funds to finance renovations for school-adjacent affordable rentals.* https://www.investatlanta.com/impact-insights/tad-funds-to-finance-renovations-for-school-adjacent-affordable-rentals.

Invest Atlanta. (2021a, July). *2021 Westside TAD program guidelines.* https://www.investatlanta.com/assets/westside_tad_program_guidelines_rev._final_p57Ovwp.pdf.

Invest Atlanta. (2021b, November 22). *Enhancing the English Avenue Corridor.* https://www.investatlanta.com/impact-insights/enhancing-the-english-avenue-corridor.

Isaf, R. (2015). *Wither the NPU?* Creative Loafing Atlanta. https://creativeloafing.com/content-232252-neighborhoods---wither-the-npu.

Jannene, J. (2014, June 10). *Finally, a new Park East plan.* Urban Milwaukee. http://urbanmilwaukee.com/2014/06/10/eyes-on-milwaukee-finally-a-new-park-east-plan/.

Jannene, J. (2015, September 22). *New Bucks arena approved.* Urban Milwaukee. https://urbanmilwaukee.com/2015/09/22/eyes-on-milwaukee-new-bucks-arena-approved/.

Jannene, J. (2017, February 24). *Bucks select apartment developer.* Urban Milwaukee. https://urbanmilwaukee.com/2017/02/24/eyes-on-milwaukee-bucks-select-apartment-developer/.

Jannene, J. (2018, May 23). *Bucks beat hiring goals on arena.* Urban Milwaukee. https://urbanmilwaukee.com/2018/05/23/eyes-on-milwaukee-bucks-beat-hiring-goals-on-arena/.

Jannene, J. (2019, March 15). *Bucks unveil master plan for Park East.* Urban Milwaukee. https://urbanmilwaukee.com/2019/03/15/eyes-on-milwaukee-bucks-unveil-master-plan-for-park-east/.

Janssen-Jansen, L. B., and van der Veen, M. (2017). Contracting communities: Conceptualizing community benefits agreements to improve citizen involvement in urban development projects. *Environment and Planning A, 49*(1), 205–225. DOI: 10.1177/0308518X16664730.

Jennings, A. (2014, November 27). Construction on Crenshaw/LAX line is hurting business, merchants say. *Los Angeles Times.* https://www.latimes.com/local/california/la-me-adv-crenshaw-closure-20141128-story.html.

Jennings, A. (2019, April 10). One of California's last black enclaves threatened by Inglewood's stadium deal. *Los Angeles Times.* https://www.latimes.com/local/lanow/la-me-inglewood-gentrification-rent-crenshaw-rams-stadium-20190410-htmlstory.html.

Johnston-Dodds, K. (2001, October). *Constructing California: A review of project labor agreements.* California Research Bureau. https://catalog.loc.gov/vwebv/search?searchCode=LCCNandsearchArg=2003387709andsearchType=1andpermalink=y.

Kahn, M. (2015a, March 19). *In shadow of stadiums, neighborhood pines for investment.* Curbed Atlanta. http://atlanta.curbed.com/archives/2015/03/19/in-the-shadow-of-the-stadium-a-neighborhood-ready-for-investment.php.

Kahn, M. (2015b, September 16). *Tech seeks city funds to spark $500M mixed-use center.* Curbed Atlanta. http://atlanta.curbed.com/archives/2015/09/16/georgia-tech-enterprise-park.php.

Kahn, M. (2015c, October 20). *In shadow of Falcons stadium, new park is a key addition.* Curbed Atlanta. http://atlanta.curbed.com/archives/2015/10/20/lindsay-street-park-english-avenue-first-park.php.

Kahn, M. (2017, November 29). *Georgia Dome replacement hotel takes a step forward.* Curbed Atlanta. https://atlanta.curbed.com/2017/11/29/16713866/georgia-dome-hotel-development.

Keating, L. (2001). *Race, Class and Urban Expansion.* Philadelphia: Temple University Press.

Keeley, S. (2016, February 22). *Seattle Housing Authority seeking bids for fourth Yesler Terrace building.* Curbed Seattle. https://seattle.curbed.com/2016/2/22/11094796/seattle-housing-authority-seeking-bids-for-fourth-yesler-terrace.

Keith, T. (2017, April 13). *Wisconsin Republicans take new swing at state's prevailing wage law, renewing clash with labor.* Fox6Now. http://fox6now.com/2017/04/13/wisconsin-republicans-launch-new-attempt-to-repeal-states-prevailing-wage-law/.

Kinney, J. (2016, March 25). *Seattle seawall project sets new bar for workforce diversity.* Next City. https://nextcity.org/urbanist-news/seattle-seawall-jobs-construction-women-minorities.

Kirchen, R. (2015, August 28). So how much will the Milwaukee Bucks arena cost you? Here's the answer. *Milwaukee Business Journal.* https://www.bizjournals.com/milwaukee/blog/2015/08/so-how-much-will-the-milwaukee-bucks-arena-cost.html.

Kirchen, R. (2016, April 22). Documents show Bucks' $524M arena cost goes beyond arena, includes professional fees. *Milwaukee Business Journal.* https://www.bizjournals.com/milwaukee/news/2016/04/22/documents-show-bucks-524m-arena-cost-goes-beyond.html.

Kirchen, R. (2018, February 9). Milwaukee Bucks agree to increased wage floor, union representation at new arena. *Milwaukee Business Journal.* https://www.bizjournals.com/milwaukee/news/2018/02/09/milwaukee-bucks-agree-to-increased-wage-floor.html.

Kirkham, C. (2015, January 20). A new effort to help black workers find higher-paying jobs. *Los Angeles Times.* http://www.latimes.com/business/la-fi-0121-african-american-employment-20150121-story.html.

KIRO 7 News Staff. (2020, June 21). *Black Lives Matter Seattle-King County launches Black-led community investment fund.* KIRO 7 News. https://www.kiro7.com/news/local/black-lives

-matter-seattle-king-county-launches-black-led-community-investment-fund/GGCAOV 5QNVDZ5FA2EEZTMXECH4/.

Kofman, Y. (2013, Fall). Building power: The Los Angeles Black Worker Center turns excluded workers into forces for change. *Progressive Planning, 197*, 4–7. http://www.plannersnetwork.org/wp-content/uploads/2013/11/PPM_Fall13pw1.pdf.

Kofman, Y., and Cuevas, L. (n.d.). *Black worker congress blueprint for addressing the jobs crisis: Labor/community dialogue, new organizing, and scaling up the worker center model.* https://www.lablackworkercenter.org/reports.

Kosla, M. T. (2014). More than members: Market revitalization in the building trades. *Critical Sociology*, 1–22. DOI: 10.1177/0896920514527847.

Kotler, F. B. (2009). *Project labor agreements in New York State: In the public interest.* Ithaca, NY: Cornell University IRL School.

Krumholz, N. (2011). *Making equity planning work: Leadership in the public sector.* Philadelphia: Temple University Press.

Kudler, A. G. (2013, July 10). *Black-owned businesses already being pushed out of Leimert Park ahead of the Crenshaw Line.* Curbed Los Angeles. http://la.curbed.com/archives/2013/07/blackowned_businesses_already_being_pushed_out_of_leimert_park_ahead_of_the_crenshaw_line.php.

Kunerth, J. (1991, February 11). Atlantans want Olympics, just not in their backyard. *Orlando Sentinel.* https://www.orlandosentinel.com/news/os-xpm-1991-02-11-9102110286-story.html.

Kussy, E. V., and Cooke, R. J. (2010). Executive order encourages project labor agreements on federal projects. *Journal of Legal Affairs and Dispute Resolution in Engineering and Construction, 2*(2), 97–99.

Langworthy, D. J. (1995). Project-labor agreements after Boston Harbor: Do they violate competitive bidding laws? *William Mitchell Law Review, 21*(1), 1103–1138.

Larsen, D. J. (2002). *Development agreement manual: Collaboration in pursuit of community interests.* Sacramento, CA: Institute for Local Self Government.

Larsen, L. (2009). *The pursuit of responsible development: Addressing anticipated benefits and unwanted burdens through community benefit agreements.* Working Paper Series Number 9. University of Michigan Center for Local, State, and Urban Policy.

League of Women Voters. (1998). *Initiative 200.* http://www.smartvoter.org/1998nov/wa/state/meas/i200/.

League of Women Voters of California. (2012, November 6). *Measure J.* http://www.smartvoter.org/2012/11/06/ca/la/meas/J/.

Lee, M. (2015, October 23). *Mayor offers land speculators journey through judicial system, restful vacation in city jail.* Creative Loafing Atlanta. https://creativeloafing.com/content-219362-mayor-offers-land-speculators-journey-through-judicial-system-restful.

Leslie, K. (2013a, November 20). Meetings over Falcons stadium community benefits erupt over surprise legislation. *Atlanta Journal-Constitution.* https://www.ajc.com/news/meetings-over-falcons-stadium-community-benefits-erupt-over-surprise-legislation/lIwoUkPrfsRAoarDCM781H/.

Leslie, K. (2013b, December 3). Atlanta council passes community benefits plan, clears path for construction. *Atlanta Journal-Constitution.* http://www.ajc.com/news/news/local-govt-politics/atlanta-council-passes-community-benefits-plan-cle/nb89x/.

Leslie, K. (2016, September 23). Reed halts plan to buy troubled investors' properties. *Atlanta Journal-Constitution.* https://www.ajc.com/news/local-govt--politics/reed-halts-plan-buy-troubled-investors-properties/gNae83owUrLJxrXHFrTMeI/.

Leslie, K., and Tucker, T. (2014, March 16). *Inside the evolving Atlanta Falcons stadium drama.* Athletic Business. http://www.athleticbusiness.com/more-news/inside-the-evolving-atlanta-falcons-stadium-drama.html.

Lesniewski, J., and Doussard, M. (2017). Crossing boundaries, building power: Chicago organizers embrace race, ideology, and coalition. *Social Service Review, 91*(4), 585–620.

Lester, T. W., and Reckhow, S. (2013). Network governance and regional equity: Shared agendas or problematic partners? *Planning Theory, 12*(2), 115–138. DOI: 10.1177/1473095212455189.

Liegeois, N., and Carson, M. (2003). Accountable development: Maximizing community benefits from publicly supported development. *Clearinghouse Review, 37,* 174–188.

Linton, J. (2022, March 18). *Most of Metro's new Crenshaw/LAX light rail line is substantially complete—Opening could be December 2022. Update: CEO "Fall 2022."* Streetsblog LA. https://la.streetsblog.org/2022/03/18/most-of-metros-new-crenshaw-lax-light-rail-line-is-substantially-complete-opening-could-be-december-2022/.

Lipsky, M. (1980). *Street-level bureaucracy: Dilemmas of the individual in public service.* New York: Russell Sage Foundation.

Lloyd, S. A. (2018, May 21). *Look inside Vulcan's Batik building in Yesler Terrace.* Curbed Seattle. https://seattle.curbed.com/2018/5/21/17377140/batik-building-apartments-yesler-terrace.

Logan, J. R., and Molotch, H. (1987). *Urban Fortunes: The Political Economy of Place.* Berkeley: University of California Press.

Lohr, K. (2011, August 4). *The economic legacy of Atlanta's Olympic Games.* NPR. https://www.npr.org/2011/08/04/138926167/the-economic-legacy-of-atlantas-olympic-games.

Los Angeles Alliance for a New Economy. (n.d.). *About LAANE.* https://laane.org/about-laane/.

Los Angeles Black Worker Center. (n.d.a.). *Black Labor Construction Council.* https://www.lablackworkercenter.org/black_labor_construction_council1.

Los Angeles Black Worker Center. (n.d.b). *Campaigns* https://www.lablackworkercenter.org/campaigns1.

Los Angeles Black Worker Center. (n.d.c). *Do you see me now.* https://www.lablackworkercenter.org/equity_transparency.

Los Angeles Black Worker Center. (n.d.d). *Equity, transparency, and accountability.* https://www.lablackworkercenter.org/equity_transparency.

Los Angeles Black Worker Center. (2014, August). *Community compliance and monitoring program report.* https://www.lablackworkercenter.org/reports.

Los Angeles Black Worker Center. (2015, March). *Community compliance and monitoring program report.* https://www.lablackworkercenter.org/reports.

Los Angeles Black Worker Center. (2016). *A special LA BWC community monitoring and compliance report: Opportunities for Measure M.* https://www.lablackworkercenter.org/reports.

Los Angeles County Metropolitan Transportation Authority. (n.d.a.). *Project map English.* https://media.metro.net/projects_studies/crenshaw/images/Crenshaw-LAX_transit_corridor_map_eng.pdf.

Los Angeles County Metropolitan Transportation Authority. (n.d.b). *System map.* http://media.metro.net/riding_metro/maps/images/rail_map.pdf.

Los Angeles County Metropolitan Transportation Authority. (n.d.c.). *Eligibility.* https://www.metro.net/projects/business-interruption-fund/eligibility/.

Los Angeles County Metropolitan Transportation Authority. (n.d.d.). *Measure R.* https://www.metro.net/projects/measurer/.
Los Angeles County Metropolitan Transportation Authority. (n.d.e.). *Project labor agreement and construction careers policy.* https://www.metro.net/about/placcp/.
Los Angeles County Metropolitan Transportation Authority. (n.d.f.). *Crenshaw/LAX transit project.* http://www.metro.net/projects/crenshaw_corridor/.
Los Angeles County Metropolitan Transportation Authority. (n.d.g.). *Business interruption fund.* https://www.metro.net/projects/business-interruption-fund/.
Los Angeles County Metropolitan Transportation Authority. (n.d.h.). *GIS data.* developer.metro.net/gis-data.
Los Angeles County Metropolitan Transportation Authority. (2012a). *FAQs.* http://media.metro.net/about_us/pla/images/frequently_asked_questions_clc.pdf.
Los Angeles County Metropolitan Transportation Authority. (2012b, December 14). *Milestone: L.A. Metro officially begins utility relocation work for major light rail project in downtown L.A.* http://www.metro.net/news/simple_pr/Metro-begins-utility-relocation-regional-connector/.
Los Angeles County Metropolitan Transportation Authority. (2012c). *Project labor agreement.* http://media.metro.net/about_us/pla/images/agreement_projectlabor_2015.pdf.
Los Angeles County Metropolitan Transportation Authority. (2014a). *Referral (hiring) process.* http://media.metro.net/about_us/pla/images/chart_placcp_hiring_2018-02.pdf.
Los Angeles County Metropolitan Transportation Authority. (2014b, June). *Targeted worker summary report.* http://media.metro.net/about_us/pla/images/C0988_Targeted_Worker_Report_June.pdf.
Los Angeles County Metropolitan Transportation Authority. (2014c, October 17). *Metro to launch Eat Shop Play Crenshaw campaign at Taste of Soul.* http://thesource.metro.net/2014/10/17/metro-to-launch-eat-shop-play-crenshaw-campaign-at-taste-of-soul/.
Los Angeles County Metropolitan Transportation Authority. (2015a). *Eat Shop Play Crenshaw/LAX.* http://www.metro.net/interactives/html/eatshopplay/#map.
Los Angeles County Metropolitan Transportation Authority. (2015b). *Project labor agreement and construction careers policy.* https://www.metro.net/about/pla/.
Los Angeles County Metropolitan Transportation Authority. (2015c, October). *Targeted worker summary report.* https://www.metro.net/about/pla/co988-crenshaw-lax-transit-corridor-designbuild/.
Los Angeles County Metropolitan Transportation Authority. (2016a, January). *Targeted worker summary report.* https://d1akjheu06qp1r.cloudfront.net/about_us/pla/images/summary_C0988_placlax_2016-01.pdf.
Los Angeles County Metropolitan Transportation Authority. (2016b, November 9). *Measure M is approved.* https://theplan.metro.net.
Los Angeles County Metropolitan Transportation Authority. (2017, December). *Metro's project labor agreement and construction careers policy.* https://media.metro.net/about_us/pla/images/policy_constructioncareers_2017-06.pdf.
Los Angeles County Metropolitan Transportation Authority. (2019, Winter). *Crenshaw/LAX transit project overview fact sheet.* https://media.metro.net/projects_studies/crenshaw/images/factsheet_crenshawlax_eng.pdf.
Los Angeles County Metropolitan Transportation Authority. (2021, March). *Metro's project labor agreement and construction careers policy.* https://media.metro.net/2021/pla-ccp-quarterly-march-2021.pdf.

Los Angeles Unified School District. (1999). *Project stabilization agreement.* http://www.laschools.org/new-site/project-stabilization/.

Lowe, N., and Morton, B. J. (2008). Developing standards: The role of community benefits agreements in enhancing job quality. *Community Development, 39*(2), 23–35. DOI: 10.1080/15575330809489728.

Lucas-Darby, E. T. (2012). Community benefits agreements: A case study in addressing environmental and economic injustices. *Journal of African American History, 97*(1–2), 92–109.

Luce, S. (2005). The role of community involvement in implementing living wage ordinances. *Industrial Relations: A Journal of Economy and Society, 44*(1), 32–58. https://doi.org/10.1111/j.0019-8676.2004.00372.x.

Luce, S. (2012). Living wage policies and campaigns: Lessons from the United States. *International Journal of Labour Research, 4*(1), 11–26.

Madrid, C. (2012, August 15). *Why is this man leaving the housing authority?* The Stranger. https://www.thestranger.com/seattle/why-is-this-man-leaving-the-housing-authority/Content?oid=14463007.

Marantz, N. J. (2015). What do community benefits agreements deliver? Evidence from Los Angeles. *Journal of the American Planning Association, 81*(4), 251–267. DOI: 10.1080/01944363.2015.1092093.

Margerum, R. D. (2011). *Beyond consensus.* Cambridge, MA: MIT Press.

Mariano, W. (2014, November 1). Betting on "The Bluff." *Atlanta Journal-Constitution.* http://www.myajc.com/news/news/fate-of-blighted-atlanta-neighborhood-in-hands-of-/nht29/.

Mariano, W. (2015a, March 14). Divine mission gives way to blighted streets. *Atlanta Journal-Constitution.* https://www.ajc.com/news/public-affairs/divine-mission-gives-way-blighted-streets/T33mrjLJrIvwWjbqSsQoAJ/.

Mariano, W. (2015b, March 27). Residents: Atlanta Falcons stadium money oversight body gets no respect. *Atlanta Journal-Constitution.* http://investigations.blog.ajc.com/2015/03/27/debate-on-atlanta-falcons-stadium-money-fractious-but-few-show-up-to-hear-it/.

Mariano, W. (2016, September 4). Atlanta speculator Rick Warren gets jail. *Atlanta Journal-Constitution.* https://www.ajc.com/news/crime--law/atlanta-speculator-rick-warren-gets-jail/BYiQ1LvXd5t6bQv0cnc6XN/?clearUserState=true.

Marklein, H. (2017, December 15). *Bang from our bucks: An update on the Milwaukee arena project.* Wisconsin Senate District 17. https://legis.wisconsin.gov/senate/17/marklein/media/weekly-columns/bang-from-our-bucks-an-update-on-the-milwaukee-arena-project/.

Marsh, L. L. (1989). Introduction. In *Development Agreements: Practice, Policy and Prospects* (pp. 2–6). Washington, DC: Urban Land Institute.

National Parks Service. (n.d.). *Martin Luther King, Jr. National Historic Park.* https://www.nps.gov/malu/planyourvisit/birth-home.htm.

Matland, R. E. (1995). Synthesizing the implementation literature: The ambiguity-conflict model of policy implementation. *Journal of Public Administration Research and Theory, 5*(2), 145–174.

Mayer, G. (2010). *Project labor agreements.* Congressional Research Service, No. 854. http://digitalcommons.ilr.cornell.edu/key_workplace/854.

Mazmanian, D. A., and Sabatier, P. A. (1989). *Implementation and public policy.* Lanham, MD: University Press of America.

McGahan, J. (2017, July 15.) L.A.'s highest-increasing home values are along Metro's Crenshaw Line. *LA Weekly.* http://www.laweekly.com/news/south-la-home-prices-are-increasing-along-metros-crenshaw-lax-line-8429372.

McGahey, R. M., and Vey, J. S. (Eds.). (2008). *Retooling for growth: Building a 21st century economy in America's older industrial areas*. Washington, DC: Brookings Institution Press.

McKean, A. (2015). Local government legislation: Community benefits, land banks, and politically engaged community economic development. *Journal of Affordable Housing, 24*(1), 133–163.

Mercedes-Benz Stadium. (n.d.a.). *Community Impact*. http://mercedesbenzstadium.com/community/.

Mercedes-Benz Stadium. (n.d.b.). *Sustainability at Mercedes-Benz Stadium*. https://mercedesbenzstadium.com/mbs-sustain/.

Millard, P. (2003, December 7). "Community" Park East plan irks developers. *Milwaukee Business Journal*. http://www.bizjournals.com/milwaukee/stories/2003/12/08/newscolumn1.html.

Miller, K. (2013, February 1). CEO Art Leahy guides MTA's transition to a community-friendly rail system. *Los Angeles Sentinel*. http://www.lasentinel.net/index.php?option=com_contentandview=articleandid=10397:ceo-art-leahy-guides-mta-s-transition-to-a-community-friendly-rail-systemandcatid=80:localandItemid=170.

Miller, L. (2017, September 17). This L.A. mall is famous for its African American Santa Claus. Can it survive gentrification? *Los Angeles Times*. http://www.latimes.com/local/california/la-me-ln-crenshaw-development-20170915-story.html.

Mudede, C. (2013, February 6). The twilight of Yesler Terrace. *The Stranger*. http://www.thestranger.com/seattle/the-twilight-of-yesler-terrace/Content?oid=15933703.

Mnookin, R. H., and Susskind, L. E. (1999). *Negotiating on behalf of others: Advice to lawyers, business executives, sports agents, diplomats, and everybody else*. Thousand Oaks, CA: SAGE.

Muhammad, C. (2018, January 12). South L.A. pushes back against gentrification. *LA Weekly*. https://www.laweekly.com/south-l-a-pushes-back-against-gentrification/.

Murphy, B. (2021, January 25). *Bucks franchise worth $1.86 billion*. Urban Milwaukee. https://urbanmilwaukee.com/2021/01/25/murphys-law-bucks-franchise-worth-1-86-billion/.

Murphy, B. (2019, April 16). *Taxpayers make Bucks, Brewers rich*. Urban Milwaukee. https://urbanmilwaukee.com/2019/04/16/murphys-law-taxpayers-make-bucks-brewers-rich/.

Murphy, B. (2015, July 14). *Why Bucks' entertainment district may fail*. Urban Milwaukee. https://urbanmilwaukee.com/2015/07/14/murphys-law-why-bucks-entertainment-district-may-fail/.

Nadler, M. L. (2011). The constitutionality of community benefits agreements: Addressing the exactions problem. *Urban Lawyer, 43*(2), 587–626.

Napolitan, F. (2007). Shifting urban priorities: The removal of inner city freeways in the United States. Master's thesis, Massachusetts Institute of Technology. https://dspace.mit.edu/handle/1721.1/40128.

National Housing Law Project. (2003, January). *Housing Law Bulletin, 33*, 1–29. https://www.nhlp.org/files/NHLP%2001_03%20Bulletin%20FINAL.pdf.

Nelson, L. J. (2014, January 21). Metro breaks ground on $2-billion Crenshaw light-rail line. *Los Angeles Times*. http://www.latimes.com/local/lanow/la-me-ln-crenshaw-line-groundbreaking-20140121,0,1889081.story#axzz2zk7wz6iD.

Nelson, L. J. (2020, April 10). Construction problems delay Metro's $2 billion Crenshaw Line opening until 2021. *Los Angeles Times*. https://www.latimes.com/california/story/2020-04-10/metro-crenshaw-lax-line-opening-date-delayed.

Newman, H. K. (1999). Neighborhood impacts of Atlanta's Olympic games. *Community Development Journal, 34*(2), 151–159.

Newman, S. (2014, July 24). Crenshaw/LAX Line doesn't guarantee Black workers employment in South L.A. *Neon Tommy.* http://www.neontommy.com/news/2014/07/just-how-many-black-workers-are-involved-crenshaw-lines-construction.html.

Newton, D. (2011, April 28). *Highlights from the Metro Board: Crenshaw grade separation, bikes on trains, bus cuts.* Streetsblog LA. http://la.streetsblog.org/2011/04/28/highlights-from-the-metro-board-crenshaw-grade-separation-bikes-on-trains-bus-cuts/.

Newton, D. (2016, September 1). *Who is lining up to fight Measure M.* Streetsblog LA. https://la.streetsblog.org/2016/09/01/who-is-lining-up-to-fight-measure-m/.

Northrup, H. R., and Alario, L. E. (1998). "Boston Harbor"-type project labor agreements in construction: Nature, rationales, and legal challenges. *Journal of Labor Research, 19*(1), 1–63. DOI: 10.1007/s12122-998-1000-8.

Nugent, J. (2017). The right to build the city: Can community benefits agreements bring employment equity to the construction sector? *Labour: Journal of Canadian Labour Studies/Le Travail: revue d'Études Ouvrières Canadiennes, 80,* 81–114.

O'Rourke, D. (2002). Motivating a conflicted environmental state: Community-driven regulation in Vietnam. *Environmental State Under Pressure, 10,* 221–244.

Oluo, I. (2015, May 21). What Seattle is losing in Yesler Terrace redevelopment. *The Seattle Globalist.* https://seattleglobalist.com/2015/05/21/yesler-terrace-redevelopment-seattle-housing-siff-hagereseb/37378.

Ostrom, E. (1990). *Governing the Commons: The evolution of institutions for collective action.* Cambridge, UK: Cambridge University Press.

Park East Milwaukee. (n.d.). *Proposal FAQs.* City and County of Milwaukee. http://parkeastmke.com/the-opportunity/proposal-faqs/.

Park East Milwaukee. (2004). *Park East Redevelopment Compact.* City and County of Milwaukee. http://parkeastmke.com/wp-content/uploads/2015/06/Attachment-Q-Park-East-Redevelopment-Compact.pdf.

Parker, B. (2005, May 9). *This land is our land: The battle for a community benefits agreement in Milwaukee.* Good Jobs and Livable Neighborhoods Coalition. http://regionalpowerbuilding.webs.com/power/downloads/Parkeast.pdf.

Parkin, J. (2004). Constructing meaningful access to work: Lessons from the Port of Oakland Project Labor Agreement. *Columbia Human Rights Law Review, 35,* 375–414.

Parks, V., and Warren, D. (2009). The politics and practice of economic justice: Community benefits agreements as tactic of the new accountable development movement. *Journal of Community Practice, 17*(1–2), 88–106. DOI: 10.1080/10705420902856225.

Partnership for Working Families. (2007, July). *Partnership in Action: Recent Victories, Future Directions.* https://www.forworkingfamilies.org/resources/publications/partnership-action-recent-victories-future-directions.

Partnership for Working Families. (2013, April 16). STAND-UP helps secure community benefits for new stadium deal in Atlanta. https://www.forworkingfamilies.org/article/stand-helps-secure-community-benefits-new-stadium-deal-atlanta.

Pastor Jr., M., Benner, C., and Matsuoka, M. (2015). *This could be the start of something big: How social movements for regional equity are reshaping metropolitan America.* Ithaca: Cornell University Press.

Pendered, D. (2013a, November 21). Community cut out of community benefits deal at Falcons stadium; Mayor Reed ready to engage. *Saporta Report.* http://saportareport.com/community-cut-out-of-community-benefits-deal-mayor-reed-says-hes-ready-to-engage/.

Pendered, D. (2013b, November 24). Falcons community benefits deal due to amidst public distrust, as attention is diverted by Braves relocation. *Saporta Report*. https://saportareport.com/falcons-community-benefits-deal-due-amidst-public-distrust-eyes-diverted-by-braves/columnists/david/david/.

Pendered, D. (2014, February 12). Lawsuit contends stadium bonds unconstitutional, violate Georgia's environmental policies. *Saporta Report*. http://saportareport.com/lawsuit-contends-stadium-bonds-unconstitutional-violate-environmental-policies/.

Philips, P. (2010). *Construction careers for our communities*. UCLA Labor Center. http://www.pacific-gateway.org/constructioncareersforourcommunities.pdf.

Philips, P., and Waitzman, E. (2021). Do project labor agreements reduce the number of bidders on public projects? The case of community colleges in California. *Public Works Management and Policy*, 1–22. DOI: 10.1177/1087724X20956662.

Porter, D. R. (1989). The relation of development agreements to plans and planning. In *Development Agreements: Practice, Policy and Prospects* (pp. 148–152). Washington, DC: Urban Land Institute.

Powell, M. (2015, August 14). Bucks' owners win, at Wisconsin's expense. *New York Times*. http://www.nytimes.com/2015/08/15/sports/bucks-new-owners-get-house-warming-gift-of-public-money.html?_r=0.

Preservation Institute. (2007). *Milwaukee, Wisconsin Park East Freeway*. http://www.preservenet.com/freeways/FreewaysParkEast.html.

Pressman, J. L., and Wildavsky, A. B. (1984). *Implementation*. Berkeley: University of California Press.

Pulido, L. (2017). Geographies of race and ethnicity II: Environmental racism, racial capitalism and state-sanctioned violence. *Progress in Human Geography*, 41(4), 524–533. DOI: 10.1177/0309132516646495.

Pulkkinen, L. (2019, January 14). *As American's first racially integrated housing project is rebuilt, ripples of displacement follow*. Next City. https://nextcity.org/features/view/americas-first-integrated-housing-project-rebuilt-ripples-of-displacement.

Purcell, M. (2009). Resisting neoliberalization: Communicative planning or counter-hegemonic movements? *Planning Theory*, 8(2), 140–165. DOI: 10.1177/1473095209102232.

Rabouin, D. (2013, December 3). *City Council unanimously approves benefits plan for communities around new Falcons stadium*. Atlanta Daily World. http://atlantadailyworld.com/2013/12/03/city-council-unanimously-approves-benefits-plan-for-communities-around-new-falcons-stadium/.

Race Forward. (2016, November). *Confronting racial bias at work*. https://www.raceforward.org/system/files/pdf/reports/RacialBiasAtWork.pdf.

Rau, N. (2019, August 22). Nashville MLS stadium costs rising, but taxpayers won't be on the hook. *Tennessean*. https://www.tennessean.com/story/sports/nashvillesc/2019/08/22/nashville-sc-mls-stadium-costs-rising-taxpayers-not-on-hook/2075347001/.

Reddy, F. (2016, November 8). *Near Atlanta Falcons stadium, new Westside jobs center comes to fruition*. Curbed Atlanta. https://atlanta.curbed.com/2016/11/18/13676950/new-center-westside-aims-create-jobs.

Redevelopment Authority of the City of Milwaukee. (2004, June 15). *Park East Redevelopment Master Plan*. http://city.milwaukee.gov/Zoning-Topics/Redevelopment-Zoning-RED/Park-East-Redevelopment-Plan.htm#.VmcY9ITEj7U.

Redfin. (2021a, March). *Crenshaw housing market*. https://www.redfin.com/neighborhood/633/CA/Los-Angeles/Crenshaw/housing-market.

Redfin. (2021b, March). *South LA Housing Market*. https://www.redfin.com/neighborhood/92255/CA/Los-Angeles/South-LA/housing-market.
Reid, D. (2015, July 15). *Bucks arena triggering more downtown deals?* Urban Milwaukee. https://urbanmilwaukee.com/2015/07/15/plats-and-parcels-bucks-arena-triggering-more-downtown-deals/.
Rihl, J. (2018, May 21). *This Pittsburgh group wants all developers getting public subsidies to agree to community benefits. Including you, Amazon*. Public Source. https://www.publicsource.org/this-pittsburgh-group-wants-all-developers-getting-public-subsidies-to-agree-to-community-benefits-including-you-amazon/.
Rodriguez, A. D. (2021). *Diverging spaces for deviants: The politics of Atlanta's public housing*. Athens: University of Georgia Press.
Rosado, R. (2015). *What will the neighbors say? How differences in planning culture yield distinctive outcomes in urban redevelopment: The example of the community benefits agreement trend*. Doctoral dissertation, University of Pennsylvania.
Rose, M. H., and Mohl, R. A. (2012). *Interstate: highway politics and policy since 1939*. Knoxville: University of Tennessee Press.
Rosen, J., O'Neill, M., and Hutson, M. (2018). The important role of government in comprehensive community initiatives: A case study analysis of the building healthy communities initiative. *Journal of Planning Education and Research*. DOI: 10.1177/0739456X18814296.
Rosen, J., and Schweitzer, L. (2018). Benefits-sharing agreements and nonideal theory: The warning signs of agreement co-optation. *Planning Theory, 17*(3), 396–417.
Rosen, J., Angst, S., De Gregorio, S., and Painter, G. (2020). *How do renters cope with unaffordability?* Los Angeles: University of Southern California Sol Price Center for Social Innovation.
Rosen, J., and Alvarez León, L. F. (2022). The digital growth machine: Urban change and the ideology of technology. *Annals of the American Association of Geographers*. DOI: 10.1080/24694452.2022.2052008.
Rosen, M. (2009, October 15). Development proposal is grandstanding. *Milwaukee Journal Sentinel*. http://archive.jsonline.com/news/opinion/64452002.html/.
Rosenberg, R. H. (2009). The changing culture of American land use regulation: Paying for growth with impact fees. *SMU Law Review, 59*, 177–264.
Rudick, R. (2015, April 22). *The 710 and Measure R2: Can Los Angeles build transit and beat its addiction to asphalt?* Streetsblog LA. http://la.streetsblog.org/2015/04/22/the-710-andmeasure-r2-can-los-angeles-build-transit-and-beat-its-addiction-to-asphalt/.
Rutheiser, C. (1996). *Imagineering Atlanta: The politics of place in the city of dreams*. Verso.
Ryan, E. (2002). Zoning, taking, and dealing: The problems and promise of bargaining in land use planning conflicts. *Harvard Negotiation Law Review, 7*, 337–388.
Ryan, S. (2004, November 15). Panel OKs Park East mandates. *Daily Reporter*. http://dailyreporter.com/2004/11/15/panel-oks-park-east-mandates/.
Ryan, S. (2005, January 5). Walker organizing anti-PERC campaign. *Daily Reporter*. http://dailyreporter.com/2005/01/05/walker-organizing-antiperc-campaign/.
Ryan, S. (2012a, February 17). Kohl's headquarters loss could help Park East corridor in long run. *Milwaukee Business Journal*. https://www.bizjournals.com/milwaukee/print-edition/2012/02/17/kohls-headquarters-loss-could-help.html.
Ryan, S. (2012b, July 20). Milwaukee to consider $1M loan for Park East Square cleanup. *Milwaukee Business Journal*. https://www.bizjournals.com/milwaukee/print-edition/2012/07/20/city-to-consider-1-million-loan-for.html.

Ryan, S. (2015a, May 8). Park East hiring, wage rules could extend to other properties. *Milwaukee Business Journal.* http://www.bizjournals.com/milwaukee/print-edition/2015/05/08 /park-east-hiring-wage-rules-could-extend-to-other.html.

Ryan, S. (2015b, June 2). Bucks owners' $400M Park East plan reveals 300-room hotel on Bradley Center site. *Milwaukee Business Journal.* https://www.bizjournals.com/milwaukee/blog /real_estate/2015/06/bucks-owners-400m-park-east-plan-shows-300-room.html.

Ryan, S. (2016a, January 14). Wangard plans 2018 openings for two more Park East apartment buildings. *Milwaukee Business Journal.* https://www.bizjournals.com/milwaukee/blog/real _estate/2016/01/wangard-plans-2018-openings-for-two-morepark-east.html.

Ryan, S. (2016b, March 21). Abele: 98% of Park East being redeveloped or under option for sale. *Milwaukee Business Journal.* https://www.bizjournals.com/milwaukee/blog/real_estate /2016/03/abele-98-of-park-east-being-developed-or-under.html.

Sager, T. (2005). Communicative planners as naïve mandarins of the neo-liberal state? *European Journal of Spatial Development,* 9544.

Sager, T. (2009). Responsibilities of theorists: The case of communicative planning theory. *Progress in Planning,* 72, 1–51. DOI: 10.1016/j.progress.2009.03.002.

Saito, L. T. (2012). How low-income residents can benefit from urban development: The LA Live Community Benefits Agreement. *City and Community,* 11(2), 129–150. DOI: 10.1111 /j.1540-6040.2012.01399.x.

Saito, L. and Truong, J. (2015). The L.A. Live Community Benefits Agreement: Evaluating the agreement results and shifting political power in the city. *Urban Affairs Review,* 51(2) 263–289. DOI: 10.1177/1078087414527064.

Salkin, P. E., and Lavine, A. (2008). Understanding community benefits agreements: Equitable development, social justice and other considerations for developers, municipalities and community organizations. *UCLA Journal of Environmental Law and Policy,* 26, 291–331.

Salkin, P. E., and Lavine, A. (2007). Negotiating for social justice and the promise of community benefits agreements: Case studies of current and developing agreements. *Journal of Affordable Housing and Community Development Law,* 17(1–2), 113–144.

Saporta, M. (2013a, August 6). *Mayor Kasim Reed: Deal reached with Friendship Baptist Church for $19.5 million; makes plea for south site.* Saporta Report. http://saportareport.com/mayor -kasim-reed-deal-reached-with-friendship-for-19-5-million-makes-plea-for-south-site/.

Saporta, M. (2013b, March 6). *New deal for Atlanta Falcons stadium will address community concerns.* Saporta Report. https://saportareport.com/new-atlanta-falcons-stadium-agreement -will-address-community-concerns/sections/reports/maria_saporta/.

Saporta, M. (2014a, April 7). *Lindsay Street Park a model of what needs to happen along Proctor Creek.* Saporta Report. http://saportareport.com/lindsay-street-park-a-model-of-what -needs-to-happen-along-proctor-creek/.

Saporta, M. (2014b, April 22). *Blank Foundation now taking grant requests for $15 million Westside fund.* Saporta Report. http://saportareport.com/blank-foundation-now-taking-grant -requests-for-15-million-westside-fund/.

Saporta, M. (2015, January 8). *Blank Foundation seeking applications for Westside funds from nonprofits.* Saporta Report. https://saportareport.com/blank-foundation-seeking-applications -for-westside-funds-from-nonprofits/sections/reports/maria_saporta/.

Saporta, M., and Wenk, A. (2013, September 13). Reed announces deals with black churches for new Falcons stadium. *Atlanta Business Chronicle.* https://www.bizjournals.com/atlanta /news/2013/09/13/reed-agreements-reached-with-church.html.

Schneider, K. (2017, October 10). In the heart of Milwaukee, a gleaming tower leads an urban renewal. *New York Times.* https://www.nytimes.com/2017/10/10/business/milwaukee-development-northwestern-mutual.html.

Schultze, S. (2013, May 31). Wisconsin governor says government will be more efficient. *Milwaukee Journal-Sentinel.* http://www.jsonline.com/news/milwaukee/scott-walker-signs-bill-to-limit-county-board-authority-b9923377z1-209735131.html.

Schultze, S., and Stein, J. (2013, May 14). Legislature passes bill to cut budget of Milwaukee County Board. *Milwaukee Journal-Sentinel.* http://www.jsonline.com/news/milwaukee/state-senate-passes-bill-to-cut-funds-for-milwaukee-county-board-u19up00-207470061.html.

Schrock, G. (2014). Connecting people and place prosperity: Workforce development and urban planning in scholarship and practice. *Journal of Planning Literature, 29*(3), 257–271. DOI: 10.1177/0885412214538834.

SCIDpda. (2014, October). *Little Saigon landmark project feasibility study.* https://www.seattle.gov/documents/Departments/OPCD/OngoingInitiatives/ChinatownInternationalDistrict/Little%20Saigon%20Landmark%20Project%20Feasibility%20Study.pdf.

Sears, K. (2017, September 22). Redoubling its efforts, an artist-lead activist group asks Vulcan for equitable development. *Seattle Weekly.* http://www.seattleweekly.com/arts/redoubling-its-efforts-an-artist-lead-activist-group-asks-vulcan-for-equitable-development/.

Seattle City Council. (2012). *City of Seattle Ordinance 123961 Council Bill 117536.* http://clerk.seattle.gov/~archives/Ordinances/Ord_123961.pdf.

Seattle Housing Authority. (n.d.). *Citizen Review Committee (CRC) Meeting Minutes.* http://seattlehousing.net/redevelopment/yesler-terrace/people/community-outreach/citizen-review-committee-crc-meeting-minutes/.

Seattle Housing Authority. (2002, December 24). *Rainier Vista lawsuit settled.* http://seattlehousing.org/news/releases/2002/rainier-vista-lawsuit-settled/.

Seattle Housing Authority. (2007a, October 26). *Section 3 program helping residents land jobs.* https://www.seattlehousing.org/news/section-3-program-helping-residents-land-jobs.

Seattle Housing Authority. (2007b). *Yesler Terrace definitions and guiding principles.* https://www.seattlehousing.org/sites/default/files/YTGuidingPrinciples.pdf.

Seattle Housing Authority. (2008, September 30). *Yesler Terrace background report.* http://www.seattle.gov/parks/projects/yesler_terrace_park/files/background_report.pdf.

Seattle Housing Authority. (2011a, May 17). *Yesler Terrace development plan.* https://www.seattlehousing.org/sites/default/files/Yesler_Terrace_Development_Plan.pdf.

Seattle Housing Authority. (2011b, April). *Yesler Terrace redevelopment final environmental impact statement.* https://www.seattlehousing.org/sites/default/files/Yesler_Terrace_Final_Environmental_Impact_Statement.pdf.

Seattle Housing Authority. (2012a, March 1). *Yesler Terrace Phase III Citizen Review Committee meeting minutes.* https://www.seattlehousing.org/about-us/redevelopment/yesler-redevelopment/citizen-review-committee.

Seattle Housing Authority. (2012b, June 27). *Yesler Terrace Phase III Citizen Review Committee meeting minutes.* https://www.seattlehousing.org/about-us/redevelopment/yesler-redevelopment/citizen-review-committee.

Seattle Housing Authority. (2012c, December 13). *$19.73 million HUD grant awarded to Seattle Housing for Yesler Terrace redevelopment.* http://www.seattlehousing.org/news/releases/2012/choice-neighborhoods-grant/.

Seattle Housing Authority. (2013a, January 3). *Community workforce agreement.* http://seattlehousing.org/redevelopment/pdf/YT_CWA.pdf.

Seattle Housing Authority. (2013b, January 30). *Citizen Review Committee (CRC) meeting minutes.* https://www.seattlehousing.org/about-us/redevelopment/yesler-redevelopment/citizen-review-committee.

Seattle Housing Authority. (2014, October 13). *Housing Authority land sale helps revitalize Yesler Terrace.* http://seattlehousing.net/2014/10/housing-authority-land-sale-helps-revitalize-yesler-terrace/.

Seattle Housing Authority. (2015). *Yesler Terrace.* https://www.seattlehousing.org/housing/public/locations/yesler-terrace/.

Seattle Police Department. (2014). *Precinct crime statistics.* http://www.seattle.gov/police/crime/14_Stats/Precincts/2014_Precinct_Crime_Statistics.pdf.

Seattle University. (n.d.). *Yesler Terrace public safety pamphlet.* https://www.seattleu.edu/media/college-of-arts-and-sciences/departments/criminaljustice/documents/YTPSP_booklet_8.5x11_English_final_web-(1).pdf.

Seattle University. (2014, December 1). *Yesler Terrace economic development project full report.* https://www.seattlehousing.org/sites/default/files/SHA_SU_IEC_Economic_Development_Study_2014.pdf.

Seattle University. (2013). *Seattle University Youth Initiative Action Plan and Activity Report.* https://yescollab.org/wp-content/uploads/2015/03/lsp_img_SUYI-Action-Plan-2012-2015-Revised-Oct-13_110315-083218.pdf.

Sebenius, J. K. (1992). Negotiation analysis: A characterization and review. *Management Science, 38*(1), 18–38.

Seigel, S. M. (2014). Community benefits agreements in a union city: How the structure of CBAs may result in inefficient, unfair land use decisions. *Urban Lawyer,* 419–505.

Selmi, D. P. (2010). The contract transformation in land use regulation. *Stanford Law Review, 63,* 591–646.

Sentinel News Service. (2018, October 4). Constructing justice: Black workers graduate from new painters pre-apprenticeship. *Los Angeles Sentinel.* https://lasentinel.net/constructing-justice-black-workers-graduate-from-new-painters-pre-apprenticeship.html.

Severin, C. (2013). We built this city: The legality of community benefits agreements for big box construction under Title VII and the Equal Protection Clause. *Columbia Journal of Race and Law, 3*(2), 215–252.

Severson, K. (2013, April 21). In Atlanta, two churches lie in new stadium's path. *New York Times.* https://www.nytimes.com/2013/04/22/us/in-atlanta-two-churches-lie-in-new-stadiums-path.html?action=clickandmodule=RelatedCoverageandpgtype=Articleandregion=Footer.

Shapiro, J. (2013a, March 18). *ATL City Council approves public funds for new Falcons stadium.* NPR Atlanta. https://www.wabe.org/atl-city-council-approves-public-funds-new-falcons-stadium/.

Shapiro, J. (2013b, September 23). *Long-running tensions on display during stadium impact meeting.* NPR Atlanta. http://news.wabe.org/post/long-running-tensions-display-during-stadium-impact-meeting.

Shapiro, J. (2013c, November 20). *Tensions erupt at Falcons stadium impact meeting.* NPR Atlanta. http://news.wabe.org/post/tensions-erupt-falcons-stadium-impact-meeting.

Shapiro, J. (2013d, November 25). *Committee approves community benefits plan related to new Falcons stadium.* NPR Atlanta. http://news.wabe.org/post/committee-approves-community-benefits-plan-related-new-falcons-stadium.

Shapiro, J. (2013e, November 26). *Falcons stadium community benefits plan clears another hurdle.* NPR Atlanta. http://news.wabe.org/post/falcons-stadium-community-benefits-plan-clears-another-hurdle.

Shapiro, J. (2013f, November 27). *Full council to vote on Falcons stadium community benefits plan.* NPR Atlanta. http://news.wabe.org/post/full-council-vote-falcons-stadium-community-benefits-plan.

Shapiro, J. (2013g, December 3). *Falcons community benefits plan clears final legislative hurdle.* NPR Atlanta. http://news.wabe.org/post/falcons-community-benefits-plan-clears-final-legislative-hurdle.

Sheikh, N. (2008). Community benefits agreements: Can private contracts replace public responsibility? *Cornell Journal of Law and Public Policy, 18*(1), 223–246.

Shelton, T., and Poorthuis, A. (2019). The nature of neighborhoods: Using big data to rethink the geographies of Atlanta's neighborhood planning unit system. *Annals of the American Association of Geographers, 109*(5), 1341–1361.

Sides, J. (2013, November 12). *The center can hold: Leimert Park and Black Los Angeles.* KCET. https://www.kcet.org/shows/departures/the-center-can-hold-leimert-park-and-black-los-angeles.

Siegel, J. M. (2001). Project labor agreements and competitive bidding statutes. *University of Pennsylvania Journal of Labor and Employment Law, 3*(2), 295–332.

Sklar, D. L. (2015, April 8). *Activists call for more jobs for black workers in L.A.* MyNewsLa.com. https://mynewsla.com/business/2015/04/08/activists-gathering-to-call-for-more-jobs-for-black-workers/.

Small, V. (2016, January 31). *Could Abele sell county parks?* Urban Milwaukee. https://urbanmilwaukee.com/2016/01/31/could-abele-sell-county-parks/.

Smith, M., and Davey, M. (2018). Wisconsin's Scott Walker signs bills stripping powers from incoming governor. *New York Times.* https://www.nytimes.com/2018/12/14/us/wisconsin-governor-scott-walker.html.

Snyder, A. (2016). *Freeway removal in Milwaukee: Three case studies.* Master's thesis, University of Wisconsin–Milwaukee. Publication No. 1249. https://dc.uwm.edu/cgi/viewcontent.cgi?article=2254andcontext=etd.

Soja, E. W. (2010). *Seeking spatial justice.* Minneapolis: University of Minnesota Press.

Sound Transit. (1999, December 1). *Project labor agreement for the construction of Sound commuter and Link light rail projects.* https://www.soundtransit.org/sites/default/files/documents/pla-20201216.pdf.

Streeter, K. (2013, September 7). Workers hoping to build Crenshaw Line rally in Leimert Park. *Los Angeles Times.* http://articles.latimes.com/2013/sep/07/local/la-me-0908-blackworkers-rally-20130908.

Stiles, M. (2015, February 24). Vulcan exec: Yesler Terrace will be "kind of like South Lake Union." *Puget Sound Business Journal.* https://www.bizjournals.com/seattle/morning_call/2015/02/vulcan-exec-yesler-terrace-will-be-kind-of-like.html.

Stiles, M. (2016, May 6). Yesler Terrace: Inside the metamorphosis of Seattle's "projects." *Puget Sound Business Journal.* http://www.bizjournals.com/seattle/print-edition/2016/05/06/yesler-terrace-inside-the-metamorphosis-of.html.

Stiles, M. (2017, January 18). New acquisition cements Vulcan's $200 million plan for Yesler Terrace. *Puget Sound Business Journal.* http://www.bizjournals.com/seattle/news/2017/01/18/vulcans-yesler-terrace-redevelopment-seattle.html.

Stiles, M., and Parkhurst, E. (2016, January 15). Vulcan buys Yesler Terrace site, plans to build 650 apartments. *Puget Sound Business Journal.* https://www.bizjournals.com/seattle/blog/2016/01/vulcan-buys-yesler-terrace-site-plans-to-build-650.html.

Stoker, R. P. (1989). A regime framework for implementation analysis: Cooperation and reconciliation of federalist imperatives. *Review of Policy Research, 9*(1), 29–49. DOI: 10.1111/j.1541-1338.1989.tb01019.x.

Stoltze, F. (2011, May 26). *MTA Crenshaw Line: Black leaders cry foul on absence of Leimert Park stop.* 89.3 KPCC. https://archive.kpcc.org/news/2011/05/26/26918/african-american-leaders-cry-foul-mta-crenshaw-lin/.

Stone, C. N. (1993). Urban regimes and the capacity to govern: A political economy approach. *Journal of Urban Affairs, 15*(1), 1–28. DOI: 10.1111/j.1467-9906.1993.tb00300.x.

Stubbs, J. (2018, May 16). *Vulcan celebrates opening of 194-unit Batik in Seattle's historic Yesler Terrace neighborhood.* The Registry. https://news.theregistryps.com/vulcan-celebrates-opening-of-194-unit-batik-in-seattles-historic-yesler-terrace-neighborhood/.

Sulaiman, S. (2013, September 9). *Hope on the horizon? The Crenshaw Line and the question of jobs.* Streetsblog LA. http://la.streetsblog.org/2013/09/09/hope-on-the-horizon-the-crenshaw-line-and-the-question-of-jobs/.

Surborg, B., VanWynsberghe, R., and Wyly, E. (2008). Mapping the Olympic growth machine: Transnational urbanism and the growth machine diaspora. *City, 12*(3), 341–355. DOI: 10.1080/13604810802478920.

Susskind, L., McKearnan, S., and Thomas-Larmer, J. (Eds.) (1999). *The consensus building handbook.* Thousand Oaks, CA: SAGE.

Swanstrom, T., and Banks, B. (2009). Going regional: Community-based regionalism, transportation, and local hiring agreements. *Journal of Planning Education and Research, 28*(3), 355–367. DOI: 10.1177/0739456X08324684.

Thompson, C. (2018, July 30). *Report: Bucks fans paying tax dollars to put private company's name on arena built using Bucks fans' tax dollars.* Deadspin. https://deadspin.com/report-bucks-fans-paying-tax-dollars-to-put-private-co-1827985159.

Tierney, M. (2012, December 15). Falcons seek new dome, not Atlanta fixer-upper. *New York Times.* https://www.nytimes.com/2012/12/16/sports/football/atlanta-falcons-not-interested-in-fixer-upper-seek-a-new-stadium.html.

Tierney, M. (2014, July 27). Saying goodbye to friendship. *New York Times.* https://www.nytimes.com/2014/07/28/sports/football/in-path-of-falcons-new-stadium-atlanta-church-awaits-demolition.html?_r=0.

Trubey, J. S. (2017, November 20). Hotel and park to transform Georgia Dome site. *Atlanta Journal-Constitution.* http://www.myajc.com/news/local/hotel-and-park-transform-georgia-dome-site/hXRf8zp0fSweQl12aRU51O/.

Trubey, J. S., and Leslie, K. (2016, March 5). Daunting task to rebuild Atlanta's westside. *Atlanta Journal-Constitution.* http://www.myajc.com/news/daunting-task-rebuild-atlanta-westside/yESA2yYnO3dg6CFm0bassO/.

The Truth About Project Labor Agreements. (2015). *About TheTruthAboutPLAs.com.* http://thetruthaboutplas.com/about-us/.

Tucker, T. (2013a, March 23). An up-close look at the Falcons stadium deal. *Atlanta Journal-Constitution.* https://www.ajc.com/news/close-look-the-falcons-stadium-deal/MCfsBYNf D1LzX96unwy9qM/.

Tucker, T. (2013b, October 25). Eminent domain in play for Falcons stadium property. *Atlanta Journal-Constitution.* https://www.ajc.com/news/local/eminent-domain-play-for-falcons-stadium-property/2CtEiFmkomJqjbBEjnUgwM/.

Tucker, T. (2013c, December 3). GWCCA approves more land purchases for Falcons stadium. *Atlanta Journal-Constitution.* http://www.ajc.com/news/news/local/gwcca-approves-more-land-purchases-for-falcons-sta/nb938/.

Turnbull, L. (2017, May 24). *Former resident recalls growing up in Yesler Terrace.* Seattle Medium. http://seattlemedium.com/former-resident-recalls-growing-yesler-terrace/.

Umhoefer, D. (2016, November 27). From Milwaukee County to Madison, Scott Walker's rise marked by union battles. *Milwaukee Journal Sentinel.* https://projects.jsonline.com/news/2016/11/27/scott-walkers-path-to-power.html.

UCLA Labor Center. (2012). *Annual report 2011-2012.* https://irle.ucla.edu/wp-content/uploads/2016/02/AnnualReport2012.pdf.

UCLA Labor Center. (2014, October 21). *Ready to work places Black workers in jobs.* https://www.labor.ucla.edu/bwc-vincent/.

Upstream Artist Coalition for Equitable Development. (n.d.). *Create equitable & inclusive development in Seattle.* https://www.change.org/p/upstream-aced-create-equitable-inclusive-development-in-seattle-s-cd.

U.S. Bureau of Labor Statistics. (2013a). *Census of fatal occupational injuries summary.* http://www.bls.gov/news.release/cfoi.nr0.htm.

U.S. Bureau of Labor Statistics. (2013b). *Current population survey, Tables 26, 40, 41, 42, 43* [Data file]. https://www.bls.gov/cps/tables.htm.

U.S. Bureau of Labor Statistics. (2014). *Occupational outlook handbook, 2014-15 edition, construction laborers and helpers.* http://www.bls.gov/ooh/construction-and-extraction/construction-laborers-and-helpers.htm#tab-7.

U.S. Bureau of Labor Statistics. (2019). *Union affiliation of employed wage and salary workers by occupation and industry.* http://www.bls.gov/news.release/union2.t03.htm.

U.S. Census Bureau. (2010). *American Community Survey 2008-2012 (5-Year Estimates), Tables SE:A00001; SE:A01001; SE:A03001; SE:A04001; SE:A04002; SE:A10003; SE:A12001; SE:A17001; SE:A1005; SE:A14001; SE:A17004* [Data file]. http://www.socialexplorer.com/.

U.S. Census Bureau. (2012). *American Community Survey 2008-2012 (5-Year Estimates), Tables SE:A00001; SE:A01001; SE:A03001; SE:A04001; SE:A04002; SE:A10003; SE:A12001; SE:A17001; SE:A1005; SE:A14001* [Data file]. http://www.socialexplorer.com/.

U.S. Department of Housing and Urban Development. (n.d.). *Section 3.* https://www.hud.gov/section3.

U.S. Department of Housing and Urban Development. (2013). *2010-2013 Choice Neighborhoods implementation grant awards.* http://portal.hud.gov/hudportal/documents/huddoc?id=implementgrantlist.pdf.

U.S. Department of Housing and Urban Development. (2015). *Choice neighborhoods.* http://portal.hud.gov/hudportal/HUD?src=/program_offices/public_indian_housing/programs/ph/cn.

U.S. Department of Transportation. (2021, May 19). *U.S. Department of Transportation announces expanded local hire and workforce development pilot programs.* https://www

.transportation.gov/briefing-room/us-department-transportation-announces-expanded-local-hire-and-workforce-development.

U.S. General Accounting Office. (1998). *Project labor agreements: The extent of their use and related information*. GAO Publication No. GAO/GGD-98-82. http://www.gao.gov/archive/1998/gg98082.pdf.

Ubaldo, J. (2014, August 19). *U.S. Labor Secretary Thomas Perez tours Crenshaw/LAX Transit Project*. The Source. http://thesource.metro.net/2014/08/19/u-s-labor-secretary-thomas-perez-tours-crenshawlax-transit-project/.

Ubaldo, J. (2016, July 15). *Twenty one women graduate from Metro/L.A. Trade Tech construction boot camp*. The Source. https://thesource.metro.net/2016/07/15/twenty-one-women-graduate-from-metrol-a-trade-tech-construction-boot-amp/.

Urbinati, N. (2010). Unpolitical democracy. *Political Theory, 38*(1), 65–92. DOI: 10.1177/0090591709348188.

Vasquez, R. (2020, October 2). *Study: Repeal of Wisconsin's prevailing wage law led to drop in wages for construction workers*. Wisconsin Public Radio. https://www.wpr.org/study-repeal-wisconsins-prevailing-wage-law-led-drop-wages-construction-workers.

Vock, D. C. (2015, March 4). *Some cities may soon make contractors hire local for transportation projects join the discussion*. Governing. http://www.governing.com/topics/transportation-infrastructure/gov-usdot-cities-require-local-hiring.html.

Vulcan Real Estate. (n.d.). *South Lake Union*. https://vulcanrealestate.com/South-Lake-Union.aspx.

Vulcan Real Estate. (2018, September 8). *Creating opportunity for all in Yesler developments*. https://vulcanrealestate.com/Stories/Creating-Opportunity-for-All-in-Yesler-Development.aspx.

Wang, D. (2013, January 22). *Vulcan bids on Yesler Terrace makeover*. KUOW. https://www.kuow.org/stories/vulcan-bids-yesler-terrace-makeover.

Weikel, D. (2012, January 26). Big Metro projects will offer jobs to disadvantaged workers. *Los Angeles Times*. http://latimesblogs.latimes.com/lanow/2012/01/big-metro-projects-will-offer-jobs-to-disadvantaged-workers.html.

Weiland, A. (2018, December 3). Avenir Apartments downtown sold for $22.3 million. *Milwaukee Business Times*. https://biztimes.com/avenir-apartments-downtown-sold-for-22-3-million/.

Weis, D. (2017, October 9). *Milwaukee Bucks retrain jobless workers to build new arena*. Association of Equipment Manufacturers. https://www.aem.org/news/milwaukee-bucks-retrain-jobless-workers-to-build-new-arena.

Weishan Jr., J. (2015, September 16). *County Board committee passes employment, environmental standards in development agreements involving county land, subsidies*. Urban Milwaukee. https://urbanmilwaukee.com/pressrelease/county-board-committee-passes-employment-environmental-standards-in-development-agreements-involving-county-land-subsidies/.

Wheatley, T. (2012a, September 6). *The stadium effect*. Creative Loafing Atlanta. http://clatl.com/atlanta/the-stadium-effect/Content?oid=6296522.

Wheatley, T. (2012b, December 20). *Community plan for new Falcons stadium takes shape*. Creative Loafing Atlanta. http://clatl.com/atlanta/the-stadium-effect/Content?oid=6296522.

The White House. (2019, October 31). *Executive Order on Improving Federal Contractor Operations by Revoking Executive Order 13495*. https://www.whitehouse.gov/presidential-actions/executive-order-improving-federal-contractor-operations-revoking-executive-order-13495/.

The White House. (2022, February 4). *Executive Order on use of project labor agreements for federal construction projects.* https://www.whitehouse.gov/briefing-room/presidential-actions/2022/02/04/executive-order-on-use-of-project-labor-agreements-for-federal-construction-projects/.

Whitely, J. (2017, August 18). *Redfin predicts the hottest neighborhoods to close out 2017.* Business Wire. https://www.businesswire.com/news/home/20170818005074/en/Redfin-Predicts-Hottest-Neighborhoods-Close-2017.

Wickert, D. (2016, June 23). Atlanta's Councilman Bond accused of 300 campaign finance violations. https://www.ajc.com/news/local-govt--politics/atlanta-councilman-bond-accused-300-campaign-finance-violations/BohByY9Te8zQqD8PIzheUI/.

Williams, D. (2014, December 19). Mayor Reed appoints board to lead West Atlanta redevelopment. *Atlanta Business Chronicle.* http://www.bizjournals.com/atlanta/blog/capitol_vision/2014/12/mayor-reed-appoints-board-to-lead-west-atlanta.html.

Wisconsin Highways. (2016). *Milwaukee Freeways: Park Freeway.* Wisconsin Highways. http://www.wisconsinhighways.org/milwaukee/park.html.

Wisconsin Legislative Council. (2013). *2013 Wisconsin Act 14.* http://docs.legis.wisconsin.gov/2013/related/lcactmemo/act014.pdf.

Wisconsin State Legislature. (2015, July 13). *2015 Wisconsin Act 55.* https://docs.legis.wisconsin.gov/2015/related/acts/55.

Wolf-Powers, L. (2010). Community benefits agreements and local government: A review of recent evidence. *Journal of the American Planning Association, 76*(2), 141–159. DOI: 10.1080/01944360903490923.

Wolf-Powers, L. (2012). Community benefits agreements in a value capture context. In G. K. Ingram and Y.-H. Hong (Eds.), *Value capture and land policies* (pp. 217–228). Cambridge, MA: Lincoln Institute of Land Policy.

WSB Web Staff. (2013, March 19). *Atlanta City Council votes yes for new Falcons stadium.* WSB Radio. https://www.wsbradio.com/news/atlanta-city-council-votes-yes-for-new-falcons-stadium/YmrviQVGFAZ8w5FhHAq0vO/.

Young, B. (2011, March 19). Seattle's Yesler Terrace faces the future. *Seattle Times.* http://www.seattletimes.com/pacific-nw-magazine/seattles-yesler-terrace-faces-the-future/.

Young, B. (2015, October 31). Some question if Yesler spirit will live on after redevelopment. *Seattle Times.* https://www.seattletimes.com/business/real-estate/some-question-if-yesler-spirit-will-live-on-after-redevelopment/.

Zapata, M. A., and Bates, L. K. (2015). Equity planning revisited. *Journal of Planning Education and Research, 35*(3), 245–248. https://doi.org/10.1177/0739456X15589967.

Zillgitt, J. (2018, October 19). How a new downtown arena saved the Bucks from leaving Milwaukee. *USA Today.* https://www.usatoday.com/story/sports/nba/bucks/2018/10/19/milwaukee-bucks-fiserv-forum-new-downtown-arena/1695685002/.

INDEX

Figures and tables are indicated by page numbers followed by *fig.* and *tab.* respectively.

accountability: agreement formulation and, 13–14, 158–62; Atlanta Falcons Community Benefits Plan and, 43, 45–49, 52, 156; benefits-sharing agreements and, 4–6, 10, 105, 224n15; community participation in oversight, 163–66, 172, 224n3; developers and, 4–6, 84, 103–6; implementation transparency and, 166–67; labor unions and, 4, 73–74; leadership transitions and, 168; Metro PLA and fragile, 5–6, 13, 113, 124–29, 135, 138–40, 155, 157; noncompliance penalties and, 159–61; oversight bodies and, 161–62; PERC and, 81, 88, 106–7, 156; strategies for, 159–71; third party expertise and, 162–63, 223n1; Yesler Terrace Redevelopment Project and, 63, 156
affirmative action, 66, 117, 188, 226n2
agreement formulation: accountability and, 13–14, 158–62; community bypass and, 13, 56, 65, 73; community oversight and, 165–66; community participation in, 116, 145, 169–71; equity goals in, 170–71; flawed negotiations and, 146; labor unions and, 116; managerial disconnect and, 13; noncompliance penalties in, 159–61, 183; nonresponsive community investment and, 13; oversight bodies and, 161–62; political division in, 86; third party expertise and, 163
Allen, Paul, 59
Aloft Hotel, 90, 91*fig.*
Arthur M. Blank Family Foundation. *See* Blank Foundation
Atlanta: civil rights movement and, 18–19; cosmopolitan vision for, 17, 19; economic inequality in, 16, 21, 23; land development in, 29; neighborhood demographics in, 24*tab.*; neighborhood planning unit structure in, 19; Olympic Games and, 19–22, 206n20; pro-growth vision, 15, 17–18; stadium construction in, 16–23, 153–54; top-down community investment approach, 17, 30, 33, 35–36. *See also* Atlanta Westside
Atlanta Braves, 18, 20–22
Atlanta Committee for the Olympic Games (ACOG), 20–21
Atlanta Falcons: Atlanta-Fulton County stadium and, 18; benefits-sharing agreements and, 15–16; Blank and, 10, 15, 22; Georgia Dome and, 19, 22; new stadium plans and, 15–17, 19, 21–22. *See also* Mercedes-Benz stadium (Atlanta Falcons)
Atlanta Falcons Community Benefits Plan: accountability and, 43, 45–49, 52, 156; Blank Foundation and, 10–11, 29–31, 34–36, 38–39, 44–46, 48–51; case study methodology, 189, 190–91*tab.*, 194–95, 195*tab.*, 196, 196*tab.*; circumvention of community committee, 15–18, 31–34; community activists and, 28–29, 32–33, 45–52, 164; Community Benefits Plan Committee and, 29–32, 38–39, 47, 51, 162, 194; community demand for legally-binding agreement, 30–31; community development and, 4, 37–38; community leverage and, 5, 47, 49, 51–52; enforceability of, 32–33, 38, 46, 50; flawed negotiations and, 47–48, 52, 146; grantmaking process in, 11, 17, 29–30, 38–39, 42–46, 209n87; implementation failures in, 10–11, 51; Invest Atlanta and, 29–31, 33–34, 38–39, 41–44, 46, 48–50; Invest Atlanta grants, 40*tab.*, 41, 41*tab.*, 42–43, 48; lack of transparency

Atlanta Falcons Community Benefits Plan (*continued*) and, 43, 45, 51; local government control of, 30–37, 46–47, 50–51; neighborhood improvement projects, 42–43; nonresponsive community investment and, 11, 15–17, 28, 37–38, 45–46, 50–52, 153–54, 162, 173; public funding and, 29, 33, 36; tokenism in, 16–17, 52; top-down community investment approach, 30, 33, 35–36, 38–39, 42, 44–46, 48–52, 208n84; workforce development in, 39, 41–42. *See also* Mercedes-Benz stadium (Atlanta Falcons)
Atlanta–Fulton County stadium, 18
Atlanta Neighborhoods United for Fairness (A'NUFF), 21
Atlanta Police Foundation, 42, 44
Atlanta United, 23
Atlanta Westside: benefits-sharing agreements and, 15–17; Black communities in, 16–21, 27; Black student organizing and, 19; city investment in, 29, 35–36; civil rights movement and, 18–19; displacement of community, 16, 36, 45, 50, 154; gentrification and, 34–35, 154; Georgia Dome impact and, 19–20; harmful impact of development and, 16–17, 20–21, 45, 173; local advocacy in, 17, 28; neighborhood demographics in, 24*tab.*; nonresponsive community investment and, 17, 37–38, 45–46, 50–51, 154; real estate speculation in, 23, 25, 27, 34; stadium construction in, 21, 23, 28–29, 34, 36, 37*fig.*; Westside Future Fund, 35; Westside Momentum, 44; Westside Neighborhood Prosperity Fund, 198–201. *See also* Atlanta; Atlanta Falcons Community Benefits Plan
Avenir Apartments, 89, 98

Barrett, Tom, 94
Bates, L., 170
benefits-sharing agreements: accountability and, 4–6, 10, 84, 158–71; advantages of, 172–74; agreement formulation and, 13–14, 56; community activists and, 2, 6–9, 143; 156; community-labor coalitions and, 143–44; community outcomes and, 139–40, 155–56; community stakeholders and, 5, 7–9, 14, 144–49, 163–66, 177; consensus building and, 9, 145; economic downturns and, 174–75; emergence of, 179–88; equity goals in, 8, 143, 170–74, 180; expedited development through, 9, 52, 67, 77, 177; foundation for, 178–79; implementation challenges, 150–53; implementation failures in, 4–6, 9–10, 13–14; land use regulation and, 9, 204n30; local government control of, 169–70; long-term neighborhood stability and, 168–69; mutually beneficial outcomes and, 146, 223n11; negotiation challenges, 145–50; neoliberalism and, 144; policy-making and, 9, 84, 115–16, 138, 171, 205n33; power asymmetries and, 13–14, 153; pro-development interests and, 4, 105–6, 135, 144; reduction of harmful development and, 172–73; urban development projects and, 2–6, 143; urban governance and, 9–10, 204n30. *See also* community benefits agreements (CBAs); project labor agreements (PLAs)
Biden, Joe, 184
Black Lives Matter, 75
Blank, Arthur: Atlanta Falcons and, 10, 15, 22; Atlanta United soccer team and, 23; benefits-sharing agreements and, 16, 49; Home Depot and, 15; neighborhood improvement projects, 51–52; new stadium plans and, 15, 18, 22–23; stadium revenue and, 23, 36
Blank Foundation: accountability and, 45–47, 52; capacity building and, 44; community benefits plan and, 10–11, 29, 31, 33–34, 37–39, 42, 45–46, 48, 51, 146; control of community investment, 29–30, 34–36, 38–39, 43–46, 48–50, 153–54, 208n84; grantmaking and, 44–46, 209n103; nonresponsive community investment and, 38, 153–54, 156, 160, 173; stadium construction and, 25, 29–31, 33–34; Westside Future Fund, 35; Westside Neighborhood Prosperity Fund, 198–201. *See also* Atlanta Falcons Community Benefits Plan
Bloom, David, 75
Bond, Julian, 15
Bond, Michael Julian, 15–16, 29, 33, 35, 47–48
Bronx Terminal Market CBA, 183
Brostoff, Jonathan, 96
Bush, George H. W., 184

Bush, George W., 184
Bus Riders Union, 112, 125

Campbell, Bill, 19
Cathy, Dan, 35
CBA. *See* community benefits agreements (CBAs)
Choice Neighborhoods Implementation Grant, 35, 55
Citizen Action of Wisconsin, 82
Clinton, Bill, 184
collaboration, 145, 222n5, 223n11
community activists: Atlanta benefits-sharing agreement and, 28–29, 32–33, 45–52; benefits-sharing agreements and, 2, 6–9, 143, 177, 179–80; leverage with officials and, 6–7, 9, 29; Metro PLA and, 114–19, 124–27, 130–35; Rainier Vista public housing redevelopment and, 55; Yesler Terrace redevelopment and, 60
community benefits agreements (CBAs): accountability and, 105, 224n15; activist leverage in, 6–7, 9, 204n18; archival documents for, 196*tab.*; community activists and, 2, 6–7, 180; community-labor coalitions and, 6, 143–44; competing narratives in, 217n84; criticism of, 182–83; defining, 2, 180; developer co-option of, 182; economic downturns and, 174–75; equity goals in, 7–8; failed distributions and, 173–74; implementation and, 4–6, 109–10; inclusive deliberations and, 180–81, 224n15; land use approval process and, 180; local government and, 180–82; power asymmetries and, 182; urban development projects and, 2–7, 217n84; value capture opportunities and, 181; workforce protections and, 204n30. *See also* benefits-sharing agreements
community organizing: accountability and, 49; agreement formulation and, 116, 145; barriers to information, 165; benefits negotiation and, 28, 149; implementation oversight and, 12–13, 150, 163–66, 224n3; local development and, 74, 106; local government resistance to, 51, 153; policy enforcement and, 152–53; for regional equity, 10
community outcomes: accountability strategies and, 159; benefits-sharing agreements and, 139–40, 155–56, 172; contractors and, 12, 71, 73, 126, 135–37,

139; implementation failures and, 4–5, 11–12, 14, 45–49, 51–52, 56, 150–51; labor unions and, 73–74, 146; Metro PLA and, 12–13, 119, 124, 129, 135–40; negotiations and, 152; power asymmetries and, 13; pro-growth resistance to, 10, 12, 17, 151–52
community workforce agreements (CWAs): community-labor coalitions and, 8, 65, 74; labor unions and, 11–12, 56, 64–65, 212n40; worker protections and, 204n30; PLAs and, 3, 8, 185, 203n8, 225n44; targeted hire initiatives, 3, 11–12, 185, 203n11; Yesler Terrace redevelopment and, 56, 64–65. *See also* project labor agreements (PLAs)
consensus building: benefits-sharing agreements and, 9, 145; collaboration and, 145; defining, 223n6; deliberative processes and, 146–47; implementation conflicts and, 120; negotiation and, 145, 147–48; power asymmetries and, 147–48
construction jobs: accountability and, 126–27; apprenticeships and, 117, 219n34; Black workers and, 115, 117, 129, 134–35, 141; core workers and, 124; discrimination in, 73, 112; diversity in, 130; female workers and, 128, 128*tab.*, 129–31, 133; impact of recession on, 69, 112; job creation and, 124; local hiring and, 112, 115, 119, 136–37; marginalized groups and, 113, 115, 117, 121; Measure R and, 112; Metro PLA and, 113–14, 119, 129–30; PERC and, 86, 100, 104; prevailing wages and, 85, 107; Residents Preference Program, 100; Southern California transportation projects and, 136–37; Yesler Terrace residents and, 64–65, 68–69, 71, 73–74. *See also* contractors
construction unions: apprenticeships and training by, 137, 185–86, 226n51; community inclusion goals, 56, 64–65, 68–69; community workforce agreements and, 56; dispatch process and, 226n45; exclusion of women and workers of color, 8, 64, 73, 115; existing lists and, 69, 74; impact of recession on, 69; PLAs and, 184; preapprenticeship programs and, 137, 186–87, 226n51; Section 3 hiring and, 74, 213n65; targeted hiring and, 213n59; Yesler Terrace Community Workforce Agreement and, 11–12, 56, 64–70. *See also* labor unions

contractors: accountability and, 128–30, 133–35; community monitoring and, 133–35; community outcomes and, 12, 71, 73, 126, 135–37, 139; community workforce agreements and, 65; core workers and, 124; implementation goals and, 72, 151; jobs coordinator and, 117, 125, 127; local hiring and, 136; Metro PLA oversight of, 12, 126, 128–30, 133–37; PERC and, 86, 97, 100; PLAs and, 3; prevailing wage provisions and, 100, 105; reputational concerns and, 136–37; SHA oversight of, 70–74; union referral process and, 137; Yesler Terrace hiring and, 67–68, 70–74

Crenshaw Line project (Los Angeles County): accountability and, 124–29, 135, 138, 140; Black neighborhoods and, 111–15, 120–23; Black workers and, 112, 117–18, 133–35, 141; construction disruptions, 122, 122*fig.*, 123, 123*fig.*; disadvantaged worker hiring and, 117–18, 128*tab.*, 129–31, 131*fig.*, 133–34, 134*fig.*; female workers and, 129–31, 222n99; gentrification and, 123, 149; implementation oversight and, 125–26, 133–40; job creation and, 124, 129; local hiring and, 114–15, 117, 129–30, 136; map of, 121*fig.*; project construction on, 120; public support for, 119; resident demographics, 120–21; South Los Angeles and, 12, 111–13, 123. *See also* Los Angeles Metro PLA

deliberative processes, 9, 146–48, 223n10
developers: accountability and, 4–6, 84, 103–6; defining, 203n1; dominance in deliberations, 182; expedited development through benefits-sharing, 9, 52, 76–77, 177; implementation failures and, 183; negotiated community benefits and, 9, 106, 150, 181; negotiated development agreements and, 177–79; PERC and, 84–85, 87–90, 94, 97; resistance to community benefits provisions, 82–84, 87, 94, 97, 105–6, 179
Dinan, Jamie, 95
disadvantaged business enterprises (DBEs), 86, 94, 185
disadvantaged workers: defining, 219n29; Metro PLA and, 117–18, 131; Port of Oakland PLA and, 3; targeted hire initiatives, 66, 117–18, 128*tab.*, 129–31, 133, 203n11, 219n31; union apprenticeships and, 186
Downtown Milwaukee Plan, 80

East Bay Alliance for a Sustainable Economy (EBASE), 8
Edens, Wes, 95
Elliot Bay Seawall project, 73
Epps, LeDaya, 131

Falcons stadium project. *See* Mercedes-Benz stadium (Atlanta Falcons)
Federal Highway Administration (FHA), 93
Federal Transit Administration (FTA), 116, 119, 220n45
Fiserv Forum (Milwaukee Bucks stadium), 98, 100
Foxx, Anthony, 218n27
freeway construction: blocking access to downtown, 79; displacement of neighborhoods and, 18, 78–79; Los Angeles Metro and, 113; Milwaukee Black communities and, 78–79; Park East redevelopment and, 79–80, 92–93, 95
Friendship Baptist Church, 27

gentrification: Atlanta Westside and, 34–35, 154, 174; community benefits as protection from, 169, 172, 175; L.A. Live project and, 7; Olympics-related development and, 21; Seattle and, 75–76; South Los Angeles and, 123, 149; stadium construction and, 30, 34–35, 174; urban development projects and, 142; Yesler Terrace redevelopment and, 75–76
Georgia Center for Nonprofits, 44
Georgia Dome: Atlanta Falcons and, 19, 22; Black residents near, 17, 23; demolition of, 36; displacement of Black community, 17, 21; failed community benefits and, 19–20, 30–31, 35, 50, 173; investment in Westside communities and, 19–20; public funding for, 206n25
Georgia STAND-UP, 28, 51
Georgia Trust Fund, 20
Georgia World Congress Center, 22–23
Georgia World Congress Center Authority (GWCCA), 27, 36, 206n25
Good Jobs and Livable Neighborhoods Coalition, 82–83, 88

Haas, G., 7–8
Hagar Civilization Training Missionary, 42–43
Hendrix, Jimi, 57
H. J. Russell & Company, 41
Home Depot Backyard, 36

Immergluck, Dan, 34
implementation: benefits-sharing agreements and, 4–6, 9–14, 110, 120, 150–52; community participation in, 170–71; data reporting and, 129–30; delayed development and, 80–81, 88, 97–101; flawed negotiations and, 52, 146, 152; fragile accountability and, 124–27, 135–40; Invest Atlanta and, 38, 43, 46; leadership transitions and, 168; limited community influence in, 4–5, 11–12, 14, 45–49, 51–52, 150–51; managerial disconnect and, 101–7; PLAs and, 187; policy approval battles and, 83–84, 97–98; political divisions and, 87, 107–8; power asymmetries and, 13, 150; pro-development control of, 150–52; SHA control of, 56, 67, 70–73; top-down enforcement and, 150, 153–55; transparency and, 166–67; urban elite influence and, 150–51
Invest Atlanta: accountability and, 43, 46–47; capital project funding and, 29; Community Benefits Plan Committee and, 29, 31, 38–39; Community Improvement Fund grants, 40*tab.*, 41, 41*tab.*, 42–43; control of community investment, 29–30, 33–34, 38–39, 42–44, 46, 48–50, 208n84; Georgia Trust Fund and, 20; lack of transparency and, 43, 45; nonresponsive community investment and, 38, 153–54, 156, 160, 173; programs and initiatives, 29, 207n44; Westside TAD neighborhood strategic implementation plan, 38–39. *See also* Atlanta Falcons Community Benefits Plan

Jackson, Maynard, 19
Jones, Yvonne, 32

Keating, Larry, 17, 28, 206n20
King, Martin Luther, Jr., 18
King County Equity Now, 75
Kohl's Corporation, 89–90, 92, 94

labor unions: accountability and, 4, 73–74; agreement formulation and, 116; apprenticeships and training by, 137, 185–86, 226n51; community coalitions and, 6, 8, 143–44, 186; community inclusion goals, 64–65; community workforce agreements and, 11–12, 56, 64–65, 69–70, 212n40; dispatch process and, 225n45; exclusion of women and workers of color, 8, 64; implementation goals and, 72, 151; Metro PLA and, 114–15; PLAs and, 3, 183–88; preapprenticeship programs and, 137, 186–87, 226n51; reputational concerns and, 69, 74; Section 3 hiring, 68–70, 73–74, 212n49; targeted hiring and, 11–12, 213n59; urban growth and, 64–65, 74, 143, 147. *See also* construction unions
LABWC. *See* Los Angeles Black Worker Center (LABWC)
L.A. Live project, 7–8, 182
land use: community activists and, 6–7; community benefits agreements (CBAs) and, 180–82; local government authority and, 204n30; negotiated development agreements and, 177–79; opposition to public financing of development, 29; power asymmetries and, 179; urban governance and, 9, 178–79
Lasry, Marc, 95
Lindsay Street Park, 42, 42*fig.*
local government: Atlanta Falcons Community Benefits Plan and, 33, 35, 41, 46–48, 50, 153, 162; benefits-sharing negotiations and, 48, 169–70, 178–79; community benefits agreements (CBAs) and, 180–82; community distrust and, 16, 20, 30–31, 50; community pressure and, 29, 132, 156, 164; marginalization of community participation and, 4–5, 17, 50–51, 83, 163; Metro PLA and, 113; mutual interdependence in negotiation, 145–46; negotiated development agreements and, 177–79; nonresponsive community investment and, 153; PERC and, 99, 101; pro-development interests and, 60, 81, 142, 144, 147. *See also* urban governance
local residents: affordable housing development and, 209n103; anti-growth interests and, 147; benefits-sharing agreements and, 175; construction jobs and, 112, 115, 119, 136–37; economic opportunity and, 111–12; hiring initiatives and, 114, 117–19, 129–30, 137, 139, 185, 218n26, 220n45, 226n45; historical exclusion of, 8; preapprenticeship programs and, 137; project harm and, 2, 7–8, 147; Yesler Terrace redevelopment and, 11, 55, 65
Lofton, Andrew, 75
Los Angeles, 114, 117, 192, 226n2. *See also* South Los Angeles

Los Angeles Alliance for a New Economy (LAANE), 7–8, 82, 114–16, 138
Los Angeles Black Worker Center (LABWC): Black worker advocacy and, 114–15, 133–35; Crenshaw Line implementation oversight and, 125–26, 133–36, 138–39, 152, 164; jobs coordinator hiring and, 127, 135; Metro PLA and, 114–16, 133–35, 137–38; preapprenticeship programs and, 137
Los Angeles County Metropolitan Transportation Authority (Metro): community alliances and, 118–19; community relationships and, 125; impact of construction on businesses, 122–23; light-rail lines and, 111–13, 118, 121–23; low-income residents and, 112–15, 118, 218n7; Measure J, 118; Measure R, 111–18, 120, 125, 128; public funding for, 118, 130; South Los Angeles and, 112; targeted hire initiatives, 115. *See also* Crenshaw Line project (Los Angeles County); Los Angeles Metro PLA
Los Angeles Metro PLA: apprenticeships and, 117, 127, 128*tab.*, 219n34; archival documents for, 196; benefits-sharing agreements and, 113, 172; case study methodology, 191–92, 192–93*tab.*, 194, 196–97; community development and, 4, 116; community outcomes and, 135–40; community stakeholders and, 12–13, 114–19, 124–27, 130–41, 164; contractor oversight and, 12, 126, 128–30, 133–37; data reporting for, 127–28, 128*tab.*, 129–31, 133, 221n74; disadvantaged worker hiring and, 117–18, 128*tab.*, 129–31, 133, 219n29; fragile accountability and, 5–6, 13, 113, 124–29, 135, 138–40, 155, 157; implementation of, 12–13, 117, 125–26, 132; lack of transparency and, 118, 129–30, 133–35; local hiring and, 114, 117–18, 128*tab.*, 129–30, 137, 139, 218n27, 220n45; as national model, 119; outcomes, 127–28, 128*tab.*, 129, 132, 134–35, 221n74; public funding for, 116–18; public narrative and, 119, 131–32; targeted hiring and, 113–18, 125, 155; top-down enforcement and, 116, 139, 155–56; worker demographics and, 127–29, 221n74; worker visibility and, 131, 131*fig.*, 132–34; workforce development in, 114–16, 119. *See also* Crenshaw Line project (Los Angeles County)
Los Angeles Staples Center, 82

Los Angeles Unified School District, 3, 114, 192

Marcoux, Rocky, 94
Marcus Theatres project, 88
Margerum, R. D., 205n34, 223n6, 223n10
Mercedes-Benz stadium (Atlanta Falcons), 37*fig.*; benefits-sharing agreements and, 28–34; construction of, 34, 36, 38; marginalization of community opposition and, 5, 11, 27–28, 153–54; public funding for, 22–23, 29, 36, 206n25; relocation of churches and, 27; stadium naming rights and, 23. *See also* Atlanta Falcons Community Benefits Plan
Metro. *See* Los Angeles County Metropolitan Transportation Authority (Metro)
Metro PLA. *See* Los Angeles Metro PLA
Milwaukee: benefits-sharing agreements and, 80, 82–84; freeway demolition and, 79; Milwaukee Bucks stadium construction, 95; neighborhood clearances in, 78–79; Park East Freeway project and, 78–79, 214n2; Park East redevelopment and, 79–86, 88–90; political divisions in, 83–85, 108; redevelopment outside PERC, 90, 92; tax incremental district and, 80, 84–85, 88. *See also* Park East Redevelopment Compact (PERC)
Milwaukee Bucks stadium: benefits-sharing agreements and, 99–100; economic impact of, 95–96; funding sources, 95–96, 216n60; naming rights sale, 100; opening of, 98; owner revenue from, 96, 100; PERC proposal, 95–96, 99; prevailing wage provision, 100; public funding for, 95–96, 100, 216n60; workforce development in, 100
Milwaukee Common Council, 82–83, 214n12, 215n16
Milwaukee County: affordable housing development, 86–87; Black communities in, 78–79; Board of Supervisors and, 83, 87–88, 97, 105–8, 194; community development and, 108; discounted land sales and, 85, 89, 93, 95–96, 101; Economic Development Division, 87, 101; enforcement and, 106–7; freeway construction in, 78–79; local hiring and, 86, 104; managerial disconnect and, 100–102, 106–9; outside agency oversight and, 93; oversight of PERC, 93, 97–109, 217n80; political divisions in, 87–88, 107–9. *See*

also Park East Redevelopment Compact (PERC)
Milwaukee School of Engineering, 89, 89*fig.*
Mitchell, Ceasar, 32
Morehouse College, 27
Mount Vernon Baptist Church, 27

National Federation of Community Development Credit Unions, 42
negotiations: accountability strategies and, 159; community bypass in, 16–17, 31, 45, 73, 146; community leverage and, 4, 16, 46–47, 143–44, 151; community pressure and, 181; community resistance to development in, 27, 174; consensus building and, 145–49, 222n4; developer opposition to community benefits in, 104–5; local government control of, 169–70; managerial disconnect and, 104; power asymmetries in, 13, 147–48, 150, 167–68; private development agreements and, 178–79; pro-growth dominance in, 56; scale asymmetry and, 169; third party expertise and, 162–63; transparency and, 166
neoliberalism, 6, 144, 204n17
neutrality agreements, 204n30
Norquist, John, 79

oaksATL Community Development, Inc., 43
Obama, Barack, 184
Obama, Michelle, 131
O'Donnell, Kristin, 62–63
Olympic Games (1996), 19–22, 206n20

Palomar Hotel and Residences, 88
Park East Advisory Committee, 88, 98–99
Park East Freeway project, 78–79, 214n2
Park East Redevelopment Compact (PERC): accountability and, 81, 88, 106–7, 156; affordable housing development, 86–87; brownfields issues and, 92, 93*fig.*, 96; case study methodology, 189, 190–91*tab.*, 194–95, 195*tab.*, 196, 196*tab.*; community advocates and, 80, 89–90, 106–7; community and economic development (CED) fund, 86, 101, 104; community development and, 4, 84–85, 88, 91, 107–8; county oversight and, 83–87, 93, 97–109, 217n80; delayed development and, 89–91, 91*fig.*, 92–94, 98, 100, 107; developer compliance and, 103–6; developer opposition to, 82–84, 87, 94, 97; developer proposals, 88–90, 90*fig.*, 91–93, 96; disadvantaged business enterprises (DBEs) and, 86; environmental remediation work and, 92, 95–96; impact of recession on, 12, 76, 80, 88–92, 94, 109; implementation failures in, 12, 84, 97, 104–5, 107–10; implementation process, 98–103; lack of transparency and, 102; local hiring and, 86, 100, 217n80; loss of original stakeholders in, 5, 76, 80–81; managerial disconnect and, 5, 12, 76, 80–81, 84, 87, 93–94, 97–104, 106–10, 154–57; marketing campaign and, 94; Milwaukee Bucks stadium and, 95–96, 98, 216n60; prevailing wage provision, 87, 94, 100, 104–5; sustainable development and, 86–87, 108; tax incremental district and, 80, 84–85, 88; terms of, 85–88
Park East Square project, 88–89, 104
Partnership for Working Families (PWF), 7–8, 28–29, 82
Peace Preparatory Academy, 43
PERC. *See* Park East Redevelopment Compact (PERC)
PLA. *See* project labor agreements (PLAs)
Port of Los Angeles, 192
Port of Oakland PLA, 3, 8, 185, 187
preapprenticeship programs, 137, 186–87
Priority Hire Ordinance (Seattle), 3
project labor agreements (PLAs): archival documents for, 196, 196*tab.*, 197; community activists and, 2; community benefits and, 185, 188; community development and, 185–86; community-labor coalitions and, 186–87; community participation in oversight, 187–88; community workforce agreements and, 3, 8, 185, 203n8, 204n30, 225n44; criticism of, 184; defining, 3, 180; economic downturns and, 186; executive orders and, 184–85; health and safety provisions, 185; implementation and, 187; labor unions and, 3, 183–88; large-scale projects and, 186; legality of, 225n40; Metro PLA and, 191–92, 192–93*tab.*, 194, 196–97; nonunion contractors and, 184, 225n36; outside compliance mechanisms and, 187–88; penalties for striking in, 183; politicization of, 184; prevention of labor delays and, 183; targeted hire initiatives, 185–86, 213n59, 225n45; third party expertise and, 163; Yesler Terrace CWA, 191–92, 192–93*tab.*, 194, 196–97. *See also* benefits-sharing agreements; community workforce agreements (CWA)

PWF. *See* Partnership for Working Families (PWF)

Quest Community Development Organization, 44
Quest Healthy Workforce Center, 39

Rainier Vista public housing redevelopment, 53–55, 62, 75
Reed, Kasim, 22, 27, 207n44
Ridley-Thomas, Mark, 113–16, 133, 136, 140

Seattle: affirmative action ban, 66, 192, 226n2; community workforce agreements and, 212n40; crime statistics in, 211n27; gentrification in, 75–76; Little Saigon, 60, 76; neighborhood density in, 59–61; progrowth interests in, 56, 58; redevelopment projects in, 53–60; South Lake Union neighborhood redevelopment, 61
Seattle Displacement Coalition, 55, 75
Seattle Housing Authority (SHA): community bypass and, 5, 53, 56; community workforce agreements and, 56, 63–74; HUD grants and, 55; internal administration of the CWA, 70–72, 156; lawsuit against, 53–54; targeted worker hiring and, 68–70, 74, 213n60; Yesler Terrace land sale and, 59–61, 66–67; Yesler Terrace redevelopment and, 11, 52–53, 58–69, 194, 212n51. *See also* Yesler Terrace Community Workforce Agreement; Yesler Terrace Redevelopment Project (Seattle)
Section 3 program: Advisory Committee, 67, 70–71, 73, 160, 213n67; construction jobs and, 68, 213n65; CWA hiring process and, 66, 69–71, 212n49, 213n60; economic targeting requirement, 68, 212n46; enforcement and, 71–72, 160–61; hiring outside Yesler Terrace, 69–70
SHA. *See* Seattle Housing Authority (SHA)
Sound Transit PLA, 187, 192
South Los Angeles: Black communities in, 111–12; Crenshaw Line and, 12, 111–13, 123; gentrification in, 123, 149; historical injustices and, 117, 133; housing costs in, 124; LABWC and, 114–15; Metro and, 12, 112; stadium construction and, 123–24
Spelman College, 27, 35
stadium construction: displacement of neighborhoods and, 123–24; economic impacts of, 22, 95, 216n60; eminent domain and, 27; Falcons stadium project, 22–23, 25, 27; gentrification and, 30, 34–35, 123–24, 174; harmful impact on Black communities, 18, 21, 28, 34, 96, 154; Milwaukee Bucks stadium project, 95–96, 216n60; naming rights revenue, 23; projects in Atlanta, 16–22; public funding for, 22–23, 29, 36, 95–96, 100, 206n25, 216n60; real estate speculation and, 23, 25, 27. *See also* Atlanta Falcons Community Benefits Plan; Mercedes-Benz stadium (Atlanta Falcons)

targeted hire initiatives: affirmative action ban, 66, 117, 192; apprenticeships and, 117, 127, 128*tab.*, 185; community workforce agreements and, 3, 203n11; defining, 219n31; disadvantaged worker hiring, 66, 117–18, 128*tab.*, 129–31, 131*fig.*, 133, 219n29; female workers and, 66, 130–31, 139, 222n99; labor unions and, 11–12, 213n59; Metro PLA and, 113–17, 127–28, 128*tab.*, 129–31, 221n74; PLAs and, 185–86, 213n59, 225n45; preapprenticeship programs and, 137, 186; Section 3 hiring, 68–70, 212n49; state/federal funding and, 116–17; Yesler Terrace Community Workforce Agreement and, 66, 68–70
TBC Industries, 41
Turner Field, 21

unions. *See* labor unions
urban development projects: benefits-sharing agreements and, 2–9, 143, 217n84; community activists and, 2, 6–7; competing narratives in, 68, 103, 119, 217n84; consensus building and, 145, 148; deliberative processes and, 146–48; elites and, 146, 150, 177; equity goals in, 8, 143, 170–71, 173–74, 180; gentrification and, 142; labor unions and, 64–65, 74, 143; low-income communities and, 1–2, 8, 142; mutual interdependence in, 145; negotiated development agreements, 177–78; neighborhood change and, 168–69; neoliberal goals and, 6, 144, 204n17; power asymmetries and, 13–14, 144; scaled up organizing and, 148
urban elites: benefits-sharing agreements and, 10, 150; control over development,

146, 150, 177; growth agenda and, 17, 142, 146–47, 149–50; implementation influence and, 150–51; local community conflicts and, 177–78; neoliberalism and, 6; public officials and, 17, 146; stadium construction and, 15
urban governance: benefits-sharing agreements and, 9–10, 204n30; consensus building and, 9, 145–46, 205n35; deliberative processes and, 9, 146, 205n34; elite dominance in, 17, 146. *See also* local government
urban growth: anti-growth interests and, 146–47; benefits-sharing agreements and, 4–6, 143; community impacts and, 6; developers and, 150; elites and, 17, 146–47, 149; labor unions and, 8, 64, 74, 142–43, 147; profits and, 142, 146
urban renewal, 1, 8, 18, 79
U.S. Department of Housing and Urban Development (HUD), 53, 55
U.S. Department of Transportation (DOT), 218n27

Villaraigosa, Antonio, 119
Vulcan Real Estate, 59, 61, 75

Walker, Scott: Act 14 and, 107–8; influence in land development, 93, 108; opposition to PERC, 12, 80, 83, 85–87, 107, 109; public funding for Bucks stadium and, 96
Walsh Shea, 128–29, 133–34, 136
Wangard, Stewart, 96
Wangard Partners, 89, 98, 104–5
Warren, Rick, 25, 34
Weishan, John, 108
Westside Future Fund, 35
Westside Heritage Owner-Occupied Rehab Program, 43
Westside Momentum, 44
Westside Neighborhood Prosperity Fund, 37
Westside TAD neighborhood strategic implementation plan, 38–39, 208n85, 209n87
Westside Works, 39
Wisconsin Department of Transportation (WisDOT), 93

Wolf-Powers, L., 91, 174
Women Build Metro LA (WBMLA), 222n99

Yesler Terrace Citizen Review Committee, 55, 59, 62–63
Yesler Terrace Community Workforce Agreement: archival documents for, 196–97; case study methodology, 191–92, 192–93*tab.*, 194, 196–97, 227n4; community bypass and, 5, 12, 52, 56, 70–73, 154, 156; community development and, 4; community distrust and, 73; implementation failures in, 11–12, 67–68, 73–74, 76; labor unions and, 65, 74, 146; lack of transparency and, 67; noncompliance and, 71–72; resident construction jobs and, 63–66, 68–70, 154; Section 3 economic targeting, 66, 68–70, 73, 212n46, 212n49, 213n60; SHA contracts and, 66–67, 69, 212n51; SHA internal administration of, 70–72; union construction jobs and, 11–12, 56, 63–67, 70; worker hiring residents, 66–67
Yesler Terrace Redevelopment Project (Seattle): accountability and, 63, 156; citizen review committee and, 54–55, 59, 62–63; 70–71; community activists and, 60; community bypass and, 74–75; community inclusion goals, 55; community opposition to redevelopment, 61–63; community workforce agreements and, 11, 63–68; crime statistics and, 62, 211n27; density in redesigned area, 59–61; displacement of residents, 62–63, 75; distrust of SHA and, 53–54; diversity in, 57, 62, 76; failed community benefits and, 56, 73, 76; flawed negotiations and, 146; gentrification threat and, 61, 75–76; land sale and, 59–61, 66–67; low-density residences in, 57–58, 58*fig.*; marginalization of community opposition and, 56; new construction, 60*fig.*; positive results of, 74–75; real estate speculation in, 61. *See also* Seattle Housing Authority (SHA); Yesler Terrace Community Workforce Agreement
Young, Ivory Lee, Jr., 35, 48

Zapata, M., 170

ACKNOWLEDGMENTS

I have so many people to thank for their support, inspiration, and belief in this project and for cheerleading me along the way. To my family and friends, thank you for the vibrancy you bring to my life, for your patience, and for your perspective. You make everything possible.

I want to thank my advisor, Lisa Schweitzer, whose brilliance and generosity shaped this work and my worldview in countless ways. I am forever grateful to you. Thanks to my dissertation committee for insightful feedback, guidance, and support: David Sloane, Malo Hutson, Tridib Banerjee, and Sandra Ball-Rokeach. I also want to specifically thank a few of the many scholars who inspired, mentored, guided, and supported me along the way, in this task and in so many others: Lisa Bates, Christine Beckman, Marlon Boarnet, Stephen Danley, Nicole Esparza, Paul Jargowsky, Robert Lake, Joan Mazelis, Gary Painter, and Deirdre Pfeiffer. I have learned so much from all of you and can only hope to pass it forward.

I am so grateful to my friends, peers, and colleagues who deeply impacted me over this time, including Sean Angst, Sarah Axeen, Michelle Carlin, Melissa Chinchilla, Jung Hyun Choi, Soledad De Gregorio, Hilary Faxon, Evan Jewell, Bryce Lowery, Sarah Mawhorter, Jocelyn Poe, Raúl Santiago-Bartolomei, Brettany Shannon, Madison Swayne, Marisa Turesky, Cynthia Wilkes, and Danielle Williams. In particular, I want to thank Vincent Reina and Luis Alvarez León, colleagues, coauthors, and friends whom I deeply respect, for sincere generosity, wisdom, patience, and kindness. To all of you, thank you for the supportive community we share.

Thank you to the institutions that made this work possible, including the Department of Public Policy and Administration at Rutgers University–Camden, the Price School of Public Policy at the University of Southern California, and the Price Center for Social Innovation at the University of Southern California. I especially want to thank those that funded this work: the John Randolph Haynes and Dora Haynes Foundation through a dissertation fellowship, the Labor Action and Research Network, and the Judith and John Bedrosian Center on Governance and the Public Enterprise at the University of Southern California. Thank you to the anonymous reviewers of this book manuscript, who encouraged me to advance this work in so many ways. Thank you to my patient and supportive editors and the publishing team at the University of Pennsylvania Press, particularly Robert Lockhart. I also want to specifically thank Edward Blum, whose insightful feedback transformed this work.

Finally, and most particularly, I thank everyone who shared their time, work, and stories with me. My sincerest hope is that in placing these stories into conversation, this book generates useful insight for people organizing to progress social change. I hope that this work effectively distills lessons and expands the possibilities that you work to create in our communities and the places we live, every day.

CPSIA information can be obtained
at www.ICGtesting.com
Printed in the USA
LVHW040605070123
736172LV00001B/1